Vice President, Licensing & Publishing Amanda Joiner
Creative Content Manager Sabrina Sieck

Editorial Manager Carrie Bolin
Editors Jessica Firpi, Jordie R. Orlando
Text Geoff Tibballs
Feature Contributors Engrid Barnett, Jessica Firpi, Jordie R. Orlando, Julia Tilford
Factcheckers Chris Lombardi, James Proud
Indexer Yvette Chin
Proofreader Rachel Paul
Special Thanks to Ripley's Video Team Steve Campbell, Colton Kruse, and Matt Mamula

Designers Rose Audette, Christopher Bigelow, Luis Fuentes, Mark Voss
Reprographics Bob Prohaska
Cover Artwork Rose Audette, Christopher Bigelow, Ron Fladwood

ISBN 978-1-60991-242-0

For more information regarding permission, contact:
VP Licensing & Publishing
Ripley Entertainment Inc.
7576 Kingspointe Parkway, Suite 188
Orlando, Florida 32819
publishing@ripleys.com
www.ripleys.com/books

Manufactured in China in May 2019 by Leo Paper
First Printing

Library of Congress Control Number: 2019936271

PUBLISHER'S NOTE
While every effort has been made to verify the accuracy of the entries in this book, the Publisher cannot be held responsible for any errors contained in the work. They would be glad to receive any information from readers.

WARNING
Some of the stunts and activities are undertaken by experts and should not be attempted by anyone without adequate training and supervision.

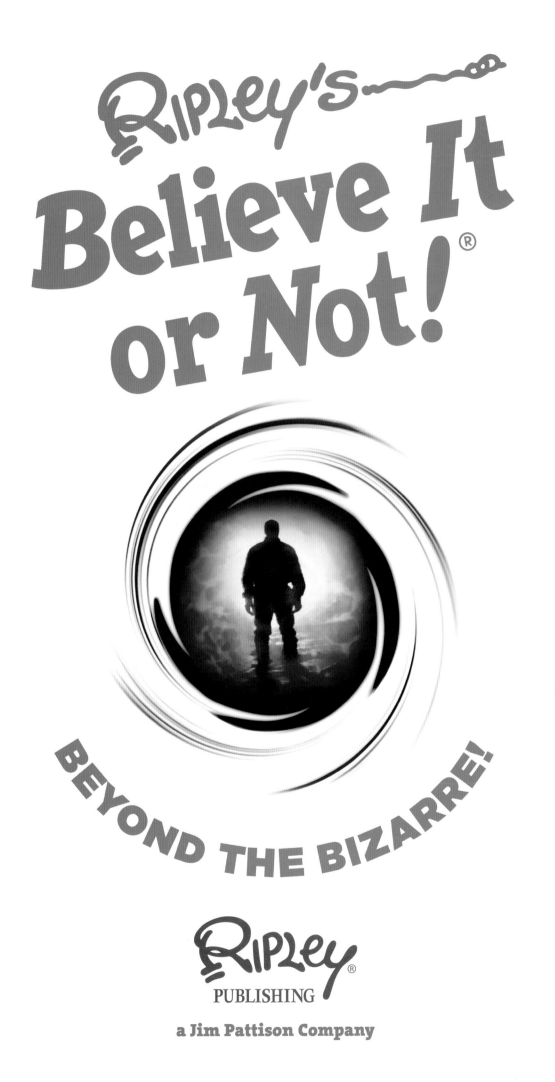

Ripley's—

Believe It or Not!®

BEYOND THE BIZARRE!

RIPLEY®
PUBLISHING

a Jim Pattison Company

CON

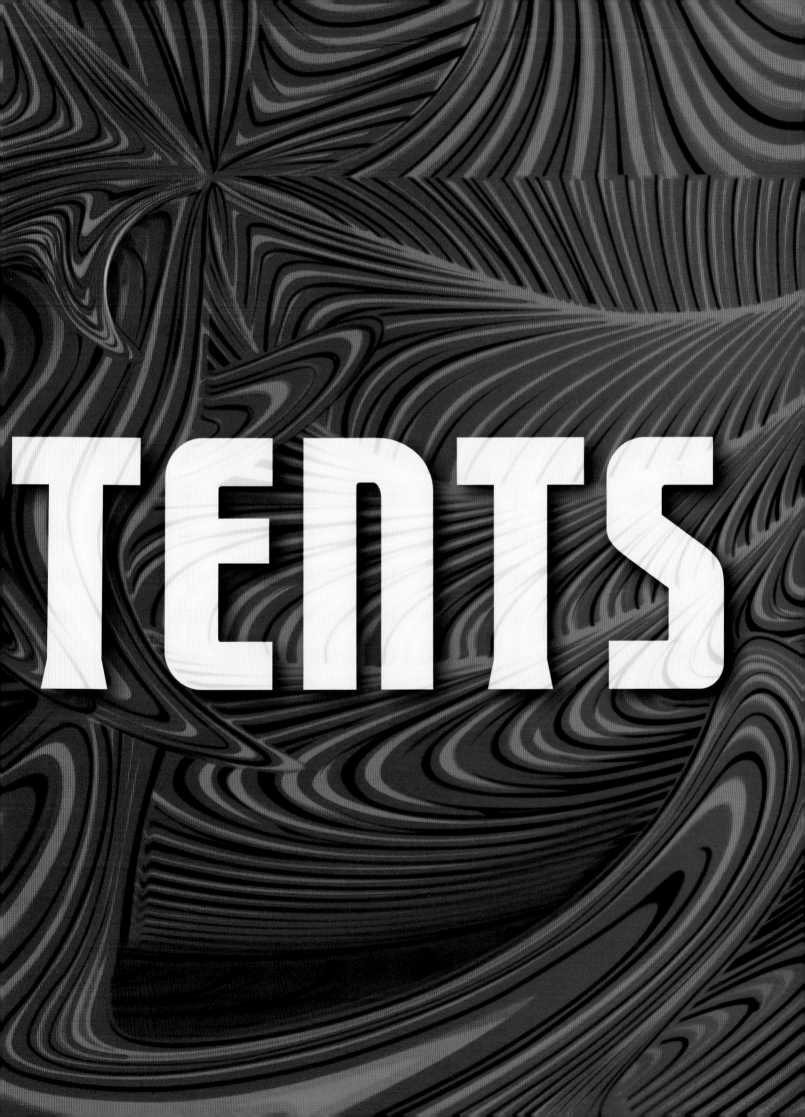

Who was Robert Ripley?

➲ It's hard to describe a man who was indescribable, but Robert Ripley was just that. Equal parts explorer, reporter, artist, and collector. He was a seeker. Just what did he seek out? The unusual.

Robert Ripley lived a life most only ever dream of, popularizing one of the most recognized and used phrases in the English language and laying the foundation for a company that carries on his unbelievable legacy.

"It is this **spirit of adventure** and the passion for sharing **amazing discoveries** that underpins everything we stand for as a company today. We are a home for **the unusual, the unbelievable**, and the many global characters and **diverse personalities** that encompasses."

Jim Pattison, Jr.
—Ripley's Believe It or Not! President

Ripley started out as a simple newspaper cartoonist depicting sporting events, but during the winter of 1918, he launched a new themed panel that eventually became the iconic "Believe It or Not" cartoon.

The runaway hit led to a life spent traveling to 201 countries in 35 years, earning him the nickname "The Modern Marco Polo." The fame of his first book gave way to a career in radio and in the new medium of television. With his extensive travels, he brought home hundreds of exotic artifacts from around the world, and in 1933, more than 2 million people visited Ripley's first museum, an "Odditorium," at the Chicago World's Fair.

Today, Ripley's Believe It or Not! is a leader in the family entertainment industry, with hundreds of attractions worldwide, including three aquariums, and 30 Ripley's Believe It or Not! museums in 10 countries filled with thousands of exhibits.

Robert Ripley holds the "Champs and Chumps" panel, regarded as the first Believe It or Not cartoon.

Robert Ripley standing with two Balinese dancers. He considered the people of Bali to be "the most artistic on Earth."

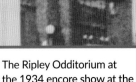

The Ripley Odditorium at the 1934 encore show at the World's Fair in Chicago.

Hollywood CHRISTMAS PARADE 2018

➲ For the second year in a row, Ripley's participated in the annual Hollywood Christmas Parade!

Complete with a custom-made upside-down Christmas tree, we celebrated our 100th anniversary by paying homage to the man who started it all: Robert Ripley. Robert Ripley was born in Santa Rosa, California, in 1890, and 100 years after "Believe It or Not!" became a household phrase, another unbelievable Santa Rosa native joined the parade route—109-year-old Art Janssen!

Ripley's guided a larger-than-life tin soldier balloon along Hollywood Boulevard, and balloon wranglers wore custom-designed Ripley's "Ugly Christmas Sweater" T-shirts. Alongside host Montel Williams, Amanda Joiner, VP of Licensing & Publishing, presented the Toys for Tots Ripley's donation of more than $100,000 worth of books.

In a segment "very near and dear to his heart," former host of the *Ripley's Believe It or Not!* television show Dean Cain introduced a brand-new addition to this year's parade. Ripley's put on a one-of-a-kind stage performance featuring unreal roller-skating feats, sword-swallowing Christmas Carolers, "bone breaker" dancers, and an extraordinary guest, Luzi Castillo, an 11-year-old girl overcoming spina bifida.

Did you know that Robert Ripley once interviewed a man by the name of Santa Clause and a woman named Mary Christmas?

Nailed It!

> He only grew the nails on his left hand; his right hand's nails were kept trimmed.

If they could be fully stretched out and laid end to end, his nails would be more than 31 ft (9.5 m) long—the height of a three-story building!

⊃ **On July 11, 2018, at the Ripley's Believe It or Not! Museum in Times Square, New York City, Shridhar Chillal cut the fingernails on his left hand for the first time in 66 years.**

The 82-year-old from Pune, India, had been growing his nails since he was scolded at school after accidentally breaking a teacher's long nail. Mr. Chillal's unusual choice didn't stop him from leading a normal and happy life. He married, has two children, three grandchildren, and enjoyed a successful career as a government press photographer. However, as he aged, his long nails made it more and more challenging to maintain an ordinary lifestyle.

In 2018, Ripley's flew Mr. Chillal from India to the United States to cut his nails and forever memorialize them in Ripley's Believe It or Not! Odditoriums. Believe it or not, a rotary tool was needed to cut through the nails! Now Ripley's owns the longest fingernails in the world.

This story and more inside Ripley's *100 Best BIONs!*

Ripley's
Believe It or Not!
100
Best BIONS

9

ON the SET

with the Trvl™ CHANNEL

⤴ Ripley's Believe It or Not! has cornered the market on the extraordinary, the death defying, the odd, and the unusual. Now, 100 years after Robert L. Ripley launched the brand, Travel Channel is rebooting the iconic TV series, hosted by veteran actor Bruce Campbell!

With all-new, one-hour episodes that will showcase the most astonishing, real and one-of-a-kind stories, the TV show was shot on location at the famed Ripley Warehouse in Orlando, Florida, and incorporates incredible stories from all parts of the globe.

"As an actor, I've always been drawn toward material that is more 'fantastic' in nature, so I was eager and excited to partner with Travel Channel and Ripley's Believe It or Not! on this new show," said Campbell. "And because amazing things happen all around the world, we should have no shortage of *unbelievable* stories to share with a fresh new audience."

Bruce Campbell

—Host of
Ripley's Believe It or Not!
TV Show

EVIL DEAD

Bruce Campbell is an American actor, producer, writer, comedian, and director. One of his best-known roles is portraying Ash Williams in Sam Raimi's *Evil Dead* film franchise.

BELIEVE IT

BORREMOSE BODY

The Borremose Body, one of three bodies found in the same peat bog, was discovered in 1946 in Himmerland, Denmark. It was so well-preserved that it was initially thought to be a recent murder victim, even though he died around 700 BC. He was strangled to death, as he was found with a slipknot around his neck.

BOG BODIES

CLONYCAVAN MAN

The Clonycavan Man was found in 2003, in County Meath, Ireland, and only his head and torso are preserved. Believed to have been in his early twenties, he was killed with a sharp object, most likely an axe, to his head and face, possibly as a ritual sacrifice. Unbelievably, he was found with remnants of primitive hair gel, made of vegetable plant oil mixed with resin from pine trees found in Spain and southwest France, still in his hair. Carbon dating has placed his death around 392–201 BC, making his remains around 2,300 years old.

OLD CROGHAN MAN

Found just three months after the Clonycavan Man, in County Offaly, Ireland, the Old Croghan Man was in his early twenties when he was killed and, based on his arm span, stood roughly 6 ft 6 in (1.98 m) tall, which was extremely rare for the time period. His manicured nails, leather armband, and last meal (wheat and buttermilk), suggest that he was of high status. Between 362 and 175 BC, he died from a stab wound to the chest and was then decapitated and cut in half.

➲ Ever since the late 1800s, a morbid sight has been turning up in peat bogs across northern Europe—prehistoric mummified bodies from as far back as 10,000 years ago.

Because of the unique conditions in the bogs, the bodies were naturally mummified, preserving their skin and even their internal organs. The bodies all date to either the Bronze Age or the Iron Age, with communities that had no written language—so no one has been able to figure out, for instance, why all the bog people were killed and placed in the bog. Men, women, and even children faced violent deaths before being laid to rest in the bog, making researchers think they may have been human sacrifices or criminals. Others think some bodies were kings held responsible for poor harvests.

A bog is a wetland area with acidic water and spongy soil, known as peat, made up of decayed plants, which can be cut out and harvested for fuel. It was when unsuspecting peat harvesters cut up the mire that the bodies started to emerge.

TOLLUND MAN

➲ Found in 1950 in Jutland, Denmark, the Tollund Man is the best-looking and best-known preserved bog body. Even today, the Tollund Man looks like he is just sleeping. He was found in almost 7 ft (2.1 m) of peat in the fetal position. He wears a cap made of sheepskin and wool on his head, and there is a noose made of braided animal hide around his neck. The short stubble on his face suggests he did not shave on the day of his death, which was back around 400 BC.

LOG CABIN
Worm

⮩ **An unusual species of moth creates its cocoon using its own silk, as well as twigs and leaves from the tree on which it hangs.**

Unlike most larvae that spin their pods with silk and hang vulnerably as they metamorphose into adult moths, the bagworm actually gathers small sticks and places them around their cocoons to camouflage and protect themselves from predators. Each species of bagworm makes a slightly different version of the stick pod, but all of them look somewhat similar to a manmade log cabin.

A closeup of the bagworm as it works to add another stick to its log cabin home.

ODD IS ART

Aquatic Dreambox
Brittany Cox

Seattle, Washington, USA
Underwater ocean scene made of 20 layers of cut paper lit from behind. 18 x 24 in (45.72 x 61 cm).

PROSTHETIC PAIN > Scientists at the Johns Hopkins School of Medicine in Baltimore, Maryland, have developed a prosthetic hand that can feel pain. The fingertips are wrapped in a thin layer of rubber and fabric, which generates pulses of electricity that stimulate nerves in the upper arm. By enabling the wearer to experience the sensation of pain, the electronic skin, known as e-dermis, helps protect the rest of the body from danger.

LUCKY NUMBERS > Francisco Rios, of Hartford, Connecticut, won $100,000 on the state lottery in 2018 by using numbers taken from a classic 1958 episode of the TV western series *Bronco*. He used the numbers 22, 2, 18, 12, and 28 because the episode was about a man who had been buried in a glacier for 22 years, 2 months, 18 days, 12 hours, and 28 minutes.

NEW LIPS > Alex Lewis, from Hampshire, England, lost all four limbs and his lips to a deadly flesh-eating infection, but has had his face transformed using skin from his shoulder to build new lips. He contracted the rare disease necrotising fasciitis in 2013, and when his lips turned gangrenous, doctors removed them and placed a temporary flap of skin on his mouth for nine months, which meant that it took him about an hour just to eat a sandwich. Eventually they were able to graft skin from his shoulder around his mouth and medically tattoo new lips onto that skin.

BELEAF IT! ⤺ Students from the China Academy of Arts used fallen gingko leaves to create a giant pair of boots in the city of Hangzhou. The shoes stand more than 13 ft (4 m) tall and 16 ft (5 m) wide, and were built to bring attention to the climate change crisis.

RARE BIRTH > In May 2018, the first baby in 12 years was born on the island of Fernando de Noronha—a remote archipelago 218 mi (350 km) off the coast of Brazil— because the 22-year-old mother had no idea she was even pregnant. There is no maternity ward on the island, so pregnant mothers are asked to give birth on the mainland instead.

CLOSE SHAVE

➲ The 1800s brought an influx of amazing inventions—like the sewing machine, the telephone, and even dynamite—but one invention basically vanished into thin hair: the mass shaving machine.

The contraption was purported to shave a dozen men at the same time, but because it couldn't alter its movements to fit different face shapes, it never took off. In October 1960, British comedian Eric Sykes brought back the invention for a pilot episode of a TV show called *Brainwaves*, which never aired.

SMOKE BOMB > A man who used a smoke bomb in an attempt to evict skunks from the crawlspace of his home in Ferndale, Michigan, ended up accidentally burning down his house. To make matters worse, firefighters found no skunk carcasses at the scene of the blaze.

LIVELY PARTY > The alcohol level in the air at a student frat party in Bethesda, Maryland, in December 2017 was so high that it registered on a breathalyzer.

SPACE KEBAB > To promote his new restaurant, Pascal Leuthold launched a kebab 124,000 ft (37,800 m) into space attached to a weather balloon in Zurich, Switzerland. The kebab crashed back down to Earth two hours later, frozen solid.

NEW TONGUE > After doctors removed a tumor on her tongue, Cynthia Zamora, from San Diego, California, was given a new tongue made from her leg. They cut a 2.4 × 3.2 in (6 × 8 cm) patch of skin and fat from her thigh and used it to shape a tongue, enabling her to speak again and taste sweet and salty foods.

SEAGULL VANDALS > Nick Burchill, from Dartmouth, Nova Scotia, Canada, was banned from the five-star Fairmont Empress Hotel in Victoria, British Columbia, for 17 years after his room was trashed by seagulls. He was taking a small suitcase full of pepperoni to some navy friends and, worried that the food would get too warm in the hotel room, he laid it out on a table near the window ledge and left the window open. When he returned from a walk, he found 40 seagulls feasting on the pepperoni and the room in a state of disarray.

LOTTERY SACRIFICE > Since 2008, Wang Chengzhou has lived under a bridge in Chongqing, China, and has cut off all communication with his family so that he could concentrate on cracking the code for the lottery. He spends more than $300 on lottery tickets every month and is convinced there is a mathematical formula behind the winning numbers.

POOP DISTRACTION > Bank robbers in Cartagena, Spain, deliberately dropped dog poop on the floor next to the front door to distract workers and cause confusion while they stole valuables.

NOT-SO-GREAT ESCAPE > A driver who tried to escape from police officers in Fairfax County, Virginia, managed to get knocked down by his own car. After being stopped by police for an equipment violation, he decided to make a run for it, but in his haste, he had forgotten to put the car in park and the moving vehicle hit him as he sprinted across the road.

SNORING CORPSE > Three doctors in Asturias, Spain, pronounced 29-year-old Gonzalo Montoya Jiménez dead until they heard him snoring four hours later on an autopsy table in the mortuary.

SHARK REPELLENT > To deter shark attacks, father and son duo Colin and Simon Brooker, of Cardiff, Wales, have developed a device that, when attached to a surfboard, slowly releases a chemical based on the scent of dead sharks. Sharks have an excellent sense of smell and can sniff out prey from nearly 2 mi (3.2 km) away.

DOG'S DELIGHT > A mix-up at the Michigan Unemployment Insurance Agency led to a dog being approved for $360 a week in benefits payments. A letter sent to "Michael Ryder" at an address in Saugatuck noted that the he had been employed at a seafood restaurant, but Ryder is actually a German Shepherd owned by attorney Michael Haddock.

WALKING DEAD > After more than 20 years working as a cook in Turkey, 63-year-old Constantin Reliu returned home to Romania in 2018 to discover that he was officially dead. His wife had registered him dead in 2016 because he had not been in contact with his family for years. He tried to prove to Romanian authorities that he was still alive, but a court in Vaslui initially refused to overturn his death certificate because his request had been filed "too late."

VINTAGE SOUP > In 2017, a food bank in Cardiff, Wales, received a 46-year-old can of soup as a charitable donation. The Heinz kidney soup flavor was discontinued more than 35 years ago.

CARDBOARD CUTOUT > Thailand's Prime Minister Prayuth Chan-o-cha avoided awkward questions from reporters at a 2018 news conference by bringing along a life-size cardboard cutout of himself and telling them to quiz that instead.

Until it was removed by surgeons, a 28-year-old man in Bahawalpur, Pakistan, had an extra nail growing on his middle finger.

FALLING FISH > Russell Hogg was relaxing with his family in an outdoor thermal spa pool in Auckland, New Zealand, when a 4.4-lb (2-kg) flounder fell from the sky and landed on his face.

RESTAURANT NAME > Justin and Jordan Garton, from Fort Smith, Arkansas, named their daughter Olivia Garton for Olive Garden, an Italian restaurant chain where they ate every day for two months.

FRUSTRATED FAN > Tranmere Rovers F.C. fan Richie Hellon spent six days walking 274 mi (438 km) from Merseyside to Dover, Kent, for an English soccer match, only for the game to be called off 90 minutes before kickoff due to a waterlogged pitch.

FLYING VISIT > Tucker Gott, from Asbury, New Jersey, flew his paramotor—a lightweight contraption featuring a parachute and a back-mounted propeller—to a McDonald's restaurant to collect a burger, which he then ate on the flight home.

CAT SMUGGLER > Some prisoners in Costa Rica train cats to sneak items into jail. A cat with a parcel strapped to its chest was intercepted while trying to enter La Reforma prison in Alajuela, and when the package was opened it was found to contain a phone, a charger, a replacement battery, and earbuds.

CHEESED OFF > Over the course of two-and-a-half weeks in 2018, Guido Grolle, a lawyer from Dortmund, Germany, received more than 100 pizzas that he had not ordered. Sometimes several different delivery men arrived at his office at the same time.

MORE THAN 14,000 FT (4,300 M) OF FABRIC!

A BIG PLUS

⟳ Every year, 24 expert climbers sway 1,300 ft (400 m) up Switzerland's Mount Säntis to secure the world's largest Swiss flag to its cliff face. The flag is a staggering 262.5 × 262.5 ft (80 × 80 m), took 600 hours to create, and weighs more than 1,500 lb (700 kg)! The tradition of hanging the flag began in 2015 to commemorate the 80th anniversary of the Mount Säntis aerial cable car. Believe it or not, a ride up the cable car gives viewers a glimpse of six countries!

CAVE *of* WONDERS

➲ During a yearly Thaipusam Festival of the god Shiva (or Murugan) in Kuala Lumpur, Malaysia, devotees celebrate inside the Batu Caves, which contain ornate shrines.

Along with piercing their bodies with metal skewers, worshippers carry pots of milk as an offering on their heads a few kilometers and up a steep, brightly painted flight of 272 steps and into the cave system.

DEVOTEES CLIMB 272 STEPS TO REACH THE TEMPLE!

LUCIFER'S FINGERS

⮑ **Against bare cliff faces in Portugal's Costa Vicentina lies a rare culinary delicacy worth braving the dangerous crashing waves to harvest— Lucifer's fingers.**

With restaurants charging around $115 (€100) for just a plate, percebes are tube-shaped barnacles that look as unappetizing as the devil's digits themselves—hence the common name "Lucifer's fingers." Although these barnacles can be found elsewhere, like Canada, they're prized in Spain and Portugal, where hunting is highly regulated.

Divers, who literally chisel the barnacles off the rock, risk their lives collecting these "truffles of the sea," with some being knocked unconscious by the pounding waves and drowning. More fortunate harvesters come away with a broken arm or cuts and bruises.

The thick claw-like trunks with diamond-shaped "feet" only grow on the rocks in between the high and low tide water mark and cannot be farmed.

CABBAGE PATCH

⊃ Ian Neale of Newport, South Wales, is a champion vegetable grower and managed to win the giant vegetable competition at the Harrogate Autumn Flower Show with his 66 lb (30 kg) cabbage! The 75-year-old champion insists there's no secret to growing giant veggies the size of a washing machine: "You do need a bit of money—for compost and fertilizer—but that's it."

COASTAL POPULATION > More than 85 percent of Australians live within 31 mi (50 km) of the coast—and in Tasmania, which covers an area of 26,400 sq mi (68,400 sq km), the figure rises to 99 percent.

TOP BANANA > Fruit farmers in Okayama, Japan, have created the Mongee banana—a special banana with edible skin.

GIANT CORNFLAKE > Hinay Lad, a student in London, England, found a 6-in-long (15-cm) cornflake in his box of cereal.

Ripley's **Rarities**

Rarity N° 173040

Spice Portrait
Portrait of actress Emma Watson made entirely from seeds and common kitchen spices, including garlic, parsley, and chili peppers, by Enrique Ramos Jr.!

METER VANDALS > More than 1,000 of the 1,167 parking meters in St. John's, Newfoundland and Labrador, Canada, have been damaged since March 2015.

HOVER CHAIR > Houston Astros fan Diego Torres cruises around the city in a hoverboard-powered tribute chair decked out in the team logos. The chair, which can travel up to 20 mph (32 kmph), has wheels on all sides and a hoverboard attached to the front.

EVEREST MAIL > There is a post office on Mt. Everest at an altitude of 17,388 ft (5,301 m) above sea level. It is located at Everest base camp on the Tibetan side of the mountain but is only open from April to August because of the weather.

BUG-COVERED CHEESE!

MITEY CHEESY ⊃ Milbenkäse cheese from Würchwitz, Germany, has a very special ingredient—mites! Mites love cheese and are sometimes used to help age and flavor the delicious dairy product, but are usually removed before consumption. When it comes to this German cheese, however, the itty-bitty arachnids are intentionally left behind to be eaten along with the cheese.

LAWN DESIGN >
After winning more than $3 million playing the lottery, Sue Richards and Barry Maddox mowed a celebratory image of a champagne bottle and two glasses into the lawn of their home in Essex, England. It took three days to create the design using three varieties of lawnmower, plus shears and scissors of different sizes.

TAXIDERMY PET >
The appropriately named Lisa Foxcroft, from Merseyside, England, takes her taxidermy fox cub, Baby Jesus, with her wherever she goes and even dresses him up in various costumes. She was given the stuffed cub as a Christmas present in 2015 after he had been killed in a car accident.

DUMB ROBBER >
A thief in Rio de Janeiro, Brazil, chose the wrong gym to rob because he ended up being chased out by several angry ju-jitsu students who had been taking a class there.

MOVIE SHOT >
A police officer in Crawfordsville, Indiana, shot at a man who appeared to be robbing a restaurant, only to discover that the man in the ski mask was actor Jeff Duff, who was filming a movie and carrying a prop gun. The movie production company had failed to notify the authorities that they were filming in public areas, so when the police received a 911 call about a robbery, they responded.

QUAINT QUR'AN
Talk about a pocketbook! Owned by Tubagus Tamyiz in Sukaraja, Indonesia, this religious text is only 0.4 in (10 mm) tall and 0.2 in (5 mm) thick! The miniscule words are printed in gold ink.

DONATED TOES >
After losing three toes to frostbite in a Yukon sled race, Nick Griffiths, from Bolton, England, donated them to the Downtown Hotel in Dawson City for its famous Sourtoe Cocktail, where customers drink from a shot glass containing an amputated human toe.

SPIDER EATER >
Daniel Roberts, from California, eats live black widow spiders. He allows the venomous spiders to crawl over his face and inside his mouth before devouring them. He carries special pills in case he is bitten by the spiders while performing his routine.

DOGGY DETOUR >
When Kara Swindle's family moved from Oregon to Wichita, Kansas, in 2018, they discovered that United Airlines had accidentally flown their dog to Japan. Irgo, their 10-year-old German Shepherd, was sent to the wrong country after a mix-up during connections in Denver, Colorado. The Great Dane, who was supposed to have gone to Kansas City, ended up in Japan.

TINY TOME
This 1895 songbook comes inside a locket with a built-in magnifying glass. Miniature books were very trendy in the 1800s. Believe it or not, Napoleon Bonaparte had his own traveling library filled with hundreds of petit volumes!

OLD
ENGLISH, SCOTCH
AND
IRISH SONGS
WITH MUSIC.

A Favourite Selection

EDITED BY
WILLIAM MOODIE

GLASGOW
DAVID BRYCE & SON

READING MACHINE

⮑ The Fiske Reading Machine makes books more portable than ever before! Well, before the 1920s, anyway.

Invented by Bradley Fiske, the handheld gadget consisted of a magnifying glass and slot for holding 2 × 6-in (5 × 15-cm) cards covered in columns of extremely small text. A reader could hold the device up to their eye, look through the lens, and be able to read the magnified words. Unfortunately for Fiske, his Reading Machine never took off, despite being able to shrink a 700-page book down to a mere 13 cards. However, the spirit of his idea lives on in today's e-readers that can carry hundreds of books in one tiny package.

FISKE
READING MACHINE
PATENTED........

A B C D
AN
ADVENTURE
WITH A
GENIUS
PAGE 1

SNOUT SNACK ➲ You can find some of the most fascinating and bizarre snacks at street market stalls in China, including these pig snouts, which have been roasted and put on display for the appetites of tourists and locals alike.

SOCK SHOCK > Chaoyi Le, of Mississauga, Ontario, tried to smuggle three live albino western hognose snakes from New York State into Canada by hiding them inside his socks.

BUNGLED EXECUTION > Before becoming president of the United States, Grover Cleveland was sheriff of Erie County, New York, for two years from 1871 to 1873, in which capacity he served as an executioner and hanged two convicted criminals. When Cleveland pulled the lever at the second execution in 1873, the 5-ft (1.5-m) drop broke prisoner John Gaffney's neck but did not kill him instantly, and it took him another 23 minutes to die.

HUMAN REMAINS > Among items donated to a Goodwill store in Vancouver, Washington, in 2018 was a wooden box filled with cremated human remains—twice!

DETECTOR SILENCED > Sixty-eight-year-old Leroy Mason, of Barton, Vermont, was charged with firing a 20-gauge shotgun to silence a smoke detector in the kitchen of his apartment.

FREAK COLLISION > On September 29, 1940, two Avro Anson airplanes from a training school collided in midair above Brocklesby, New South Wales, Australia—but instead of crashing to the ground, the planes stuck together one on top of the other and eventually made a safe landing. The collision stopped the engines of the upper plane, but those of the plane below continued to operate, allowing the pair to continue flying. The navigator and pilot of the lower plane bailed out, but Leonard Fuller, the pilot of the upper plane, miraculously managed to control the interlocked aircraft and flew for 5 mi (8 km) before making an emergency landing in a paddock.

ROYAL SOUVENIR > Teenager Edward Jones broke into London's Buckingham Palace three times between 1838 and 1841, and on one occasion was captured with Queen Victoria's underwear stuffed down his pants.

PENCIL ACCIDENT > While doing her makeup in the back of a taxi in Bangkok, Thailand, a woman got her eyeliner pencil stuck in her eye. The pencil jammed into her eye socket when the taxi crashed into the back of a slow-moving truck.

DEADLY HOOKS

➲ The devil's claw fruit of the South African grapple tree (*Harpagophytum procumbens*) is covered in fierce hooks that have been known to kill a lion. As an animal passes by, the hooks latch on to it and sink ever deeper into the animal's flesh as it tries to shake the fruit off. Lions have been reported as starving to death after touching the fruit with their mouth, because the fruit has attached itself to the lion's jaw, inflicting severe pain and preventing it from eating.

SHEDDING SKIN

⮕ Om Prakash, from Sarjupura Bachedi, India, has a rare condition called erythroderma, which causes his skin to shed every 10 days, like a snake.

He has to moisturize his skin every two hours, but the disease has left him unable to walk because the friction created by movement causes his skin to crack and bleed. He started showing signs of the condition at just five days old, and despite his bleak diagnosis, Prakash insists people treat him kindly. He spends his days making clay dolls for the village children and hopes to one day get married.

SKIN SHEDS EVERY 10 DAYS!

TOUGH AS NAILS

➔ Most tattoos are meant to stand out, but tattoo artist Eric Catalano of Hecker, Illinois, specializes in hyperrealistic pieces meant for people who have lost body parts. One of his more recent masterpieces are these fingernails he inked onto Mark Bertram, who lost the tips of his index and middle fingers. Catalano refuses payment for these kinds of tattoos, as he feels the people who need this kind of work have already been through enough.

It took Catalano just 11 minutes to tattoo these fingernails!

BEFORE

ALLERGIC REACTION > Author Martin Greenwood, from Warwickshire, England, collapsed and nearly died after inhaling microscopic spores from century-old documents. He had been poring over archives containing his late grandfather's artwork but suffered an allergic reaction to spores in the paper. He spent six days in an induced coma and took three months to recover.

SIDEWALK FIND > In 2008, Margaret Mussel, of Brick Township, New Jersey, lost her 1.1-karat diamond engagement ring while visiting her family's home in San Marco dei Cavoti, Italy—and nine years later, on a return trip, she discovered the ring nestled in a crack in the sidewalk near the house.

ODD MAN OUT > When Belgium played Tunisia in the World Cup on June 23, 2018, the only man on the pitch who played his club soccer in Belgium was one of the Tunisian team—defender Dylan Bronn, who played for Gent.

JOLLY *Holiday*

➔ Mary Poppins did return in 2018—atop the London Eye!

To celebrate the premiere of the *Mary Poppins Returns* sequel, a stunt double clad in Mary Poppins's signature clothes and umbrella stood on top of an observation pod on the 443-ft-tall (135-m) Coca-Cola Eye on the banks of the River Thames.

LOOK! IT'S MARY POPPINS!

MOOVIN' ON UP

➲ When the usual path became impassable in June 2018, farmers in the village of Spiringen, Switzerland, transported their cows in cable cars! During the summer in the Swiss Alps, farmers move their cows from valleys to smaller farms up the mountains, where the herd can graze on longer grass.

OCTOPUS SUIT > Young American Bitcoin millionaire Erik Finman built a functional version of Doctor Octopus's iconic four-arm prosthesis for Aristou Meehan, a 10-year-old Marvel Comics fan who suffers from hypermobility syndrome. Modeled on the robotic contraption worn by the mad scientist in the Spider-Man comics, the custom-made mechanical suit was built with 3D printing and features four flexible tentacles that are operated by rear-mounted microcontrollers and powered by eight motors. In addition to giving the wearer four extra limbs, the 12.5-lb (5.7-kg) suit is capable of picking up lightweight objects.

BLOWN AWAY > A real estate sign that was blown from a waterfront home in Brielle, New Jersey, by Hurricane Sandy in the fall of 2012 turned up nearly six years later 3,660 mi (5,856 km) away on a beach in Bordeaux, France.

PRACTICE BOMB > While swimming and diving in Lobdell Lake, Michigan, in May 2018, 10-year-old Paige Burnett and nine-year-old Sage Menzies found a 3-ft-long (0.9-m), century-old World War I practice bomb. A bomb squad drilled a hole into the device, but only mud came out, so it was deemed no longer active.

OCEAN DRIFTERS > After the engine on his small boat failed and a storm destroyed the radio, Polish sailor Zbigniew Reket and his cat were left drifting in the Indian Ocean for seven months. He said he survived on a month's supply of noodles and by catching fish before he was finally rescued when his boat washed ashore on the island of Réunion, off the east coast of Africa, on Christmas Day 2017.

IDENTICAL TRIPLETS > Sian Williams and Aaron Palfrey, from Cwmbran, South Wales, beat odds of 200 million to one to conceive identical triplet girls. The couple rely on different colored nail polish to tell their daughters—Jorgie, Belle, and Olivia—apart.

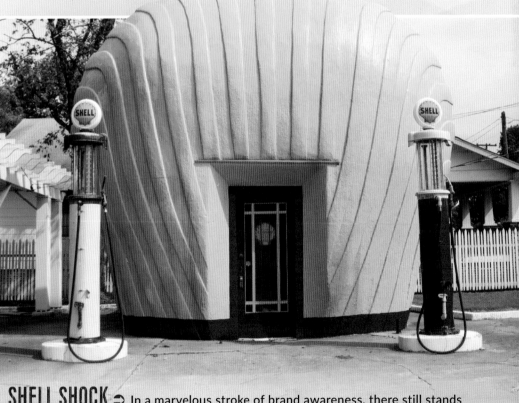

SHELL SHOCK ➲ In a marvelous stroke of brand awareness, there still stands a Shell gas station in the shape of a giant scallop shell in Winston-Salem, North Carolina. The owners of the oil company hoped to attract customers with the literally shaped building, erected in 1930. An example of novelty architecture, this last "Shell" station was listed on the National Register of historic places in 1976.

The *EVEL* LIVES ON

➲ **The grandfather of extreme sports, Evel Knievel made dancing with death America's favorite pastime during a career that spanned from 1966 to 1980 and encompassed more than 75 ramp-to-ramp motorcycle jumps.**

As famous for his epic failures as he is for his successful stunts, Knievel earned a spot in record books as the survivor of the most broken bones in one lifetime, with a purported 433 bone fractures although he personally claimed just 35. Nevertheless, when not seated on the back of a motorcycle in an Elvis-inspired leather jumpsuit with a cape, Knievel spent half the years from 1966 to 1973 in a wheelchair, on crutches, or in the hospital, a sacrifice he willingly made as he paved the way for today's multibillion-dollar extreme sports industry.

In January 1977 in Chicago, Illinois, Knievel ended his daredevil career after crashing into a cameraman on a practice run for his "Shark Jump" over a tank filled with live sharks (capitalizing on the success of *Jaws*). While Knievel had no qualms about risking his own neck, he was horrified by the thought of injuring someone else.

SOLD-OUT JUMPS ⮕ On January 8 and 9, 1971, Knievel broke another kind of record by selling more than 100,000 tickets to consecutive performances at the Houston Astrodome. For two nights in a row, Knievel jumped his motorcycle over 13 automobiles to the wild cheers of onlookers. These events helped prepare him for his world-record-breaking jump of 19 Dodge vehicles, measuring 129 ft (39 m), on February 28, 1971, at the Ontario Motor Speedway in California (shown here).

CAESARS PALACE ⮕ Thousands turned out on New Year's Eve 1967 to watch Evel Knievel jump the fountains at Caesars Palace in Las Vegas, Nevada, the longest attempted motorcycle jump—141 ft (43 m)—at the time. They watched in horror and voyeuristic fascination as Knievel failed to make the landing, sending his body in an unplanned free fall that resulted in multiple fractures yet earned him instant fame when the botched stunt aired on ABC.

SERIOUS RISK-TAKING AND A WELL-PUBLICIZED EPIC FAIL LAUNCHED KNIEVEL'S CAREER.

EPIC FAILS ⊃

Despite his improbable successes, the fame of America's first extreme athlete remained dangerously linked to his televised near-death experiences. The long-term renown that he received for events like the Houston Astrodome paled in comparison to the media coverage that followed epic fails such as the botched Snake River Canyon stunt (where he attempted to jump the canyon on a steam-powered skycycle) and his May 26, 1975, Wembley Stadium jump in London, where a crowd of 90,000 onlookers watched Knievel break his back during a botched attempt to jump 13 single-decker buses.

SNAKE RIVER CANYON STUNT!

COURAGE

- DARING PROBE OF THE UNKNOWN • THE ULTIMATE TEST!

1 Mile

"SNAKE RIVER CANYON"

EVEL KNIEVEL

WITH HIS HARLEY DAVIDSON X-2.

JET POWERED WITH "THE WATER",

WILL JUMP THE

SNAKE RIVER CANYON

— TWIN FALLS IDAHO —

WEMBLEY STADIUM STUNT!

BREAKING HIS BACK!

SOARING SUCCESS ⟹ On October 25,

1975, the "Last Gladiator" donned his iconic white leather jumpsuit with red and blue stripes at Kings Island amusement park in Ohio before successfully clearing 14 Greyhound buses, a jump 133 ft (40.5 m) in length. The high point of his career, the event was attended by 25,000 spectators, earned ABC's "Wide World of Sports" their highest ratings of all time, and resulted in a world record that would go unbroken for another 24 years.

KNIEVEL'S WORLD RECORD-BREAKING JUMP AT KINGS ISLAND MARKED THE HIGHPOINT OF HIS CAREER AS A DAREDEVIL.

GREYHOUND

LIQUIDS ONLY > In 2018, Rajendra Panchal, from Pune, India, ate solid food for the first time—at age 39. He had fallen on his face as a baby, misplacing his jaw and wedging it shut. Unable to open his mouth more than 0.6 in (1.5 cm), he was forced to exist on just a liquid diet for nearly four decades until a dentist finally released the fused bones.

ROTTEN FRUIT > About 500 students evacuated the library at a university in Melbourne, Australia, after people reported the smell of gas—but instead the foul stench turned out to be from a durian fruit that had been left rotting in a cupboard. The fruit is often banned from hotel rooms and public transport in southeast Asia because of its smell.

TELLTALE SIGN > Maria Vazquez, of Hawthorne, New Jersey, drove for about 8 mi (13 km) unaware that there was a long, metal state road sign sticking out from the sunroof of her car.

MARRIED TREE > In a special ceremony, Karen Cooper "married" a giant, 100-year-old ficus tree in Snell Family Park, Fort Myers, Florida, in the hope of saving it from being chopped down.

BUCKET WISH > A 46-year-old driver, who was pulled over for a violation by the Iowa State Patrol following a 15-minute pursuit through Des Moines, told troopers that he wanted to be chased by a police car because it was on his bucket list.

MUMMIFIED MOM > For more than 30 years, an elderly woman lived in an apartment in Mykolaiv, Ukraine, with the mummified corpse of her dead mother. Alerted by concerned neighbors, police found the body lying on a couch and dressed in a white gown, head-covering, socks, and shoes.

Luke Fox, an 11-year-old Boy Scout from West Chester, Pennsylvania, was mistakenly sent a summons by Chester County Court to appear for jury duty.

FEARS SQUASHED > In 2017, an 81-year-old man called the police to tell them he had found an unexploded World War II bomb in the garden of his home near Karlsruhe, Germany, but when officers arrived they found it was a 16-in-long (40-cm) zucchini.

CAMEL BOTOX > A dozen camels were disqualified from the beauty contest at the 2018 King Abdulaziz Camel Festival in Saudi Arabia because their owners had used Botox on their camels to make the animals look more attractive.

CIRCULAR TOUR > A 73-year-old Frenchman was arrested for drunk driving after driving 17 times around a roundabout in Brittany.

GOOSE'S REVENGE > Waterfowl hunter Robert Meilhammer, from Dorchester County, Maryland, was knocked unconscious when a dead Canada goose—shot by one of his hunting party—fell from the sky and landed on his head.

DYING WISH > Richard Lussi, from Plains Township, Pennsylvania, was granted his dying wish when his family buried him in a coffin with two cheesesteaks from his favorite sandwich shop—Pat's King of Steaks in Philadelphia.

ESCAPE FOILED > Pursued by Arizona police officers, two shoplifting suspects tried to make their escape by scaling a fence despite the presence of a large sign on an adjoining building saying "Peoria Police." They landed in the secure parking lot of the police precinct, where several officers were training at that very moment.

ROBOT CANDIDATE > Michihito Matsuda won 4,000 votes running for mayor in Tama City, Japan, as an artificial intelligence candidate on a promise to replace human public officials with humanoid robots.

DISTANT COUSINS > Meryl Streep and English actress Lily James, who play Donna Sheridan at different ages in the 2018 ABBA musical movie *Mamma Mia! Here We Go Again*, are ninth cousins three times removed. Producers had no idea they were related when casting them, but both women are descended from sons of Henry Howland, who died in Cambridgeshire, England, in 1634.

AUTO THRILLER ⊃ A new thrill ride made newspapers in 1929—the "auto thriller." Invented by Harry Rock in Los Angeles, California, the U-shaped auto roller coaster had a 2,400 ft (731.5 m) long track with undulating "humps" measuring about 10 ft (3 m) high. Adrenaline junkies would drive 40 mph (64 kmph), similar to a roller coaster, and as *The Bakersfield Californian* printed on April 15, 1929, "of course it's more thrilling because you are driving your own car."

ORANGE SNOW

⤶ Orange snow fell in parts of eastern Europe in March 2018 after snow from Siberia collided with dust-filled wind from Africa's Sahara Desert.

The strange phenomenon prompted people like Alina Smurygina of Moscow, Russia, to upload their photos to social media to share the Martian-like landscape. Believe it or not, sands from the Sahara making their way across the world is not uncommon, but it is rare for the sands to mix with falling snow.

HIGH LIVING > Gilbert Sanchez, from La Paz in the Philippines, spent three years living atop a 60-ft-tall (18-m) coconut tree. His mother regularly brought him clothes, food, and water, which he pulled up the tree with a rope. He had always refused to come down, but in 2017, local authorities ended his stay by felling the tree with a chainsaw.

LATE PAYMENT > Feeling guilty, a man finally paid a 44-year-old parking ticket to the Minersville, Pennsylvania, Police Department. The 1974 fine was $2, but the driver sent the police an apology and $5 to allow for interest accrued over the years.

EXTRA ZERO > The Norwegian Winter Olympics team accidentally ordered 15,000 eggs for the 2018 Games in PyeongChang after asking Google Translate how to say 1,500 in Korean.

STICKY SITUATION > Fadzilah Abdul Hamid was so angry at being fired from his job with a Malaysian oil company after 17 years that he superglued his hand to the floor of the company headquarters in Kuala Lumpur.

PERSISTENT GAS > In February 2018, a Transavia Airlines flight from Dubai to Amsterdam, the Netherlands, was forced to make an emergency landing in Austria when a fight broke out over one passenger's persistent and excessive personal gas.

DIFFERENT BRIDE > Dr. Ravi Kumar, a neurosurgeon from New Delhi, India, ended up marrying a different bride after his first choice unexpectedly rejected him. His family had arranged a year in advance for him to travel more than 600 mi (965 km) to Sugauli village in Bihar to marry a local girl on February 18, 2018. But the couple had never met before the wedding day, and, even though all the rituals had taken place, when the groom removed his traditional headgear just before the ceremony, the bride-to-be saw that he was balding and refused to marry him. Undeterred, his family searched the village for a replacement, and two days later he married Neha Kumari, the daughter of an impoverished vegetable seller.

WRONG TURN > An Uber driver took a wrong turn into a pedestrian walkway at a San Francisco grocery store and ended up with his car stranded halfway down an outdoor staircase.

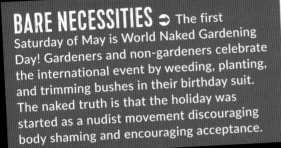

BARE NECESSITIES ⇒ The first Saturday of May is World Naked Gardening Day! Gardeners and non-gardeners celebrate the international event by weeding, planting, and trimming bushes in their birthday suit. The naked truth is that the holiday was started as a nudist movement discouraging body shaming and encouraging acceptance.

TRAIN CHAOS > A drunk man who decided to spend the night asleep on a freight train in Munich, Germany, affected the smooth running of 86 trains, causing 37 cancellations and 1,280 minutes of delays after he called the police to tell them he couldn't get out. Officials had to shut down all rail traffic and search for an hour before finding the lost man.

PROM DATE > Allison Closs arrived at the Carlisle High School prom in Pennsylvania with a full-size cardboard cutout of actor and director Danny DeVito as her date. A month later, DeVito returned the favor by posing on the set of his sitcom *It's Always Sunny in Philadelphia* with a cardboard cutout of Allison!

PIG STALKER > A man called 911 to report that he was being stalked by a pig while walking home early in the morning from the train station in Elyria, Ohio. The police assumed that the man was drunk, but when they arrived at the scene, they discovered that he was not only sober but really being followed by a pig. They managed to wrestle the pig into their patrol car before returning the animal to its owner.

HALLOWEEN COSTUME > When baby Oaklyn Selph was born on October 31, 2017, at Henry Counter Medical Center in Paris, Tennessee, she was delivered by obstetrician Dr. Paul Locus, who was dressed for Halloween as the Joker from the Batman movie *The Dark Knight*.

ICE CREAM PROCESSION > Ice cream vendor Mac Leask had worked the same area in Birmingham, England, for 46 years, so at his funeral, his coffin was followed by a procession of six ice cream trucks sounding their chimes in unison.

SELF-MUMMIFICATION > Sokushinbutsu is the outlawed Buddhist practice of self-mummification. Practitioners ate only roots and bark for three years, drank tea from the sap of the urushi tree to preserve their bodies, and were eventually buried alive.

HUNGRY RATS > Rats slipped through the back of an ATM in Tinsukia, India, and chewed their way through more than $19,000 in bills.

SAY WHAT?

⇒ Throughout the 1920s and 1930s and before the advent of radar, giant horns like these were used to listen for distant aircraft. At that point in history, airplanes were still relatively new and extremely loud, making sound amplifiers the best bet for finding out if an airborne enemy was approaching.

Cicada
CYBORG

⊃ Yuasa Riku of Osaka, Japan, created an action figure out of cicada shells!

Loudly chirping cicadas and summer go hand in hand in Japan. The hefty bugs shed their shells as they grow, leaving hollow versions of themselves behind for inventive artists like Riku to transform into something new. This particular piece is held together with pins and wood glue.

MADE FROM BUG SHELLS!

DOLLY DILEMMA > In 1998, campaigners in the United Kingdom tried to steal Dolly, the world's first cloned sheep, but gave up when they realized they could not distinguish her from the rest of the flock.

ROBOT CITIZEN > Sophia Robot, a humanoid robot designed in Hong Kong, has been granted citizenship in Saudi Arabia.

ATM RAGE > Michael Joseph Oleksik caused $5,000 of damage to an ATM at a Wells Fargo branch in Cocoa, Florida, when he punched it because it gave him too much cash.

LETHAL LAWNMOWERS > On average, 69 people in the United States are killed by lawnmowers every year.

COUNTING COINS > When a family brought 2.5 tons of old 1 and 2 pfennig coins to a bank in Oldenburg, Germany, it took clerk Wolfgang Kemereit more than six months to count them out by hand. The 1.2 million coins were worth a total of $9,400 and had been collected by the family for 30 years.

LOST VOICE > A Chinese murder suspect evaded capture for 12 years by using the false name Wang Gui and pretending to be mute, but when he was finally arrested in Anhui Province, he was genuinely unable to talk because all the years of not using his vocal cords had led to them wasting away and becoming useless.

SAUSAGE TOWN ⊃ A photo snapped in 1930 shows a peculiar town sign. Ameide, a village in South Holland, the Netherlands, covered their place name sign in smoked sausages—the phrase "rook worst dorp" means "smoked sausage village."

AMEIDE

ROOK WORST DORP

PARTY JOKE > British scientist Stephen Hawking once threw a humorous party for time travelers but deliberately chose not to send out the invitations until after the event, thus only inviting people from the future. He saw the fact that nobody had turned up as scientific proof that time travel is impossible!

STREET SAMURAI > Members of the Gomi Hiroi Samurai theater performance group dress like samurai warriors but devote their energies to collecting trash from the streets of Japanese cities. Whenever they locate and dispose of an item of garbage, they strike dramatic poses and shout menacing warnings condemning the perpetrator.

LOVERS' MEMORABILIA > Dinh Thang has set up an "Old Flames" market stall in Hanoi, Vietnam, where jilted lovers sell memorabilia, such as clothing, diaries, and letters from failed relationships.

PHONE PROPOSAL > Chen Ming, a video game designer from Shenzen, China, proposed to his girlfriend by spending more than $30,000 on 25 brand new iPhone X smartphones and arranging them in the shape of a heart.

ALIEN ATTACKS > In 2017, John and Joyce Edmonds put their 10-acre (4-hectare) desert ranch in Rainbow Valley, Arizona, up for sale because John said he had grown tired of fighting off aliens. Over 20 years, he claims to have slain 18 aliens with a samurai sword and to have fought hundreds more.

SPICY ICE CREAM

⊃ The Aldwych Café and Ice Cream Parlor in Glasgow, Scotland, released a special edition ice cream called Respiro Del Diavolo (aka Devil's Breath), and those who eat it must be at least 18 years old and sign a waiver in case of "possible loss of life." Looks can be deceiving because the harmless-looking ice cream is 500 times spicier than Tabasco sauce. The hot and cold confection is made with Carolina Reapers, the hottest chili pepper in the world!

Spin
CRUST

⮕ Meet pizza acrobatics—the delicious new sport that puts the "oh" in dough!

Every year participants from all over the globe compete for the title of World Pizza Champion at one of two competitions in Italy and in Las Vegas, Nevada. The elaborate two- to three-minute routines set to music resemble rhythm gymnastics (but with pizza dough, of course). A panel of three to five judges score based on dexterity, creativity, difficulty, if there are any drops, and transitions from trick to trick. Believe it or not, the crusty competitors practice using artificial pizza dough, not the real deal.

One contestant, Justin Wadstein, is a 14-time world pizza champion and can spin flaming pizza dough!

39

ZIT SQUEEZER > The Pop It Pal toy allows the user to recreate the sensation of squeezing huge zits. Each Pop It Pal has 15 silicone zits filled with goo that you pop to see the "pus" ooze out. The kit, which comes with a bottle of fake pus for refills, is the brainchild of South Carolina married couple Billy and Summer Pierce, who enjoy watching pimple-popping videos online.

IDENTITY THEFT > Sakorn Sacheewa, from Si Sa Ket Province, Thailand, returned home on December 17, 2017—seven months after supposedly being cremated. His family had been told by police the previous May that he had died of a digestive order, and he was subsequently cremated, even though the swollen body was difficult to identify. It turned out that he was alive and well and working away from home, the case of mistaken identity arising because a coworker had stolen his ID card.

SINK OR SWIM

⟳ Before floaties and personal flotation devices became commonplace, people had to get creative. Here a group of young people in Germany tied bike inner tubes around their bodies as a swimming aid, circa 1925.

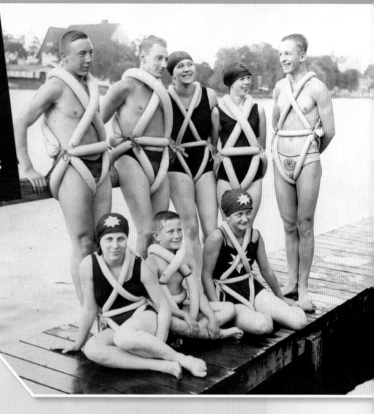

ROCKET MAN >
As part of his quest to prove that the Earth is flat, 61-year-old "Mad" Mike Hughes launched himself vertically into the air at a speed of nearly 350 mph (560 kmph) in a homemade steam-powered rocket that he had built in his garage. Taking to the skies from Amboy, California, on March 24, 2018, he reached a height of almost 2,000 ft (600 m) before pulling his parachute and making a hard landing in the Mojave Desert, breaking the rocket's nose and leaving himself with an aching back.

ALIEN COURSE > Akdeniz University in Turkey offers a course that prepares students for alien encounters, issuing them with instructions on how to welcome visitors from outer space.

PROFESSOR'S BLUNDER > Southern New Hampshire University replaced an online professor who insisted that Australia is not a proper country. She had given Ashley Arnold, a 27-year-old student from Idaho, a failing grade for an assignment on the erroneous grounds that Australia is a continent but not a country.

FACE CONES

⟳ If you were a fashionable lady living in 1930s Canada, how would you stay warm during the winter? Enter the face cone. This clear plastic mask kept the face protected against snowstorms, leaving it free from snow and ice. Pictured here, these two chic women sport the pointed look in Montreal, Canada, in 1939.

SILENT SPORTSCAST >
Annoyed at some of the referee's decisions, Russian TV sportscaster Vladimir Nikolsky abandoned his microphone and stormed off partway through a First Division soccer game between Torpedo Vladimir and Tekstilshchik Ivanovo, leaving viewers with no commentary for the rest of the match.

BROKEN TOILETS >
A Norwegian Air flight from Oslo to Munich in January 2018 was forced to make an emergency landing because of dysfunctional toilets—despite having 84 plumbers on board who were on a business trip to Germany.

SHORT VOYAGE > Colorado couple Tanner Broadwell and Nikki Walsh quit their jobs and sold everything they owned in order to buy a 49-year-old, 28-ft-long (8.5-m) boat, *Lagniappe*, and sail off on an epic voyage on the open seas. They had been planning it for two years, but just two days after setting off from Tarpon Springs, Florida, in February 2018, their boat sank.

WRONG ROUTE > Unknown Eritrean-born Italian athlete Eyob Faniel won the 2017 Venice Marathon after the leading six runners followed a guide motorcycle down the wrong route and lost about two minutes.

AMPHIBIOUS BIKE

Debuting in Paris in 1932, the Cyclomer was the world's first amphibious bike. With the alleged ability to run on land and on water with a maximum load of 264 lb (120 kg), the bizarre-looking ride featured hollow wheels and floats. Unfortunately, it didn't work out, as it couldn't get enough traction on land or in the water. Other amphibious bikes have since come up to take its place.

CROSSED WIRES > After partying with friends in Morgantown, West Virginia, New Jersey native Kenny Bachman thought he had called an Uber to take him back to where he was staying near the West Virginia University campus, but somehow wires became crossed, and instead he woke up two hours later in the passenger seat to find that the driver was taking him home to New Jersey 300 mi (480 km) away and that the fare was $1,635.

MODEL BABIES > Russian company Embryo 3D offers parents gold-plated, 3D-printed models of their soon-to-be-born babies based on images obtained from ultrasound scans.

LOFTY VIEW > After being banned from the stadium of his favorite Turkish soccer team, Denizlispor, for a year, fanatical supporter Ali Demirkaya spent hundreds of dollars renting an industrial crane to watch the game from a lofty perch outside the stands.

SKATING WITH FATE

The 1920s saw inventions like washing machines, the jukebox, assembly lines, and even television, but common sense might have been thin on the ground. In St. Moritz, Switzerland, in 1926 a mother is captured casually ice skating while pushing her newborn sitting up in a pram on skis. Today, skating moms opt to push a regular stroller—without skis—and strap their child in with a seatbelt.

VOLCANO
on the GREEN

In May 2018, a group of golfers kept playing the game even as a volcano erupted behind them.

Hawaii's Mount Kilauea volcano sent a plume of ash up into the air just as a man held his finish. Photojournalist Mario Tama drove to the club hoping to get great photos of the eruption when he was surprised to find players on the green. The Volcano Golf and Country Club course itself is located on the rim of the active volcano, 4,000 ft (1,219 m) above the Pacific Ocean. The cloud of ash was actually several miles away, and since the wind was blowing away from the course, there was no smell of sulfur.

FIRST GOLF BALL ON THE MOON FEB. 6, 1971

Rarity N° 20073
Lunar Golf Ball
Commemorative "Moonball" celebrating the first golf ball on the Moon hit by astronaut Allen Shepard on February 6, 1971.

Ripley's Rarities

HOLE IN FUN

In 1935, golf pro Alex Ednie demonstrated the power of a NEW RUBBER GOLF BALL by driving it straight through a 500-PAGE phone book.

The average golf ball has 336 DIMPLES.

Golf was BANNED by James II of Scotland in 1457 because it was distracting men from the important PRACTICE OF ARCHERY.

At the 2018 Augusta National, golfer JASON DAY sunk his shot into a SPECTATOR'S BEER!

A 2009 search for the LOCH NESS MONSTER discovered more than 100,000 GOLF BALLS but NO BEAST.

TWO ACES > Ben Tetzlaff, a 17-year-old student at Parkland High School in Allentown, Pennsylvania, recorded two holes-in-one during the same round of golf at Iron Lakes Country Club on September 18, 2017—beating odds of 67 million to one.

SCORED AGE > Golfer C. Arthur Thompson (1869–1975), of Victoria, British Columbia, Canada, scored his age while playing at the 6,215-yd (5,682-m) Uplands course in 1973—by completing the course in 103 shots at age 103.

GOLF SPRINT > Steve Jeffs completed a 500-yd (457-m), par-5 golf hole in just 1 minute 50.6 seconds at Tiverton Golf Club, Devon, England. Instead of riding in a cart, he sprinted between shots.

1,200-MILE HOLE >
Accompanied by his South African caddie, Ron Rutland, Northern Ireland golfer Adam Rolston played a 1,256-mi-long (2,011-km) hole in Mongolia, taking 80 days, 20,093 shots, and using 135 balls. Teeing off from the base camp of Khüiten Peak, the highest and most western point in Mongolia, he played in an easterly direction across the country's rough, mountainous terrain—through deserts, swamps, and frozen rivers—before finishing at the Mt. Bogd Golf Club in Ulaanbaatar. He had calculated that the hole would take 14,000 shots to complete, so his final score was 6,093 over par.

CADDIE CAGE

➲ Retrieving golf balls while a game is in play can be a dangerous job, which is why 1920s caddie Mozart Johnson is wearing this protective cage around his head and torso. Touted as "the latest safety device for golf courses," it was seen in use in California, but appears to have fallen by the wayside.

HEART ATTACK > In 2014, Danny Needham suffered a near-fatal heart attack at Norwood Park Golf Centre in Nottinghamshire, England. Four years later —almost to the day—he hit a hole-in-one on the same course.

BORDER COURSE > The Tornio Golf Club has seven holes in Finland and the other 11 in Sweden. The border between the two countries follows the Tornio River, which runs through the course. In the summer, visitors can play golf in full sunshine even at night.

FIRST ACE > Ben Bender, 93, aced the 152-yd (139-m) 3rd hole at Green Valley Golf Course in Zanesville, Ohio, to record his first hole-in-one in 65 years of playing golf.

DEFYING GRAVITY

➲ Polish pilot Luke Czepiela appeared to defy gravity in his Edge540T plane when he poured a can of Red Bull into a glass while doing a barrel roll! The seasoned flyer was 3,000 ft (914 m) above the earth but managed to get the liquid from can to glass without spilling a drop, even while upside down—but how? Like a bucket filled with water and spun in a circle from its handle, the centrifugal force Czepiela created when turning at high speeds forced the beverage to constantly change direction with him.

POURING A DRINK UPSIDE DOWN!

CONSISTENT TEAM > Mexico's national soccer team has been eliminated at the last 16 stage of the World Cup for seven tournaments straight.

DANCING BAN > For the first time in more than 65 years, it is legal to dance publicly in Fort Worth, Arkansas, on a Sunday. A 1953 ordinance, which later became known as the "Footloose" ordinance after the movie about a town that banned dancing and rock music, was finally repealed in 2018.

SHARK PAPERS > In 1799, an American privateer warship, the *Nancy*, was seized by a British warship, the *Sparrow*, in the Caribbean, a region forbidden to American ships at the time. Anticipating capture, the *Nancy*'s skipper, Thomas Briggs, threw the American papers overboard and replaced them with Dutch forgeries. Charged in Jamaica with smuggling contraband, Briggs looked set to walk free for lack of evidence until, toward the end of the trial, another British warship, HMS *Ferret*, arrived in port. The *Ferret* had caught a large shark off the coast of Haiti, and inside the shark's stomach were the incriminating American papers that Briggs had deposited in the ocean.

METAL FOIL > Gerrard McClafferty paid weekly visits to just six hairdressers in New South Wales, Australia, over a period of eight months to collect the thin scraps of aluminum foil that are used and then discarded in the hair dyeing process—and ended up with one ton of metal.

SCATTERED BILLS > On May 2, 2018, the rear doors of a Brinks armored truck suddenly swung open as the vehicle was traveling down Interstate 70 in Indianapolis, Indiana, scattering $600,000 in cash across the highway. Some drivers stopped their vehicles and hurriedly stuffed their pockets with 20-dollar bills.

SMALL WORLD > On June 1, 2018, New Jersey Trooper Michael Patterson stopped retired police officer Matthew Bailly for a minor motor vehicle violation in Kingwood Township—and discovered during the course of their conversation that, as a rookie cop in Piscataway, Bailly had delivered him as a baby 27 years earlier.

BUNGLING BURGLARS > Two burglars' attempts to break into a store in Shanghai, China, ended in frustration when one man hurled a brick at a window in a bid to smash it, only for the brick to rebound off the glass and hit his accomplice in the face, knocking him to the ground.

SMARTPHONE LANE > The Chinese city of Xi'an has created a special sidewalk lane designed for "phubbers"—people who walk while staring at their smartphones.

ICE FLOWER ➲

Flower ice (also known as *hair ice*) is a type of natural phenomenon that can occur when cold yet humid nights meet with a fungus known as *Exidiopsis effusa*. Ice is often formed on wood and on the ground, but without the activity of the fungus, it creates a harder, crust-like appearance. When the fungus interacts with the frost, however, it results in wispy strands of ice that sometimes look like hair or flowers. This is often mistaken for garbage—that is, until the individual is able to get up close and personal with the ice itself!

SCREWED ON RIGHT

⟳ Artist Andrew Myers creates arresting 3D portraits using between 8,000 and 10,000 individual screws drilled into plywood at varying heights and then individually painted to enhance the realistic look.

Born in Germany and raised in Spain, Myers doesn't rely on computer software while placing each screw. Instead, he eyeballs the placement of each one as he goes along, which makes his stunning portraiture all the more unbelievable.

MORE THAN 8,000 SCREWS!

Dirty CAKES

⮕ **Chef Ben Churchill from Hertfordshire, England, makes some of the world's most mind-boggling desserts: gross-looking confections that actually taste amazing.**

Churchill worked as a professional chef for several years before he became fascinated by pastries and desserts. At first, he wanted to make items that looked like fruits and veggies and contained their flavors—carrot cakes shaped like carrots and so on—yet he soon found a desire to produce even stranger "food illusions." Churchill began making desserts that looked absolutely disgusting: popsicles that looked like they'd been dropped on the ground, sponges with soap on them, and ashtrays filled with cigarettes. Every one of these confections, however, tastes heavenly. Churchill had so many comments on his social media about the food being inedible that he started posting videos of himself making the desserts to prove that you could, in fact, eat them.

ALL EDIBLE AND YUMMY!

GHOST TOWN > The town of Colma, California, outside of San Francisco, has more dead people than living people. With limited space to bury the dead in the Bay Area, most of San Francisco's dearly departed were buried in Colma, and now the dead outnumber the living 1,000 to 1.

PHANTOM WEDDING > In 2017, Amanda Teague, from Drogheda, Ireland, "married" the ghost of an 18th-century Haitian pirate named Jack who was executed for his crimes 300 years ago. She says they had been in a relationship for over six months before Jack proposed. The wedding took place in international waters on a boat with 12 of her friends and family members on board. Jack said "I do" through a medium and was physically represented at the ceremony by a skull and crossbones flag.

PASSENGER SCAN > A woman traveling by train from Dongguan, China, with a bag full of money was so worried that someone would steal her luggage that she climbed onto the station's X-ray security machine on all fours and went through the scanner with the bag.

HOMER LICENSE > A motorist stopped by police officers in Milton Keynes, England, presented a driver's license bearing a photo and signature of Homer Simpson. He was reported for driving without a proper license.

CAR TRADE > Twenty-three-year-old Florida resident Katie Samuels offered to trade her 2003 Honda Accord car for some Necco Wafers after learning that the colorful candies could be discontinued. She has been eating them since she was a child and offered the car in return for wholesaler Candystore.com's entire stock of the wafers.

TRASH CRUSH > When the dumpster in which he had been sleeping was lifted onto a garbage truck in Philadelphia, Pennsylvania, a man ended up buried beneath trash in the compactor section of the truck for more than two hours before he was eventually rescued by firefighters.

NEGATIVE IMAGE > Russian-born Londoner Adam Curlykale has tattooed his entire face gray and dyed his beard white so that he looks like a photographic negative version of himself. He has had more than 90 percent of his body inked—including his eyeballs—over the past 12 years.

WRONG CALL > Playing for German soccer club MSV Duisburg in February 2018, Dutch goalkeeper Mark Flekken conceded a goal because he chose the wrong time to have a drink. Thinking play had been halted, he leisurely turned around to take a gulp from a bottle that he kept in the back of his net, and while he wasn't looking, opponents Ingolstadt raced up the pitch to score.

AFGHAN TRUMP > Sayed Asadullah Pooya, a teacher from Kabul, Afghanistan, named his son Donald Trump because he thought it would bring him good fortune. He chose the name after reading a translation of Trump's 2004 book *How to Get Rich.*

LUCKY SNAIL ⟳ In Luton, England, a snail was found alive after it had been eaten and regurgitated by an owl. A man named John McEvoy discovered the snail, and after he noticed its shell had a strange look to it, decided to have it analyzed. The analysis concluded that the shell was covered in dried owl vomit, as the snail had been a meal for an owl but had managed to survive part of the digestive process.

STUDENT ANALYSIS > The No. 11 Middle School in Hangzhou, China, uses facial recognition technology to make sure students are paying attention in class. Three hi-tech cameras scan their faces every 30 seconds and feed the information to software that analyzes the students' expressions to determine whether they are enjoying lessons or if their minds are wandering. The software can pick up seven different emotions—neutral, happy, sad, disappointed, angry, surprised, and scared.

NEARLY BLINDED > Theresa Lynch, from Sydney, Australia, almost went blind because she did not remove her mascara for 25 years. Lynch ended up suffering from eye irritation and large black lumps under her eyelids.

TOOTH AND NAIL > Nail Sunny, a nail bar in Moscow, Russia, has created fingernails that look like teeth. The nails are painted white and shaped like teeth, complete with realistic-looking fillings!

STORK BILL > A Polish environmental group that was using a GPS transmitter to track the migratory movements of an adult stork received a $2,650 phone bill after the bird went missing in Sudan and someone began using the transmitter's SIM card in their own phone to make 20 hours' worth of calls.

INTERNATIONAL TAG > As part of their ongoing game of international tag, Georgina Wilkinson made an 8,000-mi (13,000-km) round trip from the United States to the United Kingdom just to tell her friend Drew McEwan "You're it!" She flew for eight hours from North Carolina to Loch Lomond, Scotland, where, disguised as a gardener, she surprised McEwan at his niece's christening. Wilkinson then ran off and flew back home on the same day. The pair and eight others have been playing the game since 2014.

➲ People in Masatepe, Nicaragua, have participated in a strange tradition for more than 130 years.

Every Good Friday, the citizens dress up in costumes and disturbing masks; some represent Roman soldiers while others represent Judas Iscariot. The Judases are chained, dragged, and symbolically beaten as they are marched through the town. Some citizens say they participate to thank God for all his blessings, while others do so simply to keep the tradition alive.

THE CHAINED

Although the procession looks aggressive, participants are dragged by chains but don't touch the ground, and they are only symbollically beaten.

ENTER
the Dragon

↪ **With a crouching tiger and a not-so-hidden dragon, the Dragon and Tiger Pagodas are colorful twin temples at Lotus Lake in Kaohsiung, Taiwan.**

Built in 1976, the seven-story towers feature yellow walls, red pillars, orange tiles, and of course, the giant, auspicious tiger and dragon. Inside there are paintings and murals of Buddhist and Taoist characters and stories. But visitors be warned: you must enter through the dragon's mouth and exit through the tiger's jaws—otherwise, it's believed to bring bad luck.

More than just one of the 12 Chinese zodiac signs, dragons symbolize power and strength, which is why Chinese emperors used the dragon as their own symbol and stitched it onto imperial robes.

ENTER

EXIT

Tigers are considered the king of all beasts (much like the lion is considered king of all animals in Western culture) and symbolize prowess, righteousness, and harmony.

SMASHING STUNT

⮕ A motorcyclist smashed through a wall of fluorescent light tubes at the Royal Calcutta Golf Club in Kolkata, India! The explosive stunt was part of a two-day show celebrating Vijay Diwas, or Victory Day. Military personnel go to extremes and perform tricks involving horses, helicopters, dogs, and of course, motorcycles for a crowd of hundreds.

SUBWAY SKIN > Fifteen percent of the air on the New York City subway contains human skin.

CREEPING CACTUS > The creeping devil cactus (*Stenocereus eruca*) is able to move across the Mexican desert at a rate of up to 2 ft (0.6 m) per year by killing part of itself. It survives by detaching itself from its major shoot and self-cloning. The cactus grows horizontally, parallel to the ground, and once the tip has rooted in the sandy soil, the old stem dies and rots to provide nutrients for the new stem to grow in its new location.

MAKESHIFT ISLAND > When a New Year's Eve alcohol ban was imposed for the Tairua estuary on New Zealand's North Island in an attempt to curb excess drinking, a group of friends found a loophole by building a makeshift island. They constructed it out of sand at low tide, making it just big enough to accommodate a picnic table, and because it was technically in international waters, they were excluded from the ban.

CAN TOWER > Built in 1933 by gas station owner Max Taubert, North Dakota landmark the Casselton Can Pile—a 45-ft-tall (13.7-m) tower made up of thousands of oil cans—stood for over 75 years.

SEWAGE BEER > The New Carnegie Brewery in Stockholm, Sweden, makes beer from recycled sewage water.

WEIRD FLAVORS > At his ice cream parlor in Kent, England, Nejmi Hassan makes both ketchup-flavored and pea-flavored ice creams.

$100 MILKSHAKE > Chef Joe Calderone of New York City restaurant Serendipity 3 has created a $100 milkshake. Served in a glass adorned with more than 3,000 Swarovski crystals, the LUXE milkshake's ingredients include Tahitian vanilla ice cream, Madagascan vanilla beans, 23-karat edible gold, Devonshire luxury clotted cream, donkey's milk, Venezuelan cocoa, and Luxardo Maraschino cherries from Italy.

CAR BURIED > In 2018, a brand-new car was lowered by crane into a concrete-lined hole and buried in the town square of Ojinaga, Mexico, where it will remain for half a century. The car is the first prize in a time capsule raffle, to be used by the winner's descendants in 2068.

BUS HOTEL > Airbnb offers accommodation on a double-decker bus in Dorset, England. The refurbished bus has three beds, a fully equipped kitchen, and room for six people.

STRANGE LAW > In Topeka, Kansas, it is illegal to sing the alphabet on the streets at night.

BORDER CROSSING > A fierce storm on January 4, 2018, blew a historic fishing-industry building from Maine to Canada. The blizzard tore the shed from its mooring at McCurdy's Smokehouse off Lubec, Maine, and caused it to drift to nearby Campobello Island in New Brunswick.

SOLAR TRAIN > A refurbished, 70-year-old train is the world's first solar-powered locomotive. It made its maiden voyage on a 1.8-mi (3-km) stretch of line in Byron Bay, New South Wales, Australia, in 2017. The two coaches have flexible, curved solar panels on their roofs to feed the train's onboard batteries.

OLD CEREAL > In 2018, Josiah and Anthea Carelse, from Lakewood, Colorado, unknowingly bought and ate a box of granola cereal that had an expiration date of 1997. The cereal was a decade older than the couple's daughter.

CONTRASTING STATES > The highest point in Pennsylvania is lower than the lowest point in Colorado. The top of Mount Davis, Pennsylvania, is 3,213 ft (980 m), while Colorado's lowest spot is the Arikaree River at 3,315 ft (1,011 m) above sea level.

PINK SAND > The beach on Budelli, a tiny Italian island in the Mediterranean Sea, has pink sand thanks to the presence of pieces of crushed coral, crystals, and the skeletons of dead shrimp.

LUXURY SUITE > A hotel suite overlooking Lake Geneva in Switzerland costs more than $70,000 a night. The 12-bedroom penthouse covers the entire eighth floor of the Hotel President Wilson, and its features include a Steinway grand piano, a private elevator, and perfumed wardrobes.

MONSTER PIZZA > Mallie's Sports Grill and Bar in Southgate, Michigan, has created a monster, 72-in (182.9-cm) pizza at a base price of $300 plus extra for toppings. In addition to being on the restaurant menu, the pizza is available for delivery, as it can just fit through a front door.

FLIPPING ROBOT > The CaliBurger restaurant in Pasadena, California, employs a robot, Flippy, to flip its burgers—and it can turn 300 patties an hour. Flippy requires a human helper to put the patties on the grill, but the robot then takes over the cooking duties and can also be programmed to wash spatulas and scrub the grill clean.

ARCTIC SOCCER

↺ Who says you need grass to play soccer, or even a field for that matter? The crew aboard patrol vessel KV *Svalbard* played a little game in the arctic ice offshore of Greenland in March 2018.

The players, made up of Norwegian Navy privates and scientists from the Norwegian Institute of Marine Research, had armed guards to protect them from potential polar bear attacks. In the town of Svalbard, Norway, which is also in the Greenland Sea, the population consists of 2,300 people and 3,000 polar bears. Worldwide, there are one to three instances of polar bear attacks a year.

HOLY SMOKE!

GO HAYWIRE

⟳ Drivers in Joypurhat, Bangladesh, often have their workers load as much hay as possible atop their trucks, since the more they haul, the more money they earn. This makes for a shocking sight as hayloads weighing as much as 22,046 lb (10,000 kg) are stacked precariously high. Overloading the trucks often leads to accidents, although some workers don't mind smoking a cigarette while sitting beside the fire hazard.

VANISHING CARS > On February 14, 2018, a 30-ft-wide (9-m) sinkhole swallowed up six cars on a street in Rome, Italy.

INTESTINAL HOTEL > Dutch artist Joep Van Lieshout built a hotel in the shape of a giant human intestine in a Belgian field. The CasAnus Hotel is sculpted with bulging veins and painted dark red to make it look realistic, while inside it contains a double bed, shower, and central heating so that guests can spend the night there.

BUG BURGERS > Swiss supermarket chain Coop sells burger patties made from ground-up mealworms instead of beef.

TRACTOR DAY > Fremont High School in Michigan has an annual Drive Your Tractor to School Day. Up to 50 students take part in the event—the younger ones on lawn tractors—and some journeys can take two hours from home to school.

COLD SPOT > The average January temperature in the Siberian village of Oymyakon is –58°F (–50°C), yet 500 people still live there. It was so cold in January 2018 that the village's new electronic thermometer broke after recording a bone-chilling –80°F (–62°C).

WATCHING FOR POLAR BEARS!

ROCKY RISK ⟳ Near the town of Bajina Bašta, Serbia, sits a tiny house precariously built on a rock in the middle of the Drina River. The shelter was built in the late 1960s by a group of young men and has managed to withstand the test of time, even surviving multiple floods and extreme winds.

TEA IN BLOOM

⊃ Flowering teas take an experience that's usually reserved for your taste buds and turn it into a feast for your eyes. While the history of flowering teas is unknown, they are thought to originate in Yunnan, China, and are made up of a variety of tea leaves and flowers stitched into a ball that gently blooms when placed in hot water.

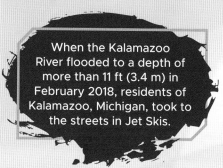

Flowering teas have a weaker taste than regular tea, as the blooms lose potency when they are baked to make them hold their shape.

REMOTE LODGE > The Ultima Thule Lodge in Alaska is 100 mi (160 km) from the nearest paved road. Guests arrive by helicopter or private plane.

OLD TICKET > John Walker, of Greensboro, North Carolina, was able to use an airplane ticket in 2018—even though it was 19 years old. He had bought the ticket to travel to his brother-in-law's wedding in December 1998 but never used it, and it was only when he found it under his bed nearly two decades later that he wondered whether it was still valid. Although the ticket was nonrefundable, United Airlines gave him its value in flight vouchers—worth around $378.

ROMANTIC BURGER > For Valentine's Day 2018, customers at Pauli's, a restaurant in Boston, Massachusetts, were able to order a burger that came with an engagement ring. The $3,000 Big Boy Burger had a diamond and gold ring nestled in the bun.

EXPENSIVE SHOT > On March 21, 2018, businesswoman Ranjeeta Dutt McGroarty spent $14,168 on a single shot of 1894 Rome de Bellegarde cognac—the world's oldest cognac—at the Hyde Kensington bar in London, England.

HISTORIC FRUITCAKE > Although the tin in which it had been kept for more than a century had badly rusted, a 106-year-old British fruitcake found in the Antarctic in 2017 was in excellent condition—and was considered almost edible. The cake was discovered in Antarctica's oldest building, a hut built in 1899, which was used in 1911 by explorer Captain Robert Falcon Scott before his ill-fated race to the South Pole. It is believed that Scott's team left the cake behind.

When the Kalamazoo River flooded to a depth of more than 11 ft (3.4 m) in February 2018, residents of Kalamazoo, Michigan, took to the streets in Jet Skis.

SLED HOTELS > Visitors to Kilpisjärvi, Finland, can stay in three small mobile hotels on sleds that are then towed around the Arctic region by snowmobile to find the best locations to see the spectacular Northern Lights. Each two-person cabin, which has a clear roof to provide an unobstructed view of the night sky, is 8 ft (2.4 m) wide and 15 ft (4.6 m) long and contains a bed, a gas heater, a small table, and an external dry toilet.

THEMED ROOMS > The Fantasyland Hotel in Edmonton, Alberta, Canada, has dozens of different-themed rooms, giving guests the experience of spending the night in an igloo, in outer space, in the wilds of Africa, or in the back of a pickup truck.

PRIZED CRICKETS > Cricket fighting has been a popular sport in China for 1,500 years, and crickets found in fields around Sidian, Shandong Province, are so prized for their large size and aggressiveness that they can sell for more than $1,500 each.

PRIVATE STREAM > A $2 million house in Miami, Florida, built in 1968 by American architect Alfred Browning Parker for himself, has a 90-ft-long (27-m) stream running through its three connecting buildings, allowing the owners to swim or float between rooms.

SHOP TREE > The trunk of a sacred neem tree grows right through a family sweet shop in Varanasi, India. Deepak Tadaw and his family used to sell sweets from a cart parked beneath the tree. Each day, as they worshipped the tree and left it offerings, business boomed. Since the Hindu tradition would strictly prohibit cutting down the tree (seen as the embodiment of Shitala, the goddess of disease), they built their shop around it.

EXCLUSIVE WINE > A bottle of exclusive AurumRed Gold wine costs a cool $30,000. It is produced by Hilario Garcia on a small vineyard in La Mancha, Spain, and is made from Tempranillo vines that are over 100 years old. Its creation incorporates ozone therapy, an alternative medicine treatment, and once uncorked, the wine retains its freshness and flavor for two years.

TOILET BREAK > On December 2, 2017, a Delta Air Lines flight from New York City to Seattle had to make an emergency stop in Billings, Montana, after the plane's toilets broke down, leaving several passengers in urgent need of a bathroom break.

UNDERGROUND FIRE > An underground fire in the Changshou district of Chongqing, China, has been burning for more than 60 years. Leftover fuel from an abandoned gas well keeps flames rising all year round from a 13 ft (4 m) square patch of land. Twice a day, villagers use the fire to boil water, a process that only takes about five minutes.

BURNING CATHEDRAL

➲ Russian artist Nikolay Polissky and 20 workers spent three months assembling hundreds of dry tree branches to form a massive Gothic cathedral—and then burned it down to celebrate Maslenitsa, a Slavic religious holiday.

The impressive structure was built in a park near Moscow and stood 100-ft-tall (30-m) before it was reduced to ash.

NET-Works

➲ A man was saved by a giant net hanging off the side of a cliff when his truck careened off a dangerously narrow expressway near the Yunnan province of China.

Sometimes called "death road," the Kumming-Mohan Expressway claimed many lives before the net was installed. So far, the ingenius device has saved at least five motorists. In the rescue pictured here, the truck driver was driving down the Yuxi section of the expressway and tried to make an emergency stop before careening down the runaway truck ramp. The cabin of his truck rolled off the side of the road, causing him to fall out and land safely in the net.

This 33-ft-long (10-m) log came from a 1,900-year-old tree felled in 1938 that once towered 267 ft (81 m) high.

Rarity № 17809
c.1938
Redwood House
A 4-room house hand-carved from a giant redwood log. Outside the St. Augustine, Florida, Odditorium.

Ripley's Rarities

TRUCK DRIVER THAT WAS SAVED →

TWO CELEBRATIONS > New Year's Day is celebrated twice in the country of Georgia—on January 1 and also on January 14, which is known as "Old New Year" according to the dates of the Julian calendar.

FLOORBOARD DIARY > When the new owners of the Château de Picomtal in Crots, France, decided to renovate the flooring, they discovered a hidden diary that was more than 135 years old written on the floorboards. The 72 entries were written in pencil by carpenter Joachim Martin and were dated over several months from 1880 to 1881.

BURGER FEAST > Following a six-course meal, guests at Andrew and Nancy Tadrosse's wedding in Terrey Hills, New South Wales, Australia, were treated to 400 cheeseburgers, collected from a nearby McDonald's.

FIREFLY SHOW > Nanacamilpa, a small town in Mexico, attracts over 100,000 visitors each year between June and August to watch the magical display of fireflies.

MONTHLY ALARM > Every first Monday of the month in the Netherlands, sirens sound across the country at midday for 1 minute 26 seconds as a practice alarm in case there is ever a major disaster.

HIGHEST POINT > The highest point in Latvia is Gaizinkalns hill at just 1,023 ft (312 m) above sea level, but in order to surpass Suur Munamägi, the highest point in neighboring Estonia at 1,043 ft (318 m), the Latvians built a tower on top.

MUD VOLCANOES > Azerbaijan has more than 400 mud volcanoes—nearly a third of the world's total number. When dormant, the volcanoes bubble with noxious gases, and when they erupt, they shoot flames up to 0.6 mi (1 km) into the air.

ZIPLINE COMMUTE > The only way that people can reach the mountain village of Lazimi in China's Yunnan Province is via a zipline across a raging river. As the Nu River is too dangerous to cross by boat and the nearest bridge is 12 mi (19 km) away, local people must use the zipline to get to work, go to shops, or attend church.

PRIZED MELONS > Two melons grown in the prized region of Yubari, Japan, sold for a combined price of nearly $30,000 at the Sapporo market in 2018.

GROWING UP

➲ An enormous banyan tree has been growing quietly through and alongside the wall of a residential building in Guangzhou, China, for the past 40 years. While the tree has been developing there unencumbered for decades, authorities are concerned about the issue, while tenants of the building say it doesn't cause any problems. The branches of the tree were recently pruned in order to ensure resident safety, but the tree itself has not been removed.

DESERT SKI RESORT

⮐ Snowboarders, skiers, and tourists alike can all enjoy the one and only ski resort in the mostly desert country of Lesotho, Africa. Afriski sits over 10,571 ft (3,222 km) above sea level in the Maluti Mountains and has a slope that's more than 0.5 mi (0.8 km) long! Because the area doesn't experience much snow that sticks to the ground, Afriski employees use manmade snow to keep the party going. From a distance, the slope looks like a long strip of winter wonderland in the otherwise barren desert.

HIDDEN EGG > Scott Stockman, a farmer from Queensland, Australia, found an unusually large hen's egg with a smaller egg inside. The large egg weighed more than 6 oz (170 g)—three times the weight of a regular chicken's egg.

TALKING BREAD > There are more than 3,200 different types of bread in Germany—and a talking loaf of bread named Bernd is a popular character with German children.

LONG STREET > Colfax Avenue in Denver, Colorado, is a continuous street that stretches for 26.8 mi (43 km)—longer than the distance of a marathon. It first appeared on Denver maps in 1868 as a dirt road.

BARBIE RACER > Edwin Olding, from Sandpoint, Idaho, modified a pink toy Barbie car so that it could reach a speed of 72 mph (115 kmph). He and his friends fitted the little car with the components from an old go-kart and the engine from a Honda dirt bike.

27-YEAR DIG > Starting when he was 15, Shyam Lal spent 27 years single-handedly digging a pond for his home village of Saja Pahad in India to solve a local water shortage. The pond, which is 15 ft (4.6 m) deep and covers one acre, now provides all of the villagers with enough rainwater to feed their cattle and irrigate their crops.

LITERALLY BANNED > In January 2018, the Continental Bar in Manhattan's East Village banned customers from using the word "literally." Bar owner Trigger Smith posted a sign warning that anyone heard saying the word would be given five minutes to finish their drink before being asked to leave.

A Category 3 hurricane releases more energy in just 10 minutes than all the world's nuclear weapons combined.

SELF-DRIVING SLIPPERS > The ProPilot Park Ryokan, a hotel in Hakone, Japan, has teamed up with car manufacturer Nissan to make self-driving slip-on shoes for its guests. Each slipper features two tiny wheels, a motor, and sensors to drive across the wooden floor of the hotel lobby. The slippers park themselves at the hotel entrance ready for arriving guests to slip them on, and when the guests have finished with them, the slippers drive themselves back to their original position.

QUICK FREEZE > Temperatures on Neptune can drop to −373°F (−225°C), meaning that a person exposed to its atmosphere would freeze solid in less than two seconds.

WISCONSIN WATERWAYS > If laid end to end, Wisconsin's 12,600+ rivers and streams would stretch for 84,000 mi (135,185 km)—more than three times the Earth's circumference.

PRISON LIFE > A former prison in Karosta, Latvia, is now a hotel where guests can opt for the "full prisoner experience." This includes spartan, cell-like rooms with iron bars, uniformed officers, verbal abuse, organized physical exercise, and the same meals that the inmates used to eat.

ACTIVE GEYSERS > There are more than 300 active geysers in Yellowstone National Park—that's about half of the total number of geysers in the entire world.

TECHNICOLOR TEMPLE

⮕ The Meenakshi Amman Temple in Madurai, India, has 14 towers up to 170 ft (52 m) tall, whose walls are covered with around 33,000 colorful sculptures depicting animals, gods, and demons.

To keep the temple in peak condition for the more than 15,000 people who visit each day, the sculptures need to be repainted and repaired every 12 years.

CLOWN CHURCH

➲ **Inside an unassuming church in London is a museum dedicated to clowns!**

Since December 1959, Holy Trinity Church, Dalston, has also been known as the Clown's Church due to the three small rooms inside known as the Clowns' Gallery and Museum. It was previously exhibited at St. James's Church in Islington, which is the burial place of famous clown Joseph Grimaldi, for whom there is a memorial service every February. The service has become so popular that it was moved to the larger All Saints Church in Haggerston.

Ceramic eggs painted with individual clowns' make-up serve as informal copyrights for their designs.

Dozens of clowns attend the Grimaldi Memorial Service every February.

EMMETT KELLY

ALBERT FRATELLINI

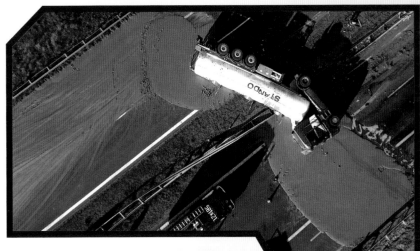

CHOCO TRIP

⊃ In May 2018, a truck carrying around 12 tons of liquid chocolate overturned on a Polish highway, covering six lanes of traffic! Thankfully, no one was gravely injured, but the cleanup proved incredibly difficult as the chocolate began to harden in the cool air.

WINE FREEZE > In January 1205, it was so cold in England that wine and ale froze and were sold by weight rather than volume.

MULLET CONTEST > After its largest business closed in 2012, the town of Kurri Kurri in New South Wales, Australia, used tourism to boost the local economy by staging Mulletfest, an international contest to find the best mullet hairstyle.

SKIN BOOK > Among the exhibits at the History of Surgery Museum in Edinburgh, Scotland, is a book bound with the skin of William Burke, who had been hanged and dissected in 1829 after being convicted of murder and grave robbing with his partner in crime, William Hare.

EYE-POPPING DRINK > Faros Tapas, a restaurant at the Museum of Old and New Art in Hobart, Tasmania, Australia, serves black margaritas garnished with the frozen eyeball of a feral pig. Customers are advised to drink the margarita as quickly as they can to prevent the eye from melting into it.

MEDICAL CITY > One out of every six doctors in the United States receives medical training in Philadelphia.

GOLDEN WINGS > New York City restaurant The Ainsworth serves gold-plated chicken wings. The deep-fried wings are tossed into a metallic gold sauce and then sprinkled with edible gold dust.

BLUE SOUP > Kipposhi, a restaurant in Tokyo, Japan, serves bright blue soup. The clear chicken and noodle soup is made with blue ramen and has no food coloring or artificial additives. Although chef Mr. Koizumi keeps the recipe a secret, it is believed that his blue ramen gets its distinctive color from phycocyanin, a natural pigment derived from *Spirulina* algae.

DONKEY LAW > In the French village of Saint-Léger-des-Prés, it is illegal to slander donkeys by using terms such as "jackass" or "dumb ass." Anybody breaking the law is required to offer their apologies to all local donkeys in the form of carrots or sugar lumps. The law was introduced in 1991 by the mayor, who was very fond of donkeys.

SHORT RACE > The Boerne 0.5K run—a charity road race for "underachievers"—was staged at Boerne, Texas, on May 5, 2018. The course was only 0.3 mi (499 m) long, and for an entry fee of $25, participants received free beer at the start and finish. Those not wishing to expend any energy at all could pay an extra $25 to have an old bus transport them the length of the course.

FOOT KISSING > On St. Spyridon's Day (December 12) on the Greek island of Corfu, thousands of pilgrims pay homage to the island's patron saint by kissing the slippered feet of his 1,650-year-old mummified body.

ABANDONED ITEMS > Among items found on New Jersey beaches in 2017 were a lawn mower, a bird cage, two fire extinguishers, a plastic statue of the Hindu god Vishnu, and a box containing a human tooth.

WINE DRINKERS > Vatican City, in Rome, Italy, has the highest consumption of wine per head of any country in the world, with each resident drinking an average of 74 liters of wine (equivalent to 105 bottles) per year.

Rarity № 173601

Ripley's Rarities

African Wooden Headrest

Used like a pillow in parts of Africa. This example is decorated with cowry shells and silver beads.

EQUATORIAL BULGE > Because the Earth bulges at the equator, measurements taken from the center of the planet rather than from sea level show that the 20,561-ft-high (6,268-m) Chimborazo Volcano in Ecuador—and not the 29,029-ft-high (8,848-m) Mount Everest—is the point on Earth that is closest to the Sun.

NATURAL DIVERS

⊃ The Bajau people of the Philippines are natural divers and can hold their breath underwater for as long as 13 minutes while diving as deep as 200 ft (60 m)—70 ft (21.3 m) deeper than the standard depth limit for recreational divers!

The seafaring Bajau live on houseboats, venturing onto land only occasionally, and research has found that their spleens are up to 50 percent larger than those of the Saluan people who live on the mainland in Indonesia. The spleen contracts when you dive underwater, which helps conserve energy when the body cannot obtain more oxygen. Because the Bajau spend more than half their day underwater—fishing, collecting shellfish from the ocean floor, and diving for other useful items—they signal a mutation that has built up over many years, giving them their aquatic advantage.

FEELIN' HOT HOT POT

⟶ At a hot spring hotel in Hangzhou, China, tourists are able to both enjoy hot pot and be a hot pot. While soaking in a warm spring filled with vegetables, people can partake of delicious meals of bubbling broth where they are able to cook their choice of ingredients—while also cooking themselves.

ROAD DIGGER > Despite being barely able to walk or move his right hand following an accident, 63-year-old Melethuveetil Sasi worked alone for three years to carve a 660-ft-long (200-m) dirt road through a hill in front of his home in Kerala, India. Using only basic tools such as shovels and pickaxes, he worked an average of six hours a day digging the road so that he could ride along it on a scooter to the nearest town and find a job to support his family.

MOVING DAY > For more than 100 years and even right up until World War II, almost everyone who moved out of their apartments in New York City did so on May 1, or, as it became known, "Moving Day." On February 1 each year, landlords informed their tenants what their new rent would be after the end of the quarter, and, three months later on May 1, the leases expired at 9 a.m., causing as many as 1 million people to change residence simultaneously.

WAR TREATY > New Hampshire is the only U.S. state where a foreign war has been formally ended. The Treaty of Portsmouth, signed in 1905, marked the conclusion of the Russo-Japanese War. President Theodore Roosevelt moderated the talks and won the Nobel Peace Prize for his efforts.

BOOMBOX BUILDING ⟶ A building in Shenyang, China, received a fancy facelift in the form of a giant boombox. Included are faux knobs, speakers, and even what appears to be a cassette player—but good luck finding a tape large enough to play!

The Roaring 20s

○ Every year on the second Monday in January, thousands of young adults converge in city centers to take part in Seijin-no-Hi, otherwise known as **Coming of Age Day.**

The holiday, which itself is hundreds of years old, celebrates all the teenagers that turned 20 during the previous year, welcoming them into adult society. Nearly all the young women wear elaborate, colorful silk kimonos, which are so expensive to own that most rent the fine clothing just for the occasion. The young men wear Western-style suits or men's kimonos with hakama (i.e., traditional Japanese pants that resemble a wide skirt). Did we mention the flamboyant hairstyles and make-up?

A *furisode* is a long-sleeved kimono for unmarried young women.

Slippery SLOPE

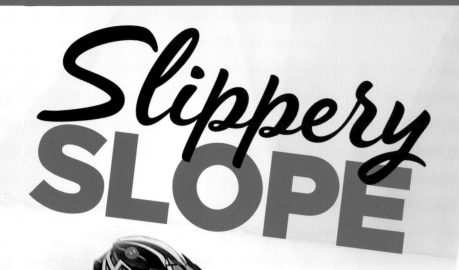

➲ For more than 40 years, participants and spectators have turned out for a wooden sled race called Hornschlittenrennen in Garmisch-Partenkirchen, Germany—the biggest traditional sled speed race of its kind.

The first week of January sees more than 360 daredevils race down a slope nearly 4,000 ft (1,219 m) in length while a few thousand people cheer them on. The teams of four reach speeds of up to 62 mph (100 kmph), and their daring maneuvers and speed often cause accidents. The sleds are 6.5 to 9.8 ft (2 to 3 m) long, and some are more than 60 years old.

CREEPY BURGER > For one day only on Halloween, Australian fast food chain Huxtaburger offered a creepy Bugstaburger at its Melbourne restaurant—a burger featuring roasted mealworms, ant mayonnaise, and served on a blue bun.

REMOTE LOCATION > Point Nemo in the South Pacific Ocean is located so far from land that the nearest humans are often astronauts. The International Space Station orbits Earth at a maximum altitude of 258 mi (413 km), while the nearest inhabited landmass to Point Nemo is more than 9,942 mi (16,000 km) from the nearest land.

DEEP CAVE > A 4,000-year-old underwater cave on Mexico's Yucatán Pensinula is 216 mi (346 km) long—greater than the distance from New York City to Washington, D.C.

TREE DATING > The Bridegroom's Oak, a 500-year-old tree near Eutin, Germany, has its own postal address and receives about two to three letters a day. It acts chiefly as a woodland dating service, as most of the letters are sent by love seekers from around the world, in the hope that a stranger will read their letter and reply.

BARKING TRAINS > Japanese researchers have developed new technology that can make trains bark like dogs and snort like deer in the hope of scaring the animals away from railroad tracks.

THEFT DETERRENT > The Beer Wall, a bar in Bruges, Belgium, has installed alarm sensors on all of its beer glasses to stop customers stealing them. Each of the 1,600 different beers sold at the bar is served in its own specially designed glass.

SURPRISE CATCH > During floods in Australia's Northern Territory in January 2018, Damien Monck caught a fish on what is normally dry land. He cast his line from a waterlogged road near Batchelor, south of Darwin, and landed a barramundi in a flooded park.

TWISTY TREES

↪ Along with all the square watermelons and baby-shaped pears, China has gone one step further, molding full-sized trees to look like a twisty braid. They also resemble a popular street food, called *mahua*, which consists of a fried dough twist.

EXPENSIVE YACHT > Mike Ludgrove, from Devon, England, spent 12 years hand-crafting a 60-ft (18-m) yacht, *Helena*, out of antique wood. The hull is made of Canadian Douglas fir, and the decking is teak salvaged from a 160-year-old Indian cotton mill, which was due to be demolished. The project cost him $1.8 million—almost three times more than he anticipated—and he had to sell two homes and his health food business to pay for it.

SMALL HOTEL > Guests pay Mohammed Al-Malahim $55 a night to stay in his hotel—a stripped out VW Beetle. The car, which forms the smallest hotel in the world, sits on piles of stones but overlooks beautiful scenery in the desert village of Al Jaya, Jordan. No more than two people can stay in the hotel at a time, and Al-Malahim prepares breakfast for his guests in a nearby cave, which also serves as his hotel's lobby.

SOLO FLYER > On October 22, 2017, author Karon Grieve, from Ayrshire, Scotland, was the only passenger on a 189-seater airplane from Glasgow to the Greek island of Crete. The only other two people who were booked on the Jet2 flight failed to turn up.

SLIDING AT SPEEDS UP TO 62 MPH (100 KMPH)!

OUCH!

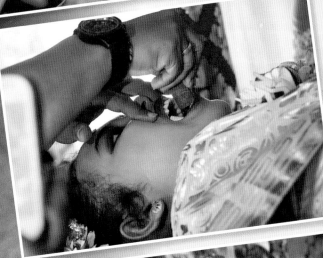

The files used in the ceremony are cleaned in between filings with the same toothbrush.

Tooth-Filing CEREMONY

➲ Every July in Balinese culture, teenagers have their teeth filed by a high priest in a complex coming-of-age ceremony that is more than 2,000 years old.

Entire villages gather for the special occasion, which marks the transition from childhood to adulthood, and both the boys and the girls are adorned with intricate, colorful costumes and headdresses. Only close friends and family are allowed at the ceremony, because at certain stages it is believed that the teen is vulnerable to the forces and influence of evil. The sharp canines and incisors are thought to represent the savage, uncivilized aspects of the soul and so are filed down—without anesthetic—to the same level as the surrounding teeth. It is said that if a Balinese person does not file down their teeth, they might be denied entry into heaven because they are considered an animal.

THE TOOTH-FILING CUSTOM PREDATES THE ARRIVAL OF HINDUISM IN INDONESIA IN 5 BC.

GILDED BATHROOM > A humble gas station in Quezon, the Philippines, has a restroom that is decorated to look like a medieval throne room. It features gilded wall and ceiling decorations, a chandelier, a gilded mirror, and an ornate wooden throne frame around the toilet bowl.

LONELY TREE > A Sitka spruce that is more than 100 years old is the only tree on Campbell Island, New Zealand, and is 139 mi (222 km) away from its nearest fellow tree, on the Auckland Islands.

CHICKEN BEER > The Veil Brewing Company of Virginia teamed up with New York–based Evil Twin Brewing to produce a beer made with fried chicken.

PIPE HOMES > Architect James Law designs space-saving homes in Hong Kong from concrete pipes. Each pipe weighs about 22 tons, is 8 ft (2.4 m) in diameter, and offers 1,000 sq ft (93 sq m) of living accommodation—enough room to fit two people.

VITAL RAINFORESTS > Even though rain forests occupy less than 0.3 percent of the total land area of Australia, they hold half of the country's total plant species and a third of its birds and mammals.

DWARF VOLCANO > Monte Busca in Emilia-Romagna, Italy, is nothing more than a small pile of rocks just 4 ft (1.2 m) high on a hill, but it was once thought to be a volcano. It has no crater and does not expel lava but has a constant flame because it acts as a natural vent for hydrocarbon gases below the surface, which burn when they come into contact with oxygen in the air.

LIGHTS UP MY HEART!

SCENE OF HEARTS

⮑ Two hours away from Tokyo sits a piece of rare natural beauty that is wild at heart. Just twice a year, near the spring and autumn equinoxes, light floods through Kameiwa Cave in Chiba prefecture, Japan, reflecting off the serene water to create the image of a heart.

PICKING UP STEAM

⮑ On May 27, 2018, chefs at a steamed dish competition in Tianmen, Hubei Province, China, steamed more than 1,000 dishes in a giant wooden food steamer. The steamer itself measured 9 ft (2.7 m) in diameter and 5.2 ft (1.6 m) high.

SNAKES ON A STICK

⟳ Feeling adventurous? Many people who visit Cambodia are either repulsed or excited by the idea of eating some of the most interesting market foods in the world, including insects, snails, and grilled snakes on a stick. The need to eat whatever one could find crawling or slithering on the ground was something many Cambodians faced during the brutal Khmer Rouge regime in the 1970s, but now these kinds of meals have become a part of their culture, as well as a way to attract tourists.

CRIME FREE > Crime in the village of Eibenthal, Romania, is virtually nonexistent. People there are so trusting that they leave money unattended in bags on the streets to pay the bread delivery man, and in more than 20 years not one has ever been stolen.

SECOND WIDEST > With a distance of 1,523 mi (2,451 km) from east to west (Kure Atoll to Big Island), Hawaii is the second widest state in the United States, behind Alaska.

UNDERGROUND HOMES > Three thousand people in Sanmenxia in China's Henan Province live in underground homes called *yaodongs*. The rectangular dwellings, many of which are equipped with running water and electricity, are sunk into the ground to a depth of about 23 ft (7 m), ensuring that they remain cool in summer and warm in winter. The site dates back to the Bronze Age, when people in the region lived in deep pits.

TREE TREATMENT > An 800-year-old banyan tree in Mahabubnagar, India, was treated against a termite infestation using an intravenous drip. Scientists hooked hundreds of bottles with a diluted pesticide to the tree and injected the liquid into the bark like a hospital saline drip.

WET DAY > On July 27 each year, homes across Finland mark National Sleepy Head Day, when the last person in the house to get out of bed in the morning is traditionally thrown into a lake, a river, or the sea. In the city of Naantali, a Finnish celebrity is chosen to be thrown into the sea at 7 a.m.

FIRM FOUNDATIONS > When Great Falls High School was built in Montana in 1896, a herd of sheep was driven 100 times around the foundation's backfill in order to compact the soil.

MULTIPLE NAMES > The city of Leeuwarden in the Netherlands has been known by 225 different variations of its name since the 10th century, including Ljouwert, Liwadden, Leewadden, Luwt, Leaward, and Leoardia. It is popularly known as the "City of 100 Names."

ROTATING HOUSE > Ethan Schlussler, from Sandpoint, Idaho, has built a two-story tree house that rotates 360 degrees. The house is fixed to a western larch tree by a custom steel bracket and rotates with the help of a system of chains and an old car steering wheel.

PORK DESSERT > In 2018, Windy Brow Farms, of Fredon Township, New Jersey, launched a pork roll–flavored ice cream. The speciality dessert mixes in French toast with pieces of pork roll.

ANCIENT PINE > A Heldreich's pine tree in Italy's Pollino National Park is at least 1,230 years old and is still growing.

POO PAPER ⟳ Looking for a last-minute gift for the wild animal lover in your life? Now you can actually purchase tissue paper made from the feces of real giant pandas! The panda poo—along with food waste consisting mainly of discarded bamboo bits—is supplied to a Chinese paper company by the China Conservation and Research Centre for the Giant Panda.

These huge disks representing money were used on the set of the 1954 movie *His Majesty O'Keefe*, filmed on location on Deuba Beach, Yap.

STONE
CURRENCY

➲ **Although the national currency of Yap in Micronesia is the U.S. dollar, islanders sometimes use giant limestone discs, which can weigh more than a car!**

There are about 13,000 rai stone discs in circulation on Yap, ranging from 12 in (30 cm) to 11 ft (3.5 m) in diameter. Since the stones are usually too large to move, buying an item with one simply involves verbally agreeing that ownership has changed.

SUBMERGED TOWN > For most of the year, the abandoned town of Mansilla de la Sierra in northern Spain lies underwater buried beneath a reservoir, but toward the end of summer, the water level often drops sufficiently for explorers to be able to walk around the old streets. The town's 600 residents moved out in 1959 before the area was flooded to create a larger reservoir.

NAKED DINING > At O'Naturel, a restaurant in Paris, France, customers leave their clothes in a cloakroom and dine naked.

SURPLUS ZUCCHINI > August 8 each year is National Sneak Some Zucchini onto Your Neighbor's Porch Day. The holiday is the brainchild of Pennsylvanians Tom and Ruth Roy who, looking for helpful ways to dispose of surplus zucchini at that time of year, suggested quietly delivering any unwanted, freshly picked squash to a neighbor in the dead of night.

FORT BLUNDER > An abandoned fort on Lake Champlain is popularly known as Fort Blunder because when it was built in 1816, it was accidentally located half a mile (0.8 km) north of the Canadian border instead of in New York State.

HOUSE MOVE > Gao Yiping, a farmer from Jiangxi Province, China, moved his entire three-story house a distance of 130 ft (40 m) to avoid it being demolished to make way for the construction of a new road. The moving process took six weeks and was carried out using a system of strong ropes and winches and 1,000 wooden support beams.

FASTEST WAITER > Nearly 500 waiters take part in an annual race in Buenos Aires to find Argentina's fastest waiter. They must carry trays loaded with bottles and drink glasses over a distance of 5,250 ft (1,600 m)—15 blocks—without spilling any.

ROOFTOP TRUFFLE > In 2017, a 25-gram (0.88 oz) winter truffle was found growing in the roof garden of a hotel near the Eiffel Tower in Paris—the first wild truffle ever found in the French capital. Truffles are usually found in southern Europe and are so rare that prized specimens sell for thousands of dollars per kilo.

DIVIDED VILLAGE > Known as "Little Berlin," the German village of Mödlareuth, which straddles the border between Bavaria and Thuringia, is still divided between west and east almost 30 years after the country's reunification. There are just 15 households, but the two halves have different mayors, dialects, dialing codes, and schools.

NINE-HOUR RAINBOW > A rainbow in Taipei, Taiwan, on November 30, 2017, lasted around nine hours from 6:57 a.m. to 3:55 p.m. Most rainbows last for less than one hour.

PIG POPULATION > Pigs outnumber people in Denmark by more than two to one. There are 215 pigs to every 100 human residents.

MOUNTAIN POOP > Between 1951 and 2012, 36,000 climbers on Alaska's Denali deposited up to 215,000 lb (97,610 kg) of poop onto the Kahiltna Glacier.

LANDFILL PAYMENT > The Methane Gas Canteen, a restaurant in Semarang, Indonesia, is located at a landfill and allows customers to pay for their food with recyclable plastic garbage.

PRINTED BRIDGE > A 3D-printed concrete bridge spanning 26 ft (8 m) over a waterlogged ditch in Gemert, Netherlands, is so strong that it can take the weight of 40 trucks. The bridge, which was created by scientists at Eindhoven University of Technology, has 800 printed layers.

TIME CHANGE > It takes brothers Roman and Maz Piekarski more than 14 hours to change the time twice a year for British Summer Time on their 700 cuckoo clocks at their Cuckooland museum in Cheshire, England.

THRILLING RIDE > A zip line that opened in Ras Al-Khaimah, United Arab Emirates, in 2018 stretches for 1.76 mi (2.8 km). Riders on the Jebel Jais Flight set off from a launch pad on the country's highest mountain peak 5,512 ft (1,680 m) above sea level and sweep down past rocky terrain at speeds of up to 94 mph (150 kmph).

DESERT REFUGE > A community of about 20 households in the quiet desert town of Snowflake, Arizona, acts as a refuge for people who are allergic to modern life. Many suffer from multiple chemical sensitivity (MCS), a chronic disorder in which they struggle with exposure to everyday chemicals and technologies, such as fragrances, synthetic fabrics, pesticides, and Wi-Fi. To combat this, some of the houses in Snowflake have been built with aluminum foil–lined walls.

HOLLOW WHEEL

The Bohai Eye of Weifang, China, is the world's largest spokeless Ferris wheel! The impressive feat of engineering is 475 ft (145 m) tall and holds 36 carts, each of which can hold a maximum of 10 passengers. Incredibly enough, the wheel is built as part of a bridge and offers views of the city and Bailang River.

MOROS
vs
CRISTIANOS

Loud and bright parades, battle reenactments, music, and costumes dominate the Moros y Cristianos festivals held throughout the Valencia and Alicante regions of Spain.

The festivals usually last several days and recreate the unlikely victory of a Christian army over the Moors during the Middle Ages. The first day sees both armies arrive in spectacular fashion early in the morning, with sometimes thousands of people lining up to watch. The celebrations end with a bang, as intense battle reenactments, including swords, gunpowder, muskets, and fireworks, rage on!

WATER FIGHT > Toby Evans, owner of the 3Sheets waterfront restaurant in Perth, Western Australia, placed a free water gun on every outdoor table so that customers could fend off annoying seagulls.

GLASS BEACH > A beach in Omura City, Japan, is made of recycled colored glass. The area used to be covered in foul-smelling algae, so the authorities decided to cover the beach with pulverized glass to prevent the algae from growing.

CORKSCREW MUSEUM > Le Musée du Tire-Bouchon in Ménerbes, France, is home to more than 1,200 wine bottle corkscrews, some dating back to the 17th century, and includes corkscrews that have been incorporated into a walking stick, a ring, and even a revolver.

PHONE BOOK > The first telephone book was issued on February 21, 1878, in New Haven, Connecticut, and featured only 50 names.

POOP LIGHT > A street lamp in Worcestershire, England, is powered by dog poop deposited by pet owners. Dog walkers drop the waste in an anaerobic digestor attached to the lamp, where it is broken down by microorganisms to produce methane for the light. Ten bags of poop can power the light for two hours.

SPREAD OUT > Montana is the only U.S. state with rivers that drain into the Gulf of Mexico, Hudson Bay, and the Pacific Ocean.

What a Relief

⊃ On the grounds of the Barony Castle Hotel in the Scottish Borders lies the Great Polish Map of Scotland, which is exactly what it sounds like.

Former Polish soldier Jan Tomasik designed and built (along with a small group of Poles) a detailed, 3D relief map of Scotland to scale in the 1970s—the largest terrain relief model in the world. The concrete map took Tomasik five years to build and measures more than 160 × 130 ft (50 × 40 m).

BIKE GRAVEYARD

⮌ All over China, millions (that's right, *millions*) of abandoned bicycles are being collected in humongous piles, referred to as bicycle graveyards. These broken or deserted bikes are mostly the result of bikeshare companies going bankrupt and leaving their product behind. While the companies have disappeared, the local governments are having a hard time deciding what to do with the leftover bikes, which are currently being stripped for parts, crushed down into cubes, or in many cases, simply discarded in large heaps.

DECEPTIVELY MILD > Despite its name, temperatures in Iceland on average do not drop as low as New York City's in winter.

FRIENDLY FIRE > A South African plant, *Leucospermum cordifolium*, relies on the smoke from wildfires to germinate its seed and in turn produce new plants.

CONFUSING HATS > Panama hats originally came from Ecuador. When President Theodore Roosevelt visited the construction of the Panama Canal in 1904, he admired the hats worn by the workers. He called them *Panama hats*, making them famous apparently without knowing that both the workers and their hats hailed from Ecuador.

CAVE CHAMBER > Gaping Gill in North Yorkshire, England, has an underground cave chamber that is 476 ft (145 m) long, 82 ft (25 m) wide, and 115 ft (35 m) tall, making it large enough to fit a cathedral inside.

BEERY BEARDS > It is estimated that 24,568 gal (93,000 l) of beer—equal to 195,419 pints—are lost in facial hair each year in the United Kingdom alone.

SPARSELY POPULATED > Pittsburg, New Hampshire, is the largest town by area in New England, covering about 300 sq mi (777 sq km), but it has a population of under 1,000.

FREE TACOS > In 2018, Houston, Texas, real estate agent Nicole Lopez began offering $250 in free tacos with the purchase of properties.

WOMEN ONLY > Only women live on SuperShe Island off the coast of Finland. Men are not allowed on the 8.4-acre (34,000 sq m) island resort, which is the brainchild of American entrepreneur Kristina Roth.

TERRIFYING TREE > Australia's gympie gympie tree (*Dendrocnide moroides*) contains a toxin so powerful that simply brushing against it can leave victims with burning sensations for as long as two years. The whole plant is covered in stinging hairs, the pain from which has been compared to being sprayed with hot acid and has even driven some people to suicide, including one man who mistakenly used the tree's leaf as toilet paper.

ROBOT BARISTA > A robot barista named Sawyer greets customers and makes and serves coffee at the Henn-na Café in Tokyo, Japan.

MYSTERY LADDER ⮌ An old, wooden ladder has rested under a window on the outside of the Church of Holy Sepulchre in Jerusalem for more than 200 years. No one knows why—none of the six churches that govern the site can agree on who owns it—and people refuse to move it. The "Immovable Ladder," as it is known, has only been moved twice in more than two centuries.

BEAR PARADE

➲ **Every December, groups of Romani people parade around dressed in bearskins to ward off evil spirits.**

In the town of Comănești, Romania, villagers keep a long tradition alive of wearing bearskins and marching through streets before every new year. This parade is also known as Ursul and began with the Geto-Dacian tribe, which believed bears to be sacred animals with the ability to heal and protect humans. The tradition is also based on when Romanies used to lead bears on leashes for the entertainment of European crowds. The parades exist all over Romania, and after marching through the streets, the bears all pretend to die and then spring back to life, which symbolizes the transition from winter to spring.

It is customary in Chinese culture for each child to be assigned an animal at birth that the family believes represents their personality.

FISH TREAT > The McDonald's Filet-O-Fish sandwich was created in 1962 by Lou Groen, a McDonald's franchise owner in Cincinnati, Ohio, to sell to Roman Catholics who could not eat red meat on Fridays.

SKINNY PANTS > The Museum of Icelandic Sorcery and Witchcraft in Hólmavik, Iceland, houses a replica of 17th-century Nábrók, or necropants. Made from human skin, necropants were sliced whole from the deceased by sorcerers to bring wealth.

ENDLESS SUNSET > Venus rotates so slowly that if you were to walk across its surface while watching the sunset, it would never end.

REPLICA VILLAGE > In Paju, South Korea, a few miles from the border with North Korea, is a reproduction of a typically English village, complete with red mail boxes, a pub serving fish and chips, and even a replica of Stonehenge.

NO VOLCANOES > Australia is the only continent without an active volcano. The most recent volcanic activity there was the eruption of Mt. Gambier in South Australia, more than 4,500 years ago.

ALCOHOLIC CLOUD > A gas cloud 10,000 light years away in the constellation Aquila holds enough alcohol to make 400 trillion trillion pints of beer.

Rarity № 169973

Chinese Cat Shoes
Children's slippers made into cat-like faces with white whiskers, white and red eyes, green ears, and a question mark-like tail.

Ripley's Rarities

SINGING ROAD > A highway in the Dutch village of Jelsum played the local Friesland regional anthem when cars drove along it at the correct speed of 38 mph (60 kmph), thanks to a series of rumble strips embedded in the road. However, villagers complained that speeding cars at night resulted in the anthem being played too fast and that the cacophony was keeping them awake.

PALACE LIFE > There are 40,000 light bulbs, 1,514 doors, 775 rooms (including 78 bathrooms), and more than 300 clocks in Buckingham Palace, the official London residence of the British royal family. The palace also has its own post office, police station, doctor's office, swimming pool, and movie theater.

PLANTED DOLLS > Neville Daytona, from Wiltshire, England, bought several dolls in a charity shop and planted them in large road potholes to show the local council how deep the holes were. The dolls not only drew attention to the poor state of the highway, but also warned his fellow motorists about which parts of the road to avoid.

MULE MAIL > The only place in the United States where mail is delivered by mule is the village of Supai, Arizona, located at the bottom of the Grand Canyon. The village, which has more than 600 inhabitants, is 8 mi (13 km) from the nearest road, and is only accessible by hiking, helicopter, or riding an animal.

CHECKMATE

➲ A king at the World Chess Hall of Fame in St. Louis, Missouri, stands 20 ft (6 m) tall, has a base of 9.1 ft (2.8 m), and weighs 10,860 lb (4,930 kg)—more than five tons. The giant chess piece, which was unveiled in April 2018, was hand-carved from mahogany wood.

⊃ Opening in June 2018, the Golden Bridge on Ba Na hill near Da Nang, Vietnam, features two giant hand structures seemingly holding up the walkway.

The uniquely designed bridge has attracted tons of tourists, who enjoy taking selfies on the gold-painted pedestrian pathway, walking among the purple flowers lining the path, and taking in the breathtaking views of the surrounding countryside. According to Reuters, the bridge's design is meant to represent the "giant hands of gods, pulling a strip of gold out of the land." Believe it or not, the hands are not carved stone but actually made of fiberglass over sculpted steel mesh.

HOOF IT!

⊃ In May 2018, the traditional sport of oxen racing got some fresh competition within spitting distance—camels joined the race!

The German town of Taufkirchen in Bavaria held the race in celebration of a fraternity's 125th anniversary, but when they couldn't find enough race-ready male oxen to compete, they brought in the humps. Eight oxen and four camels participated in the 100-meter (328-ft) race—a first in Bavarian history.

The oxen don't always cooperate with their riders, sometimes choosing instead to get pets from spectators on the sidelines.

GIANT AVOCADO > Pamela Wang found a 5.23-lb (2.4-kg) avocado under a tree in Kailua-Kona, Hawaii—the fruit was as big as her head.

WHISKEY POWER > A car driven around the campus grounds at Edinburgh Napier University, Scotland, was fueled solely by whiskey residue biofuel.

SNOWBALL FIGHT > A mass snowball fight involving 9,000 people, which was scheduled to take place at the Six Flags Great Adventure theme park in Ocean County, New Jersey, on December 16, 2017, was canceled because of too much snow.

STURDY APPLE > Canadian company Okanagan Specialty Fruits spent 20 years creating the Arctic Apple, a genetically engineered apple that does not turn brown after being cut or bruised.

SNOW LOAD > On February 3, 2018, Swiss police stopped a Swedish bus that was traveling along a highway near Oensingen with more than 1.6 tons of snow on its roof. The snow on the bus roof was 16 in (40 cm) deep.

112 CHEESES > Taso Vitsas, the manager of Crown Pizza in Waterford, Connecticut, cooked a 42-in (106.7-cm) pizza with 112 different cheeses.

WITCHCRAFT LAWS > In Canada, practicing witchcraft is legal, but pretending to practice it is a punishable offense.

SILENT DRIVER > In 2017, Dipak Das, a chauffeur from Kolkata, India, won a special award for not honking his car horn once in the previous 18 years. The Manush Sanman award is designed to reduce noise pollution in Indian cities.

CHEESE TEA > Cheese-topped iced tea is so popular in China that people spend up to five hours in line to get a cup.

NATIONAL PARK > The Wrangell-St. Elias National Park and Preserve in Alaska covers 13.2 million acres, making it the same size as Yellowstone, Yosemite, and Switzerland combined.

The Buc-ee's car wash in Katy, Texas, is 255 ft (78 m) long and can hold 16 cars at a time—the world's longest car wash.

FUNERAL CAFÉ > The Kid Mai Death Café in Bangkok, Thailand, has a funeral theme. Funeral wreaths are used as floral decorations, photos of funerals line the bar, and if customers can lie down in a full-size coffin with the lid on for three minutes, they can get a discount on their food and drink.

DISPUTED ISLAND > Hans Island is a disputed Danish and Canadian territory. Both countries claim the tiny, 0.5-sq-mi (1.3-sq-km) island and offer gifts during border exchanges. Denmark leaves a bottle of schnapps, while Canada provides whiskey.

SCOTTISH LANDOWNERS > Nearly 500 residents of Scotland, Connecticut, each own 1 sq ft (0.09 sq m) of land in Scotland, United Kingdom, and boast the courtesy title of Lord or Lady of Glencoe.

SPIT WINE > Peter Bignell, a distiller from Tasmania, Australia, took wine that had been deliberately spat out into a bucket at a Sydney wine-tasting festival and turned it into a spirit drink. He has called the drink "Kissing a Stranger" and says it tastes like fruity brandy.

RESCUE BUS > During December, when a lot of Japanese companies hold end-of-year drinking parties, the Nishi Tokyo Bus Company runs a special rescue bus to pick up drunk train passengers who fall asleep and miss their stop.

SNOW RARITY > A rare phenomenon called a *snowbow* is a rainbow produced on cold, wintry days when sunlight is refracted through snowflakes in the same way as rain. For a snowbow to appear, the sun has to be low in the sky at the same time as snow is falling.

OLD YELLOW

➲ In May 2018, Swiss artist Felice Varini glued 15 bright yellow aluminum strips across a medieval castle in Carcassonne, France. The art installation, called *Concentric Eccentric Circles*, was done to celebrate the 20th anniversary of the location being listed as a UNESCO World Heritage site. The yellow circles have sparked outrage among those who think the artist has vandalized Carcassonne Castle, which is France's second-most visited tourist attraction after the Eiffel Tower.

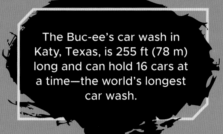

ELDER TREE ➲ A 402-year-old almond tree stands proudly in the middle of a road in Nanning, Guangxi Zhuang Autonomous Region, China. Located on a large green patch of grass along the road, the tree was originally going to be moved to make way for the road's construction. It was only when they discovered dry rot and insect pests that they left the now endangered elder tree where it was.

402 YEAR OLD TREE!

LIBRARY ASHES > The Osler Library at McGill University in Montreal, Canada, is also a mausoleum, with the ashes of physician William Osler and his wife Grace residing in a specially created niche among the books.

MACE BEER > The Dogfish Head Brewery of Milton, Delaware, created a limited-edition beer that is partially brewed with oleoresin capsicum, the active ingredient in mace pepper spray. "In Your Mace" is a dark, roasty beer that numbs the mouth. In its raw form, the pepper oil used in the beer is so fierce that the team needed to wear protective gear during the brewing process.

CHEETOS MENU > For three days in August 2017, a New York City pop-up restaurant, The Spotted Cheetah, offered Cheetos-themed cuisine. Dishes on the three-course menu created by chef Anne Burrell included Cheetos Crusted Fried Pickles and Cheetos Sweetos Crusted Cheesecake. The restaurant sold out instantly and had a waiting list of 1,000 people.

> Margaret Arnold, the first wife of Benedict Arnold, is buried here.

WHAT LIES BENEATH

➲ Buried beneath a church in New Haven, Connecticut, are the remains of more than 1,000 people! They belong to the town's earliest founders and settlers, who were buried in the local cemetery between 1638 and 1796. About 137 are identified, thanks in part to the headstones that were preserved when the church was built over them in 1812.

Here lyeth the Body of Mrs Lydia Rofewell Relict of Mr Richard Rofewell Who dyed Decently A°... I 31 ... year of her Age

HAUNTED ROOM > For 30 years, Stateroom B340 at The Queen Mary hotel in Long Beach, California, remained unoccupied because it was said to be haunted. The $499-a-night room aboard the former luxury cruise liner finally reopened to guests on Friday, April 13, 2018, with added amenities including a Ouija board, tarot cards, a crystal ball, and ghost-hunting equipment.

SNOW PENTHOUSE > In January 2018, Michael Koenigs built a 5-ft-tall (1.5-m) snow fort penthouse out of snow that had fallen on the balcony of his New York City apartment. He then offered it as an accommodation on Airbnb for $250 a night "for a limited time because it will melt."

EGG-LAYING CLIFF > A cliff near Gulu, Guizhou Province, China, is said to "lay" mysterious egg-shaped stones every 30 years. Part of Mount Gandeng, Chan Da Ya—Mandarin for "egg-producing cliff"—is 20 ft (6 m) high and 65 ft (20 m) wide. It has an uneven surface, and every three decades erosion causes each hollow to emit an oval-shaped, perfectly smooth rock, which eventually falls to the ground, like a hen laying an egg. These are quickly collected by villagers who believe the stones bring good luck.

HANDMADE ROAD > Working eight hours a day for two years, Jalandhar Nayak, from Orissa state, India, single-handedly constructed a 5-mi (8-km) stretch of road with just a pickax, a chisel, and a garden hoe so that his children, who live away at boarding school, can visit him more often. Without the hand-built road, the journey from the school in Phulbani to their home in Gumsahi village takes them three hours because they have to trek over five hills.

Rehab

Rehab
PARLIAMENTARY
PANCAKE RACE
Supported by
LYLE'S GOLDEN SYRUP
Mims
Davies 7
PancakeRace.co.uk

Flipping OUT

➲ Every year on Shrove Tuesday, a charity race in London, England, has competitors running laps while flipping pancakes in frying pans.

The bizarre tradition started because Shrove Tuesday, the last day before Lent, is customarily the time when people clean out things like milk, butter, and eggs—foods that are fasted for Lent and all key ingredients in making the delicious breakfast staple. With Shrove Tuesday falling between February 3 and March 9, races are held all over the city, with one in particular taking place outside the Houses of Parliament, pitting politicians against journalists.

HOOKED

Every year during the Panguni Uthiram festival, Hindu worshippers show their devotion to Murugan, the God of War, by using metal hooks to pierce their skin—sometimes even dangling from cranes.

The festival takes place from mid-January to February, and devotees hope to bring many blessings on themselves by participating in this ritual: from good luck to forgiveness. In some extreme cases, worshippers will actually hang on JCB machines or cranes from the hooks piercing their skin and spin in circles with the help of others. While some participants have been interviewed about the intense acts associated with the festival, many say they do not experience the pain but rather the hope that they will find favor with their deity.

PULLING THE CRANE!

FireFETUS

○ In Bolivia, dried llama fetuses are set ablaze as an offering to the goddess Mother Earth, Pachamama.

Usually sold on the streets, and famously in a witches' market in the mountain city of La Paz, the llama fetuses are the result of miscarriages and still births. It is integral to traditional indigenous beliefs to make offerings—candy, herbs, figurines, colored yarn, and most importantly, the llama fetus—to Pachamama, which are done in August, on the first Friday of every month, and whenever constructing new buildings.

UNBORN BABY LLAMA READY FOR FIRE OFFERING!

FETUSES SOLD ON STREET

TREE TUNNEL ⮞ The road in the village of Asahduren in western Bali goes through a hole in the middle of the roots of a banyan tree, which is wide enough for two cars to pass through side by side. When the road was being built, the topography made circumnavigating the tree—called Bunut Bolong—impossible, and because the Banyan is sacred and can never be cut, the road was built through the center of its huge, aerial roots without disturbing the tree itself.

ILLEGAL POTATOES >
Potatoes were illegal in France for 24 years. They were banned by the French parliament in 1748 in the belief that they caused leprosy and were only declared edible by the Paris Faculty of Medicine in 1772 thanks to the work of army medical officer Antoine-Augustin Parmentier, who while held prisoner by the Prussians during the Seven Years War, had eaten potatoes and experienced no adverse effects.

TONGUE TWISTER >
Webster Lake in Webster, Massachusetts, is also known as Lake Chargoggagoggmanchaug-gagoggchaubunagungamaugg. The 45-letter name means "lake divided by islands" in Nipmuc, a language of the indigenous Algonquian peoples.

SNOW CAR > Simon Laprise, of Montreal, Canada, built a full-size replica car out of snow on the street outside his home—and it was so realistic that a passing police patrol car even pulled over to write a ticket for the "illegally parked" vehicle.

COLLAPSING PLANT > The slightest touch causes the sensitive plant (*Mimosa pudica*) of South America to collapse in one-tenth of a second. When touched, the cells surrounding the base of the leaflet stalks rapidly lose water, resulting in the collapse of the entire stalk, but within 10 minutes, as the cells reabsorb water, it returns to its normal upright position. The plant's sudden wilting mechanism deters grazing animals from eating it.

SYMBOLIC NUMBER >
The number 96 is very significant in Hungary. In 896, the crowning of Arpad as first king of the Magyars (the Hungarian people) marked the beginning of the Hungarian state. Budapest's Metro was then built on the country's millennial anniversary in 1896. A recent law states that any new buildings in Budapest must not exceed a height of 96 meters, and the Hungarian national anthem, if performed at the correct tempo, should be sung in precisely 96 seconds.

UNIQUE COUNTY > Cimarron County, Oklahoma, is the only county in the United States that touches five states—Texas, Colorado, New Mexico, Kansas, and its home state, Oklahoma.

ROBERT RIPLEY

In 1934, Robert Ripley actually visited a Meteora monastery on a trip to Greece.

CLIFF CLOISTER

⮞ Standing atop a 1,312-ft-high (400-m) cliff in Kalabaka, Greece, is the Monastery of the Holy Trinity. The remote cloister is one of six remaining of the Meteora, which means "suspended in the air" in Greek. Each of the six monasteries was built high up on millions-of-years-old rock formations in the 14th century. Before the 1920s, the monasteries were only accessible by long ladders or large nets and baskets that hauled up goods and people.

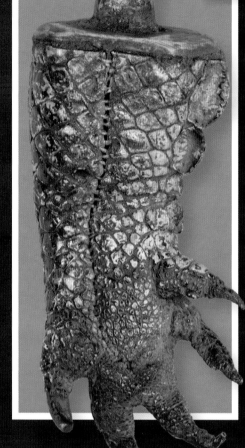

Rarity N° 9761

Crocodile War Club
Made by the Maori people of New Zealand and was probably used in ceremonies as a rattle. About 14 in (36 cm) long.

MAILED BRICKS > To build a bank in Vernal, Utah, in 1916, William H. Coltharp arranged for more than 15,000 bricks to be mailed to the town via the U.S. Postal Service's new Parcel Post. Coltharp devised his ingenious scheme because the nearest brick works was 125 mi (200 km) away in Salt Lake City and the cost of transporting the bricks by rail to Vernal would have been prohibitive. To stay within the permitted 50-lb (23-kg) weight limit per package, the bricks were individually wrapped in paper and divided into crates of 10, with up to 40 crates, weighing nearly a ton in total, sent from the brick factory each day and delivered to Vernal by postal workers. About 37 tons of bricks were mailed to Vernal at a cost of just 54 cents per crate.

UNDERWATER BALLROOM > Witley Park, in Surrey, England, has a 30-ft-tall (9-m) underwater ballroom, built directly beneath one of the estate's three artificial lakes. Before the mansion was destroyed by fire, the secret ballroom, with its glass-paneled, dome-shaped roof, was accessed via spiral steps and a 400-ft-long (122-m) corridor.

TRUCK CAKE > The Pandora Cake Shop in Hong Kong created a remote-controlled, edible truck cake that features a working horn and flashing lights. Its load is a pile of crumbled cookies.

JOB RUSH > When Indian Railways launched a recruitment drive in 2018, more than 28 million people applied for jobs.

STATE ANOMALY > Martinsburg, West Virginia, is closer to five other state capitals than its own. The state capitals of Virginia (Richmond), Pennsylvania (Harrisburg), Maryland (Annapolis), Delaware (Dover), and New Jersey (Trenton) are all nearer than Charleston.

TUMBLEWEED INVASION > In April 2018, 60 mph (96 kmph) winds left up to 150 homes in Victorville, California, submerged in tumbleweeds.

SOUVENIR BILLS > To celebrate the 200th anniversary of the birth of philosopher and economist Karl Marx, his hometown of Trier, Germany, sold more than 5,000 worthless 0-euro bank notes for 3 euros ($3.50) each.

PINBALL MUSEUM > Hungary's Budapest Pinball Museum houses Balázs Pálfi's collection of more than 130 classic pinball machines, including bagatelles from the 1880s and a 1920s table hockey game.

B·E·A·T·I·N·G
GHOSTS

➲ Tibetan Buddhist monks at the Yonghe Temple in Beijing dress up as demons and participate in elaborate dances meant to expel evil spirits and defend against trouble.

Known as Da Gui, or "Beating Ghost," the religious ceremony is an important part of Tibetan New Year, or Losar, celebrations, which last for three days. Because Tibetans follow the lunar calendar, Losar starts on a different day each year, usually sometime in February or March.

ANIMALS

FROG BUTT

→ When threatened, the Cuyaba dwarf frog (*Physalaemus nattereri*) from South America inflates its butt to scare off predators with its false eyes!

The defensive 1- to 1.5-in (3- to 4-cm) frog lifts its rear up for maximum effect, hoping that the spots on its body look like the large eyes of a snake. If the attacker decides to strike anyway, there are toxic glands beneath the fake eyes, with each frog containing enough poison to kill 150 mice.

SWEET TOOTH > A black bear smashed a window to break into baker Christine Allen's car in Rockaway Township, New Jersey, and ate every one of the two-dozen chocolate, vanilla, and strawberry cupcakes that she had stored there waiting for delivery. The bear left behind only smeared icing and a telltale paw print.

PINEAPPLE RIDE > A snake hitched a 5,300-mi (8,480-km) ride from Costa Rica to a store in Edinburgh, Scotland, by hiding in the leaves of a pineapple.

SPEEDY MITE > *Paratarsotomus macropalpis*, a tiny, 0.7-mm-long mite from Southern California, has been recorded traveling at a speed of 322 body lengths per second, compared to a cheetah's 16 bl/s and Usain Bolt's 6 bl/s.

WILDFIRE HERO > When Roland Hendel and his family were forced to flee their Sonoma County, California, home to escape the wildfires that devastated the area in October 2017, they had to leave behind their dog, Odin, who refused to be parted from the family's eight goats that he guards from coyotes and mountain lions at night. The next day, Hendel returned to his incinerated home, expecting to find that Odin and the goats had perished, but found that Odin not only survived, but also managed to rescue all eight goats and some baby deer by guiding them to a clearing that was protected from the flames by high rocks.

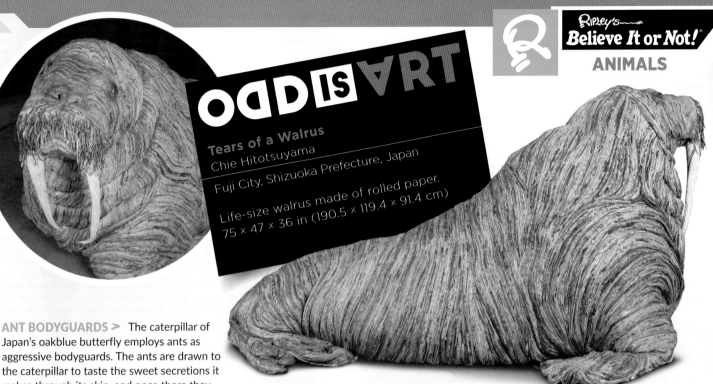

ODD IS ART

Tears of a Walrus
Chie Hitotsuyama
Fuji City, Shizuoka Prefecture, Japan
Life-size walrus made of rolled paper.
75 × 47 × 36 in (190.5 × 119.4 × 91.4 cm)

ANT BODYGUARDS > The caterpillar of Japan's oakblue butterfly employs ants as aggressive bodyguards. The ants are drawn to the caterpillar to taste the sweet secretions it makes through its skin, and once there they never leave. When the caterpillar inverts the tentacles on top of its head, a chemical in the secretions compels the ants to attack any nearby spiders or wasps, thus safeguarding the caterpillar.

LEOPARD RESCUE > After a wild leopard fell 20 ft (6 m) down a well in Madhya Pradesh, India, villagers and wildlife officials constructed a makeshift ladder from bamboo and rope and lowered it into the well so that the leopard could climb out.

BUTTERFLY RICH > Nearly a fifth of all butterfly species in the world are found in Costa Rica—a country that is smaller than Lake Michigan.

SNAKE SHOCK > While Laura Goff was driving her SUV in Warrenton, Virginia, a 2.5-ft-long (0.8-m) garter snake slithered out of the car vent, entangled itself in her phone cord, and disappeared under the seat.

ROCK CROC > Scientists named the fossil of a 19-ft-long (5.8-m) crocodile that terrorized coastal waters around Britain more than 145 million years ago after Lemmy, the hell-raising former singer of rock band Motorhead. The Jurassic-era beast was named *Lemmysuchus* by Lorna Steel, a Motorhead fan and the curator of London's Natural History Museum.

ADOPTED CHICKEN > Niv, a lonely macaque monkey at the Ramat Gan Safari Park in Israel, adopted a chicken that wandered into her enclosure. She carried the bird in her arms, hugging it and grooming it as if it were her child. The chicken responded by sleeping with Niv at night and running to her for protection if frightened.

CICADA CYCLE > Some periodical cicadas of eastern North America only emerge from belowground every 17 years. The bugs spend most of their lives underground, feeding on fluids from the roots of deciduous trees, before emerging as mature nymphs in vast numbers for a short adult life of about six weeks. After mating, they die and the newborn nymphs burrow underground to start another 17-year cycle.

MAN EATER > A single leopard—known as the Leopard of Panar—was reported to have killed and eaten more than 400 people in the Almora district of northern India over several years in the early 20th century.

SCOWLING TADPOLE

◯ The Asian horned frog (*Megophrys nasuta*) of Indonesia grows to resemble brown, dead leaves, but before this dramatic camouflage, tadpoles sport an unusual umbrella-shaped mouth. The funnel-like lips and mouth create a suction to allow feeding at the surface of water—and looks a lot like a frown or scowl.

SAD FACE!

WARTY GIRAFFE

◐ A giraffe in South Africa's Kruger National Park appears to be transforming into a tree, the result of scaly, multiplying growths sustained from the constant pecking by oxpecker birds.

While the strange wart-like mounds have the appearance of rough tree bark, they represent lesions caused by papillomavirus contracted through the constant onslaught of the bird's beaks. The hard, horn-like bumps aren't life-threatening, but they could prove itchy to the giraffe and result in infections if wounds open during tree scratching for relief.

POODLE SURGERY > A poodle named Oreo had a tumor the size of a soccer ball removed at an animal hospital in Connecticut. The tumor weighed 6.4 lb (2.9 kg)—nearly a third of the dog's body weight.

PINE CONES > When Kellen Moore, of Gaylord, Michigan, heard strange noises coming from his car's air conditioning, he opened the hood and found that squirrels had stashed 50 lb (23 kg) of pine cones there.

DARING RACCOON > Over a period of two days in June 2018, a daredevil raccoon imitated Spider-Man by scaling the exterior walls of the 25-story UBS Plaza in St. Paul, Minnesota, eventually climbing all the way to the roof.

APPROPRIATE PUNISHMENT > Convicted Missouri deer poacher David Berry Jr. was ordered to watch *Bambi* at least once a month during his year-long jail sentence.

POUNDING PRIMATES

◐ Move over, Ringo Starr! In September 2018, an adorable capuchin monkey performed a drum solo during a new show at the National Circus in Kiev, Ukraine. However, drumming primates around the world are enjoying their moment in the sun. Researchers were fascinated by groups of capuchin monkeys that aggressively drum stones against rock outcroppings to scare off predators, and a captive chimp named Barney impressed researchers when he banged on a bucket in rhythm—a trait once considered unique to human beings.

TECH-SAVVY PARROT > Petra, an African gray Congo parrot who can speak more than 300 words, has learned to operate Amazon's Alexa voice-activated device, and is able to order the virtual assistant to switch the house lights on and off at will at her owner's home in Orlando, Florida.

HORSE SIDECAR > When rancher Casey Perkins, from Shoshone County, Idaho, takes to the roads on his motorcycle, his horse comes along, too—in a homemade, single occupancy, roofless sidecar.

GOAT CADDIES > Silvies Valley Ranch in Seneca, Oregon, offers goats as caddies to players on its three golf courses. The goats wear special backpack harnesses so that they can carry clubs, tees, balls, and even beverages.

HEADLESS CHICKEN > In 2018, a chicken in Ratchaburi Province, Thailand, survived for more than 10 days after being decapitated. Although the bird had lost its head, first a veterinarian and then a group of monks kept it alive by dropping food down its neck with a syringe. If the jugular does not rupture during the beheading, a chicken can occasionally survive without its head because its brain is located in its skull at an angle. So if it is beheaded high up the neck, the rear part of the brain, which controls breathing, can remain intact. In 1945, Mike the headless chicken famously lived on a farm in Fruita, Colorado, for 18 months without his head after the axe wielded by owner Lloyd Olsen had missed Mike's jugular vein. Mike's memory is still honored every year by a festival in the town.

MOOSE CALLS > At the 2018 Skowhegan Moose Festival in Maine, more than 1,600 people simultaneously simulated moose calls.

BONE HOUSE > The exterior walls of the Bone House in Haddenham, Buckinghamshire, England, are decorated with the knuckle bones of dead sheep. The bones have been arranged to form heart and diamond patterns, as well as numbers to show the year when the cottage was built—1807.

POOP BURIAL > To treat snake bites in parts of rural India, snake charmers completely bury the victims alive for at least an hour in a mound of cow dung, in the belief that the poop will suck out the poison.

TRAINED SQUIRRELS > Rather than use CGI, director Tim Burton had 40 squirrels trained to crack nuts for the conveyor belt scene in his 2005 film *Charlie and the Chocolate Factory*.

CHISELED CHOMPERS

⮑ The crabeater seal (*Lobodon carcinophaga*) sports extravagantly serrated teeth that include multiple cusps, a bizarre feature that earned it the scientific name Lobodon, or "lobed" teeth. Ironically, crabeater seals don't eat crab at all. Instead, their teeth represent an adaptation allowing them to feast on microscopic Antarctic krill, which makes up 90 percent of their diet. With each mouthful, the seals take in krill while sieving out ocean water through those stunning choppers, their own biological colanders.

BEAVER BOURBON > Tamworth Distilling from New Hampshire launched a bourbon, Eau de Musc, that is flavored partly by castoreum, the secretion from a beaver's castor sacs.

MONKEY PAINTING > At the end of the shoot for *Pirates of the Caribbean: Dead Men Tell No Tales*, actor Geoffrey Rush was presented with a framed painting that had been done by Pablo, one of the two capuchin monkeys that played Captain Barbossa's pet, Jack.

CAT TATTOOS > Jessica Holmes, from Bullsbrook, Western Australia, has tattooed hundreds of portraits of cats onto their owners' bodies.

Eel SEAL

In 2018, a Hawaiian monk seal was photographed with an eel stuck up its nose—something that apparently keeps happening and no one is sure why.

Scientists at the Hawaiian Monk Seal Research Program thought they'd stumbled across something truly unique, but the mellow seals with stuck-up eels have continued to crop up time and time again. Researchers think there may be one of two reasons for it: either the seals are frightening eels, and the eels climb up their noses in defense, or the seals are regurgitating the eels incorrectly after accidentally eating them. In every instance, the eels have been safely removed, leaving the seals happy and healthy.

COCKROACH MILK > Scientists are developing cockroach milk for human consumption and hope that it could one day become a superfood. They think the yellow liquid that the female Pacific beetle cockroach feeds to her young is one of the most nutritious substances on the planet, containing three times the energy content of buffalo milk. However, it would take an estimated 5,600 cockroaches to produce a pint of milk.

DINOSAUR CHICKEN > Discovered as recently as 2005, the *gigantoraptor* was a 16-ft-high (5-m), chicken-like dinosaur that roamed the plains of central Asia 85 million years ago. It had a beak like a bird and probably also had feathers, but it weighed nearly two tons, making it 20 times heavier than an adult ostrich.

NO EYES > Rosie, a blind rescue pugalier (pug and cavalier King Charles spaniel mix) who lives with Jadie Cooley in Hertfordshire, England, has her own guide dog—Diesel, a 13-year-old Eurasier. Rosie was born with only one eye and then had to have that surgically removed when she was six due to a permanently blocked tear duct, leaving her with no vision at all.

LEAF BUG ⮌ Look closer at this leaf, and you'll soon realize it has legs! The *Uropyia meticulodina* moth is able to mimic a dead leaf when it reaches adulthood, a talent that protects it from getting swallowed up by predators. This moth was photographed in Nagano, Japan, but they are most commonly found in parts of Taiwan and China.

COW ART > In March 2018, cow artist Derek Klingenberg used a feed truck to herd 300 cows on his farm in Marion County, Kansas, into a formation where they spelled out the word "Hi" so that the Tesla sports car-toting SpaceX rocket could see it from space.

BIRD'S-EYE VIEW

⮌ German apothecary Dr. Julius G. Neubronner patented a pigeon camera in 1908 that allowed these birds to take images from impressive heights. Neubronner, a pigeon enthusiast, was first turned down for his patent because the patent office didn't think birds could carry the 75-g (about 2.5-oz) camera. The pigeon cams were briefly considered for the purpose of photographing battlefields for the military, but they were soon made irrelevant by airplane photography. Still, some of the pictures exist today, offering an elevated, wide-angle perspective similar to modern-day GoPros.

CLONED IBEX > After the Pyrenean ibex—a Spanish wild goat—became extinct in 2000, it had the distinction of being the first animal to be brought back from extinction by scientific cloning. A live specimen was born in 2003, but sadly it died less than 20 minutes later due to a lung defect.

NASTY NEWT > The rough-skinned newt of North America produces a chemical in its skin called *tetrodotoxin*, a poison that is 10,000 times deadlier than cyanide.

VIEW FROM PIGEON CAM!

LONE ELEPHANT > An elephant at the Imire wildlife reserve in Zimbabwe has been living with a herd of wild buffalo for nearly 50 years. When her parents were killed in the 1970s, Nzou was placed with a bull elephant and the buffalo, and when the bull died, she had grown so acclimatized to the buffalo that she refused to leave them. She looks after the buffalo herd and has developed her own way of communicating with them.

SNAKE BITE > Nala the boxer dog was bitten on the nose by a deadly Mojave green rattlesnake while standing her ground and defending her 10-year-old owner, Cole Lewis, during a walk near their home in Lancaster, California. Nala bravely faced off with the snake, giving Cole and his mother time to escape, and went on to make a full recovery from the bite.

CHICKEN OBITUARY > Stephanie Sword and her family, from College Station, Texas, were so distraught by the death of their pet chicken, Big Mama, whom they had adopted five years earlier in 2013, that they paid for an obituary for the bird to appear in their local newspaper, *The Eagle*.

Smile CROCODILE

➲ In April 2017, a crocodile at Vandaloor Zoo in Chennai, India, was photographed with a deformed snout.

The poor croc had a losing fight with a fellow crocodile two years ago, fracturing his jaw. The croc has since recovered, although the top half of its mouth is missing. Staff at the zoo rehabilitated the reptile, saying they could not even get near it to bandage the wound, instead cleaning the injury with a brush attached to a pole. It has adapted to its crooked smile and now happily lives in its own enclosure.

TAXI DRIVER > A dog took control of an electric three-wheeler taxicab and drove it through the window of a phone store in Taizhou City, China. The cab driver said he had left his dog alone in the vehicle with the engine running and that the animal must have knocked it out of park, sending it careening across the street and crashing into the phone shop.

GUARDIAN WHALE > A 25-ton humpback whale appeared to protect American marine biologist Nan Hauser from a 15-ft-long (4.6-m) tiger shark while she was swimming off the Cook Islands in the South Pacific. As the shark circled, the huge whale lifted Hauser right up out of the water with its head, then shielded her with its pectoral fin for nearly 10 minutes before pushing her through the ocean to safety while another whale warded off the shark with its tail.

TASTY TEDDIES > Veterinarians removed four half-chewed teddy bears from the stomach of Maisy, an eight-year-old St. Bernard dog owned by Jane Dickinson in West Yorkshire, England.

POTENT POISON > Although smaller than a human fingernail, the Irukandji jellyfish, which lives off the coast of Australia, fires stingers from its tentacles containing venom that is 100 times more venomous than a cobra and 1,000 times more powerful than a tarantula.

ALBINO BAT

⮑ Bats can be albino, too! The *Peropteryx macrotis* bat lives in small colonies throughout South America, and it is usually brown, gray, or even a reddish color.

SNEEZING DOGS > African wild dogs communicate with each other by sneezing. They use sneezing to decide whether or not to hunt and will only set off in pursuit of prey when enough members of the pack sneeze at a prehunt rally.

GIFT WRAPPED > The male nursery web spider (*Pisaura mirabilis*) brings a silk-wrapped insect to the female before mating, so that afterward she eats the gift instead of eating him.

EXPLODING ANT > A newly discovered species of ant from Borneo, *Colobopsis explodens*, blow their bodies apart and sacrifice their lives to protect the rest of the colony. If threatened, one or more of the ants bite down on the would-be predator, angle their butts in close, and flex so hard that their abdomens burst, releasing a yellow, sticky, toxic secretion.

LIZARD SURPRISE > After Al and Chris Brummett, from Hemet, California, ordered a bicycle online for their granddaughter, they opened the box to find that it also contained a large bearded dragon lizard, which had stowed away in the package.

CATERPILLAR ARMOR > The hermit crab caterpillar from Peru protects itself by making its own suit of armor out of leaves, which it rolls into a tube and glues together with sticky saliva. Once the tube is complete, the caterpillar squeezes its body inside and uses its mouth to drag itself along the forest floor. It even leaves a bulge in the center of the protective casing so that it can turn around inside if it suddenly needs to escape through the back entrance.

FLOATING SANCTUARY > For more than 50 years, a canal boat in Amsterdam, the Netherlands, has been a sanctuary for stray and abandoned cats—and more than 50 currently live on it. De Poezenboot (The Catboat) was started in 1966 by cat lover Henriette van Weelde, and although she died in 2005, the barge has since been maintained by volunteers. It has been modified with a cat-friendly interior and has been reinforced with wooden slats and wire to prevent any cats from falling into the water.

REPLACEMENT TEETH > Sharks typically lose at least one tooth per week, but because they always have new rows of teeth developing behind their front set, ready to move forward like a conveyor belt, any lost tooth can often be replaced within a day. Some sharks can go through more than 50,000 teeth in their lifetime.

SLOW PROGRESS > On the ground, a sloth's maximum speed is 10 ft (3 m) per minute, meaning that it would take a sloth more than half an hour to complete the 100 meters and about nine days to finish a full marathon. Yet sloths are surprisingly strong swimmers and can swim four times faster than they can walk.

COVERED IN LADYBUGS!

LADYBUG SWARM
⮑ A remote radio tower near Mount Burrin South Australia has attracted a few spotty visitors—millions of ladybugs—and no one seems to know why. Wildlife photographer Steve Chapple shared photos and video of the strange event on his Facebook page, saying that the number of ladybugs has increased over the years. The beetles swarm during the day, sometimes 4 in (10 cm) thick in places, and then take shelter at night. Experts say the mysterious swarm could be mating masses or for protection against predators.

BARNACLE BALL ⊃ A commercial skipper and her husband found a basketball that had gained a beard of barnacles after bobbing around in the ocean for what the couple concluded was almost two years. After taking a picture with the barnacle ball, they gave it back to the ocean again, maintaining that it needed to "continue its journey."

NASAL LEECH > Doctors in Beihai, China, pulled a huge live leech from a 51-year-old man's nostril, where it had been hiding and had caused him to suffer nonstop nosebleeds for 10 days.

FAKE ZEBRA > A keeper at a zoo in Cairo, Egypt, was accused of painting black stripes on a donkey in an attempt to convince visitors that it was a zebra. Suspicion was aroused when the black coloring on the animal's face began to smudge in the hot weather.

POOP SHOCK > After feeling unwell for months, Columbus Blue Jackets hockey player Carson Meyer, from Powell, Ohio, finally discovered the cause of his lethargy when he went to the bathroom and a 25-in-long (62.5-cm) tapeworm emerged in his poop. The orange parasitic tapeworm, which had been living in his small intestine for nearly a year, is caused by eating raw or undercooked fish and can grow up to 30 ft (9.1 m) long.

RETIRED PARROTS > Ken Banks, of Rockhampton, Queensland, Australia, has set up a retirement home for parrots who have outlived their owners. Some parrots can live to age 90.

TWO NOSES > Wallis, a golden retriever owned by Lana Culley, of Poole, England, was born with two noses.

COCKROACH COSTUME > To underline her concerns about an escalating insect problem along a street in Corpus Christi, Texas, university professor Patricia Polastri addressed a city council meeting dressed as a cockroach. Wearing a brown body costume complete with antennae and legs, Polastri said that newly planted palm trees have brought about an increase in the number of rodents and insects.

VOTING BEAR > A man arrived in Severobaykalsk to vote in the 2018 Russian presidential election wearing a full brown bear costume—but then found he was too big to fit inside the voting booth.

BAD LUCK > Having previously been attacked by a black bear and bitten by a rattlesnake, Dylan McWilliams, of Grand Junction, Colorado, went on vacation to Hawaii, where he was promptly bitten on the leg by a shark. All three incidents happened in the space of just over three years, at estimated odds of 893.35 quadrillion to one.

SQUID SPERM > In South Korea, a 63-year-old woman's mouth was "inseminated" by the sperm of a Japanese flying squid after she ate the undercooked seafood without first removing its internal organs. When doctors examined her, they discovered 12 sperm bags embedded in her tongue and gums.

TWO BUTTS > The Jackson County Historical Society in Maquoketa, Iowa, displays a stuffed lamb with two butts.

MAD HATTER-PILLAR

⊃ The uraba lugens, a caterpillar found in Australia, wears a stack of its old heads like a hat! When the caterpillar grows and sheds its most recent outer shell, it keeps the part that used to house its head, eventually building a stack tall enough to give it the whimsical, informal name: the mad hatterpillar.

HORSE SUES > Justice, an eight-year-old horse in Portland, Oregon, sued his former owner for neglect and claimed more than $100,000 in damages. Since 2014, the Oregon Supreme Court has ruled that animals have legally protected rights and can be victims of crime.

SUPPORT PEACOCK > New York–based performance artist and photographer Ventiko tried unsuccessfully to take her emotional support peacock, Dexter, on a flight from Newark, New Jersey, to Los Angeles, California. She bought a ticket for the therapy bird so he could enjoy his own seat, but United Airlines turned the feathered passenger away because of its size.

TRUCK SWARM > Beekeeper Wallace Leatherwood drove 40 mi (64 km) with 3,000 bees loose in the cab of his truck—and was not stung once. He was transporting 18,000 bees to his home in Waynesville, North Carolina, when some escaped from their container.

DEAD ANTS > Ashwini, an 11-year-old girl from Belthangady, India, had over 60 dead ants pulled from her eyes in 10 days—and doctors had no idea how the insects got there. Her parents had taken her to a hospital after she had complained about a severe pain in her eyes.

BURNING BIRD > A burning bird set fire to a field in Rostock, Germany, during a prolonged dry spell in July 2018, torching 17 acres (6.8 hectares) of land. More than 50 firefighters tackled the blaze, which was ignited when a bird landed on an overhead electric line before catching fire and falling in flames onto the parched ground.

STUBBORN COCKROACH > Katie Holley, from Melbourne, Florida, had a cockroach stuck in her left ear for nine days. It crawled in while she slept, and she woke up to discover two bug legs sticking out of her ear. Her husband tore those off with tweezers but the rest of the roach wriggled deeper into her ear canal. So she went to the hospital, where doctors killed the bug and pulled out three small pieces, confident that they had removed everything. But she continued to experience ear pain and a loss of hearing until nine days later, when another doctor removed six more pieces of carcass—the head, upper torso, the remaining limbs, and the antennae.

HUNGRY PUP > A seal pup was found in a garden 4 mi (6.4 km) from the sea in Norfolk, England, after traveling up a drainage system in search of food.

OCTOPUS WHISPERER > Eighty-four-year-old Wilson Menashi, from Lexington, Massachusetts, is known as the "octopus whisperer" because for more than 25 years he has been able to interact with octopuses at the New England Aquarium in Boston, rubbing their backs and playfully wrestling with them.

SNOW HOME > The Ussurian tube-nosed bat of Japan survives harsh winters by creating a small "igloo" in the snow and hibernating there. The bat makes a small depression in the fresh snow, cozies down in it, and is then covered by more snowfall that insulates its body against the cold.

BLEEDING HEARTS

⊙ The *Gallicolumba luzonica* is commonly called the "Luzon bleeding-heart dove"—because it looks like its chest is covered in blood.

While its body is a kind of iridescent gray that can turn different varieties of green, purple, and blue in the light, the red patch often runs from its chest down to its belly, making it look like blood has actually trickled down its feathers. The dove is most commonly found in Luzon, an island in the Philippines.

Smooth OPERATOR

In 1881, a baboon named Jack was trained to operate railway signals in South Africa, and in nine years, he never made a mistake!

Peg-legged railway signalman James Edwin Wide bought Jack after seeing the baboon driving an oxcart. Jack helped his double-amputee owner to and from work, and also helped him with household chores. Soon Jack was trained to handle the rails—when trains approached the station, they'd blow their whistle a certain number of times to let Jack know which tracks to manually change. Jack operated the switches so well that he was given an official employment number and paid 20 cents a day and half a bottle of beer weekly.

Jack the baboon never made a single mistake when operating the switches.

ROAR FLOOR

⮕ The king of the jungle was found hiding in plain sight on a boardwalk at Green Cay Wetlands and Nature Preserve in Boynton Beach, Florida. Lynda Christison looked down at the unassuming wood planks and spotted the familiar visage, the knots and grain in the wood resembling the big cat.

TRIPLE YOLKS > A pet chicken named Lucky, owned by Lauren Mayes, of Norfolk, England, beat odds of 25 million to one by laying two eggs with triple yolks over the course of one month.

KILLER CROC > Gustave, a crocodile living in the Ruzizi River in Burundi, Africa, is believed to have killed more than 300 people. He weighs over 2,000 lb (908 kg), is more than 20 ft (6 m) long, and is thought to be at least 70 years old.

TEN-YEAR WAIT > Debra Suierveld and her family were reunited with their black Labrador mix Abby in 2018—10 years after the dog had disappeared from their home in Apollo, Pennsylvania. Abby showed up on a front porch in Lower Burrell 10 mi (16 km) away, and when she was returned to the Suiervelds, she still remembered commands they had taught her a decade earlier.

OUT OF BOUNDS > In January 2018, a wallaby was captured uninjured by Australian police officers after bounding across Sydney Harbour Bridge. The marsupial somehow negotiated the bridge's eight lanes of traffic before turning off down an expressway.

CAT CUDDLER > The Just Cats Veterinary Clinic in Dublin, Ireland, employs a professional cat cuddler to comfort its feline patients.

LOUD CLICKS > When diving deep in the ocean, a mother sperm whale communicates to her calf on the surface by a series of clicks delivered at 230 decibels—more than double the noise level of a jackhammer and easily enough to burst a human's eardrums.

DRUNK OPOSSUM > A thirsty opossum broke into a liquor store in Fort Walton Beach, Florida, and got drunk after consuming a whole bottle of bourbon. Store owner Cash Moore found the animal next to a broken, empty bottle of bourbon that it had knocked off the shelf while jumping down from the rafters. After sobering up, the opossum was released unharmed.

STRONG JAW > The titan beetle (*Titanus giganteus*) of South America can grow up to 7 in (17.5 cm) long, and its jaw is so strong it can break a wooden pencil in half.

LONG HORNS > A longhorn bull named Cowboy Tuff Chex, owned by Richard and Jeanne Filip of Fayetteville, Texas, has an incredible horn span of 8.4 ft (2.6 m).

PUPPY SHARE > A mother pig on a farm in Korat, Thailand, allowed a hungry puppy to nurse alongside her similarly sized piglets.

WONDER WEB > By feeding a solution of graphene—the world's strongest material—to spiders, scientists at the University of Trento in Italy found that the resulting spider webs produced silk that was five times tougher than usual, making it strong enough to carry the weight of a human.

HEAVILY PREGNANT > A 14-ft-long (4.3-m) Burmese python that was captured in Florida's Everglades in 2017 weighed 62 lb (28 kg) and was carrying 73 eggs inside her.

HURRICANE ESCAPE > A female hawk escaped Hurricane Harvey by taxi. When William Bruso stopped for food in Houston, Texas, on August 25, 2017, the hawk hopped onto the passenger seat of his taxi cab and remained there while he drove her out of the storm before releasing her.

MASS MIGRATION > Each year in a mass migration, more than 10 million giant fruit bats fly between the Democratic Republic of Congo and Zambia's Kasanka National Park—the largest mammal migration on Earth!

FLYING FROG

⮕ Deep in the tropical jungles of Malaysia and Borneo lives a bright green 4-in (10-cm) frog that not only hops and swims but also flies! Wallace's flying frogs (aka parachute frogs) live in the trees, and when threatened or in search of food, will leap from branch to branch. The membranes in their webbed feet and loose skin flaps on the sides of their bodies help them glide as far as 50 ft (15.2 m).

SNAKE BOY > Seven-year-old Devesh Adivasi, from Madhya Pradesh, India, goes into the jungle near his village almost every day and returns with venomous snakes. He then bathes the snakes, sleeps with them, and massages them with oil before releasing them back into the wild. He has never once been bitten.

MOOSE PRANK > Woken in the middle of the night by the sound of their doorbell ringing, Kyle Stultz and Allie Johnstone, of Anchorage, Alaska, found nobody there—but when they checked their security footage, they discovered that the culprit was a moose.

STOWED AWAY > Baloo, a tabby cat owned by Jacqueline Lake of Dartmouth, Nova Scotia, jumped into a box and ended up being mailed 700 mi (1,120 km) to Montreal, Quebec.

SHOCK DISCOVERY > Searching for her missing cat in Pascagoula, Mississippi, Brooque Snow looked down a storm drain and saw a 7-ft-long (2.1-m) alligator.

DINNER SNAKE > A new species of snake—*Cenaspis aenigma* (the mysterious dinner snake)—was first discovered inside the stomach of a Central American coral snake in Mexico.

HOSPITAL VISITOR > In January 2019, a moose wandered through automatic doors into the Alaska Regional Hospital in Anchorage and ate the plants in the atrium.

VAMPIRE BIRD > The vampire ground finch, which is native to the Galápagos Islands, drinks the blood of other birds.

SPIDER BEACH

⟳ **In the fall of 2018, a beach in Aitoliko, Greece, became almost completely covered with more than 900 ft (274 m) of spider webs.**

The webs, created by the over-abundant *Tetragnatha* spider, made the normally beautiful beach in Western Greece look abandoned, as they covered almost every plant and tree on the coastline. However, experts unfortunately promised this was actually normal, stating the weather conditions (high temperatures and humidity) combined with easy access to food made the nightmarish spider boom possible. When colder temperatures arrive, the spiders will simply die off, leaving the beach to thrive again.

JELLYFISH BANDAGES > Adhesive bandages made from the barrel jellyfish can assist in the healing of chronic wounds. The material extracted from the jellyfish is rich in collagen, a protein also found in human skin, which helps new tissue to grow and speeds up the healing process.

LION CAFÉ > In 2018, Mevzoo, a café in Istanbul, Turkey, kept a live lion on the premises to entertain customers.

ACTUAL SIZE!

JURASSIC MOSQUITO

➲ An enormous mosquito 10 times larger than those encountered by most humans was found in China in 2018. The mosquito has a wingspan greater than 4 in (10 cm), and its body is about 2 in (5 cm) long. The insect belongs to the *Holorusia mikado* family, but it is about a third longer than the average mosquito in its species. No need to worry, though—unlike its annoying cousins, this large insect doesn't drink blood and is mainly interested in nectar.

CAMERA SWARM > Nearly 20,000 bees swarmed over a New York City surveillance camera on June 17, 2018, at the junction of 42nd Street and Broadway.

COLOSSAL COW > Knickers, a huge 6.33-ft-tall (1.9-m) Holstein Friesian steer on a farm in Myalup, Australia, weighs more than 3,000 lb (1,362 kg), towers over the rest of the herd, and is too big for the slaughterhouse.

HOME INVASION > A 65-lb (30-kg) kangaroo jumped through the window of a house in Melbourne, Australia, while Mafi Ahokavo and his family were asleep and locked itself in the bathroom.

GUARD PIG > An attempted burglary at a home in Indianapolis, Indiana, was foiled when the thieves came face-to-face with the owner's pet pig, Dumplin.

49 CLONES > Miracle Milly, a chihuahua owned by Vanesa Semler of Kissimmee, Florida, was so tiny at birth she could curl up inside a teaspoon—but her genes have since been used to create 49 genetically identical dogs in an attempt to discover why she is so small.

RED SWEAT > Hippopotamus sweat is red, and the red pigment not only acts as a sunscreen—it also kills bacteria on the hippo's skin.

LUCKY FROG > Jamie Chapel, a snake catcher from Townsville, Queensland, Australia, performed CPR to save a green tree frog that had been regurgitated after being eaten by a snake.

BIG MOUTH > The mouth of the frogfish can expand to 12 times its resting size, allowing it to catch and eat other fish.

YOUR UPLOADS

Duck Tongue?

Benjamin Hicks of Perth, Western Australia, recently let us know about this Pacific black duck living in Busselton, Western Australia, with a bizarre growth. Hicks believes it to be "an extra foot growing next to its beak." Luckily, the appendage does not appear to impact its health, since workers at the Bayview Geographe Resort have frequently seen it on the property for the last two years.

Glow HOME

COMMUNAL NESTS > Social weaver birds of southern Africa build communal nests that are so large they can pull down mature trees. Each structure can weigh more than a ton, measure 20 ft (6 m) wide and 10 ft (3 m) tall, and be made up of more than 100 separate nesting chambers. Successive generations of the birds refurbish and reuse these individual compartments, often for more than 100 years.

HERBAL MEDICINE > Orangutans in Borneo chew the leaves of a plant—*Dracaena cantleyi*—into a lather and then rub it into their upper arms or legs for up to 45 minutes to relieve aches and pains. They use the leaves as an ointment, even though this particular herbal medicine is not yet known to humans.

FROZEN SOLID > Alligators survive harsh winters in frozen swamps by entering brumation—a state of dormancy—and sticking their snouts through the ice so that they can keep breathing. They appear to know instinctively when the water is about to freeze and position their bodies accordingly, remaining frozen in place until the ice melts.

CAFFEINE OVERDOSE > A baby long-tailed macaque monkey in Bangkok, Thailand, collapsed and passed out for 10 hours because it suffered a caffeine overdose after stealing a tourist's strong coffee.

HUNTING AID > A cheetah's inner ear is structured to help the animal keep its head perfectly still, even when pursuing prey at speeds of 60 mph (97 kmph). By keeping its head still and its eyes fixed, the cheetah is able to focus better on the animal it is chasing.

FARMING RETRIEVER > Rambo the golden retriever drives a tractor on Albert Reid's farm in County Down, Northern Ireland. He sits on the tractor wearing a high-visibility vest and helps his master plow the fields and cut down corn. He also assists with hedge trimming and grass cutting.

CONSTANT GROWTH > A beaver's teeth never stop growing, and if they didn't continually wear their teeth down on trees, the constant growth would prevent them from being able to feed and would therefore eventually kill them.

A tiny tree frog discovered at a supermarket in Lancashire, England, accidentally traveled 4,200 mi (6,720 km) from the Dominican Republic in a bunch of bananas.

PUPPY CLONES > Singer Barbra Streisand has two dogs, Miss Scarlett and Miss Violet, that are clones of one of her previous pets, Samantha, a curly haired Coton de Tulear who died at age 14 in 2017. Cells were taken from Samantha's mouth and stomach to create the identical pups.

GAS ADDICT > At the end of their day, workers in Panipat, India, returned to their motorcycles in a parking lot, only to find that they had been drained of gas—by a monkey! Waiting until nobody was around, the monkey had removed the fuel pipes before drinking the gas.

SPIDER HORN > A new species of tarantula was discovered in Angola—*Ceratogyrus attonitifer*, Latin for "bearer of astonishment"—with a flimsy horn on its back!

FACELESS TOAD > An adult American toad found in a Connecticut state forest was hopping around with a healthy body and legs—even though it had no face.

SWALLOWED SLIPPER > Veterinarian Josh Llinas, of Mount Ommaney, Queensland, Australia, performed surgery to remove a slipper from the stomach of a carpet python. The snake had slithered into someone's home and swallowed the slipper, which showed up on an X-ray of the reptile. As the footwear was too big to be manually coaxed up the digestive tract and out of the snake's mouth, it had to be removed by a gastrotomy procedure.

FREE RIDE > A bobcat survived a 50-mi (80-km) ride in the grill of a car after being hit on a road in Gloucester County, Virginia. Despite being stuck in the grill for more than an hour, the animal emerged from its ordeal with just a few scratches.

WEIGHT DIFFERENCE > The female blanket octopus can be 40,000 times heavier and almost 100 times larger than the male. The female reaches nearly 7 ft (2.1 m) in length, whereas the male is less than 1 in (2.5 cm) long.

NOT EXTINCT > A 2017 expedition to Guatemala's Cuchumatanes Mountains rediscovered Jackson's climbing salamander (*Bolitoglossa jacksoni*), an amphibian feared to have become extinct because it had last been seen 42 years earlier in 1975.

Grant's golden mole is the only known iridescent mammal!

GOLDEN EYES

⮕ Grant's golden mole of southwestern Africa has eyes but is completely blind! Their peepers sit useless beneath a layer of skin and fur. This isn't a problem for the golden mole, however, since it hunts at night using its incredible sense of hearing. The tiny critter will submerge itself in the sand and, thanks to its slick fur, "swim" through the desert, listening for prey to eat.

NEW FROG > A new species of frog—the jaguar-snouted tree frog (*Scinax onca*)—was first discovered on a stretch of abandoned highway in Brazil.

BIG MEAL > A Burmese python at Collier-Seminole State Park, Florida, ate an entire white-tailed deer—a prey amounting to 111 percent of the snake's body mass. The 11-ft-long (3.3-m) snake weighed 31.5 lb (14.3 kg), compared to the deer's 35 lb (15.9 kg).

EXTERNAL LUNG > The alkali fly (*Ephydra hians*) is able to breathe underwater because the hair on its body helps create an air bubble, which serves as an external lung. Its major breeding area is the highly alkaline Mono Lake, California, where the water is three times saltier than the ocean. At the height of summer, there are up to 100 million alkali flies around the lake.

REPAIRED WING > Romy McCloskey, a costume designer from The Woodlands, Texas, raises monarch butterflies as her hobby—and even fixed the broken wing of one butterfly so that it could fly again. Finding a monarch with a badly damaged left wing, she cut it off and replaced it with the left wing of another monarch butterfly that had recently died of natural causes. The new wing was carefully attached using glue, tweezers, a wire hanger, a toothpick, and a cotton swab.

POOL RESCUE > An 800-lb (363-kg) heifer that had been grazing nearby had to be rescued after accidentally falling into Burt Thornburg's swimming pool in Newton, North Carolina. The cow had walked across the pool cover, thinking it was solid ground.

TUNNEL DRAMA > Firefighters in Chandler, Arizona, helped rescue Toby Passmore's Scottish Schnauzer dog, Ticklish Rubin, after it had chased a cat into a garden tunnel dug by his giant tortoise. Armed with shovels, they excavated the 6-ft-deep (1.8-m) tunnel and then held Passmore by his ankles while he squeezed in headfirst and pulled the dog out.

KITTEN ALERT > When Alexis Guerrero and Alfred Griffin's dog Little Momma kept barking and growling at the bedroom wall of their home in Houston, Texas, they decided to investigate and heard the sound of a kitten. They cut through the wall to rescue the trapped kitten, which they named Angel.

PIPE PYTHON > Rescuers pulled a 20-ft-long (6-m) python weighing 65 lb (29.5 kg) from the toilet of Chalida Thawephol's home in Chonburi Province, Thailand. Her five-year-old son had told her that there was something unusual in the toilet bowl.

STATION RITUAL > A stray dog walked alone to Kanjurmarg station in Mumbai, India, every night for more than two months and waited on platform one to greet the late-night train bound for Kalyan. She always waited outside a coach that was reserved for women passengers, peered inside, and when nobody she knew got off, chased the train as it pulled away.

TOAD MUSEUM

⮕ On the banks of the Thuan River in Yasothon, Thailand, sits a giant toad. The five-story building houses the Toad King Museum (Phraya Khan Khak Museum), and it celebrates the story of Praya Kankak, the Toad King, who battled the god of rain to save mankind from flooding. The top floor, in the toad's mouth, has an observation platform to view the river.

DEFLATED DOG!

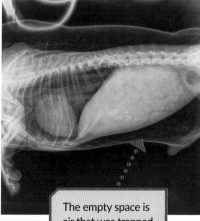

The empty space is air that was trapped under Trevor's skin.

BALLOON DOG

➔ When a hole in his windpipe caused air to become trapped under his skin, Trevor, a four-year-old wiener dog owned by Fran Jennings of Cheshire, England, ballooned to three times his normal size! Veterinarians were successfully able to carry out an operation to deflate him.

The Last Straw

⤷ **Giant straw animals are sculpted every year for the Wara Art Festival in Japan's Niigata Prefecture.**

The art festival was born in 2008 out of necessity for farmers to find a way to use their leftover rice straw, or wara, after the harvest. Art students, professional artists, and even amateur artists from areas nearby enjoy creating their own sculptures with the use of wara and the wooden frames that provide a sturdy base. Currently in its 11th year, the festival has seen some amazing sculptures, from crocodiles and gorillas to mammoths, hippos, and sabre-toothed tigers.

FEATHERS SPILLED > A tractor-trailer that rolled over north of Tacoma, Washington, dumped 40,000 lb (18,100 kg) of chicken feathers across Interstate 5.

LAP OF LUXURY > Troy Good rented a $1,500-a-month studio apartment in San Jose, California, just for his daughter Victoria's two cats, Tina and Louise.

MARATHON RUN > Stormy, a stray dog, completed the 13.1 mi (21 km) of the 2018 Goldfields Pipeline Half-Marathon in Kalgoorlie, Western Australia, alongside human competitors. He finished in around 2 ½ hours, similar to the average time of the 97 runners.

JAZZ FANS > A study by Australian scientists at Macquarie University shows that sharks prefer jazz to any other form of music.

CHOCOLATE TREATS > A family of bears broke into a car in Asheville, North Carolina, and ate 49 chocolate bars that were being stored there for a fundraiser.

HOME BODY > Hermit crabs with large, desirable shell homes have developed larger penises—more than half the length of their bodies—so that they can mate without leaving their shell and risking it being stolen by a rival.

FALSE ALARM > Fire crews in Northamptonshire, England, rushed to what they thought was the sound of a fire alarm, only to discover it was Steve Dockerty's African gray parrot Jazz mimicking the alarm noise.

LAST SNAIL > When George, a Hawaiian tree snail, died on New Year's Day 2019 at the age of 14, the species *Achatinella apexfulva* became extinct.

HORSE MUSTACHES

⤷ A breed of horse known as Irish Cobs can actually grow hair right beneath their noses, making it look like they have tiny mustaches. These mustaches sometimes curl up on their own, but some horses are lucky enough to have their facial hair styled by their loving owners.

OVEN SHELTER > Loukoumakis, a four-year-old poodle mix, survived devastating wildfires in Mati, Greece, by hiding inside an outdoor oven for two days.

RUN, RUN REINDEER > At just one day old, baby reindeer are faster than Olympic sprinters and can keep up with the rest of the herd running at top speed.

HOLDING ON > Some Caribbean lizards can cling on to objects in the face of 109 mph (174 kmph) winds, enabling them to survive hurricanes.

TINY SEAHORSE > A new species of pygmy seahorse—*Hippocampus japapigu*—discovered off the coast of Japan is no bigger than a grain of rice.

BRICKED IN > Dexter, a tabby-Bengal cross cat owned by Rosy Clark of Devon, England, emerged unscathed after being bricked up inside the foundations of a neighboring new-build house for more than two weeks.

PRIZED CARP > A female red and white koi carp measuring 3.4 ft (101 cm) long sold for $1.8 million at a fish auction in Hiroshima, Japan.

FELINE MAYOR > The village of Omena, Michigan, elected a nine-year-old local cat, Sweet Tart, as its mayor in 2018. Sweet Tart, who had previously served as vice mayor, defeated competition from 13 dogs, another cat, a goat, a chicken, and a peacock.

QUICK THINKING > To escape a pod of hungry killer whales in Frederick Arm, British Columbia, Canada, a seal jumped on board a passing tourist boat, the *Yellowfin Swan*.

COW COMPANION > For his graduation photo at the University of Missouri, senior animal sciences major Massimo Montalbano brought along Amelia, his favorite cow.

ODD GREETING > White-faced capuchin monkeys say "hello" by sticking their fingers up each other's noses.

HOTEL GUEST > In August 2018, a black bear opened the door of the Stanley Hotel in Estes Park, Colorado (the hotel that inspired Stephen King to write *The Shining*), wandered into the lobby, and climbed over furniture while 300 guests slept.

TRASH COLLECTORS > The Puy du Fou theme park in western France has trained six crows to pick up cigarette butts and other trash.

POOP DIET > Koala bear babies eat their mother's poop and toxic eucalyptus leaves.

BEAR BITE > The bite of a grizzly bear is so powerful it can crush a bowling ball.

MOUSE COSTUME > To help Rupert the Dalmatian dog bond with him before undergoing surgery, veterinarian Mike Ferrell, from Hertfordshire, England, dressed up in a full, one-piece, gray mouse costume.

SNAKE BUS

In northern Australia during a severe rainstorm, 10 cane toads were spotted riding atop an olive python as the snake was moving toward higher ground. While the toads were originally thought to be hitching a ride to take shelter from the storm, it turns out they were just a little overeager for mating season. Believe it or not, cane toads are highly poisonous, and animals such as crocodiles and snakes have been killed by eating or mouthing the amphibians.

OXYGEN TUBE!

RODENT RESCUE ➲ Firefighters in Lacey, Washington, responded to a mobile home fire and managed to save the family—that is, the hamster family—inside. They revived the baby hamsters, referring to their "Pet Emergency Pocket Guide" and then administered oxygen through a tiny pipe.

CHOPPER CRASH > A low-flying helicopter was brought down by a leaping elk in the mountains of Wasatch County, Utah, in February 2018.

SIX-LEGGED CALF > A mutant calf was born in Chongqing, China, in 2018, with two legs and a butt hanging from its stomach. Although it struggled to walk properly with its extra limbs, the animal weighed a healthy 33 lb (15 kg) and soon became a tourist attraction.

CARDBOARD LOVE > Grape-kun, a 20-year-old Humboldt penguin that lived at Tobu Zoo in Miyashiro, Japan, fell in love with a cardboard cut-out of Hululu, an anime character in a penguin dress, that had been placed in the enclosure as part of a promotion. He stared longingly at her every day for six months, and keepers even had to remove Hululu temporarily so that the penguin could be persuaded to eat.

CHANCE DISCOVERY > The Vangunu giant rat (*Uromys vika*) was only discovered when loggers felled a 30-ft-tall (9-m) tree on the South Pacific island of Vangunu and the large rodent came crashing down with it. For years, people in the Solomon Islands had spoken of huge treetop-dwelling rats weighing more than 2 lb (0.9 kg) and growing up to 1.5 ft (45 cm) long—four times larger than city rats—but nobody had ever proved that they actually existed.

DETERMINED SQUIRREL > A squirrel made repeated attempts to board a small plane that was preparing for takeoff from Beverly Regional Airport, Massachusetts. After hiding inside the hangar, it ran out to the plane and jumped into the engine compartment. Despite being removed, it then made several efforts to climb into the passenger area before eventually giving up and running off.

LONG-LOST MONKEY > When monkey expert Laura Marsh spotted a live specimen of Vanzolini's bald-faced saki (*Pithecia vanzolinii*) in Brazil in 2017, it was the first time that one had been seen in the wild for more than 80 years.

GREAT SHAKES > Dogs can shake 70 percent of the water out of their fur in four seconds, generating more G-force than Formula 1 drivers experience when taking tight corners.

BUSINESS BRAIN > In 1999, Raven the chimp became the 22nd most successful money manager in the United States after choosing stocks at random, generating a 213 percent gain and outperforming more than 6,000 professional Wall Street brokers.

WHALE ROUTE > Every year, gray whales swim more than 10,000 mi (16,000 km) while migrating between their winter breeding grounds off the coast of Mexico and their summer feeding grounds in the Arctic.

WILD TURKEYS > In January 2018, mail carriers in Rocky River, Ohio, found their routes blocked by a gang of aggressive wild turkeys, with the result that 30 homes were unable to receive any mail for three weeks. After the birds started attacking the carriers, homeowners were instructed to go to the post office to pick up mail.

28 TOES > Paws, a polydactyl cat owned by Jeanne Martin of Northfield, Minnesota, has 28 toes—10 toes more than an ordinary cat.

PAINTING SQUIRREL

➲ Meet Winkelhimer Smith—the painting squirrel! Owner Shyla M. of Louisiana saved Winkelhimer from a cat attack as a baby, nursing her back to health before discovering her hidden artistic talents. A video of the rescue rodent showing off her skills went viral on YouTube, and now all proceeds from the sale of the squirrel's masterpieces are donated to charity. (Every painting comes with a picture of Winkelhimer as she's working on the piece, as well as glued-on molted fur from her tail as proof of authenticity.)

CAUTION: WET PAINT!

CAT JOCKEY > Louis, a Siamese cat, often rides on the back of Comet, a Connemara pony, near their owner Emma Massingale's home in Devon, England. Louis sits on the pony's back while he walks along country lanes, and when he gets bored, he simply jumps off. If Louis wants Comet to stop, he bites his mane.

SNAKE ATTACK > Melissa Butt's protective pit bulls Slayer and Paco saved her grandchildren from an attack by a venomous snake in the garden of her home in Brandon, Florida. Zayden, 4, and Mallory, 1, were playing in the garden when the dogs began barking at something in the grass. As the children were hurriedly taken indoors, the dogs continued to stand guard and, although both were bitten by the snake, they recovered after veterinary treatment.

REGURGITATED ROOSTER > After chicken breeder Nut Wattana noticed that two of his champion roosters were missing from their coop in Pathum Thani, Thailand, he spotted a 15-ft-long (4.6-m) python hanging from the roof with an enormous bulge in its stomach. The snake was caught and placed on the ground, and eventually it regurgitated one of the roosters, which emerged dead and covered in slime. The other bird was found dead nearby.

A MOTHER'S EMBRACE

➲ Despite having a scary appearance, centipedes can make great moms!

In some centipede species, the mother will curl up around her eggs to protect her babies before and after they hatch, forgoing food until her young are ready to be alone. Believe it or not, even though their name literally means "one hundred legs," there are no centipede species with 100 legs!

PROTECTING HER BABIES!

BADGERED ANTELOPE

⭢ Honey badgers are notorious for picking fights with just about anyone, no matter how big or strong they are, but this one got more than it bargained for when it decided to attack a South African oryx.

The photographer who witnessed the event, Dick Theron, said the badger attacked the oryx, a type of antelope, at a watering hole in Etosha National Park, South Africa. The oryx responded by picking the badger up between its horns and tossing it 16 to 19 ft (5 to 6 m) through the air. Unperturbed, the badger went back several times, getting thrown each time, before deciding to back down.

BABOON VANDAL >
A baboon wandered into a power station and tampered with machinery in Livingstone, Zambia, leaving 40,000 people without electricity for five hours.

FAKE TESTICLES >
Gregg Miller, from Kansas City, Missouri, has become a millionaire by selling fake dog testicles that allow neutered male dogs to retain their masculine appearance. He has sold more than 500,000 of the silicone implants called Neuticles in around 50 different countries worldwide since the product was launched in 1995 and has expanded the business to provide fake testicles for cats, horses, and bulls.

NUCLEAR COWS >
Animal lover Tani Sakiyuki risks her life every day by venturing into Japan's Fukushima radiation zone to feed a herd of 11 cows abandoned there after the 2011 nuclear disaster. She even changed jobs from Tokyo to a location closer to the exclusion zone and switched to a night shift so that she could care for the cows by day.

FIRST STARLINGS >
European starlings were introduced to North America in 1890 by William Shakespeare fan Eugene Schieffelin who wanted New York's Central Park to become home to all the songbirds mentioned in Shakespeare's plays, the starling featuring briefly in *Henry IV, Part 1*. Schieffelin initially brought in 80 starlings, and now there are 200 million in North America.

DESTRUCTIVE DONKEY >
A donkey in Schlitz, Germany, ate the rear bodywork of Markus Zahn's $280,000 luxury McLaren sports car, causing considerable damage and leaving the animal's owners with a $6,800 fine. The police speculated that Vitus the donkey may have mistaken the orange car parked next to his enclosure for a giant carrot.

PLAYFUL BEARS > In October 2017, a family of bear cubs wandered into the backyard of Tim Conklin's home in East Granby, Connecticut, and played with the family's swing set.

MUSICAL ELEPHANT > Using its trunk, Andaal, an elephant at a conservation park in Coimbatore, India, can play the harmonica.

KOALA RIDE > A koala survived a 10-mi (16-km) journey across Adelaide, South Australia, while clinging to the wheel arch of a four-wheel drive vehicle. The driver only realized the animal was there after being flagged down by other motorists.

MEAT EATERS > Globally, spiders eat twice as much meat as humans each year—800 million tons of insects compared to humans' 400 million tons of meat and fish.

DACHSHUND MUSEUM

↪ The Dackelmuseum in Passau, Germany, contains more than 4,500 items of dachshund-related memorabilia, including a toy Waldi, the mascot for the 1972 Olympic Games in Munich. The museum was founded by former florists Josef Küblbeck and Oliver Storz, who collected wiener dog toys, salt shakers, beer mugs, and plates over a period of 25 years.

EAGLE INVASION > In Unalaska, Alaska, bald eagles are as common as pigeons are in other cities. The city is home to 4,700 people and 600 bald eagles.

DUAL FUNCTION > The mouth of the hammerhead worm is also its anus. The worm uses the same orifice, located in the middle of its body, for both eating and excretion.

ADOPTED NARWHAL > Since 2016, a young male narwhal has been spotted swimming with a pod of about 50-60 beluga whales in Canada's St. Lawrence River—about 600 mi (966 km) south of where narwhals typically live.

TOUGH BEETLES > Click beetles can withstand 40 times more G-force than a fighter pilot. When threatened by a predator, the insect contracts a hinge that holds together two segments of its body and explodes into the air at 380 times the force of gravity.

EATING CHOICE > In March 2018, Pancho and Lefty, a live rat snake with two functional heads, went on display at the Cameron Park Zoo in Waco, Texas. The snake can eat using either of its heads, and sometimes takes food with both heads simultaneously, although the left head is more dominant.

ODD IS ART

Peacock Feather Painting
Luke Winebrenner

Cat. No. 170833

Strange Mail Contest submission. Portrait of a young girl and boy painted on peacock feathers.

INLAND SHARKS > Aggressive, 11-ft-long (3.4-m) bull sharks live in Nicaragua's Lake Nicaragua, even though it is freshwater, inland, and does not connect to the nearby Pacific Ocean. Instead, the sharks reach the lake by swimming almost 120 mi (192 km) up the San Juan River from the Caribbean Sea. In 1937, a bull shark traveled up the Mississippi River as far as Alton, Illinois, about 700 mi (1,120 km) from the ocean.

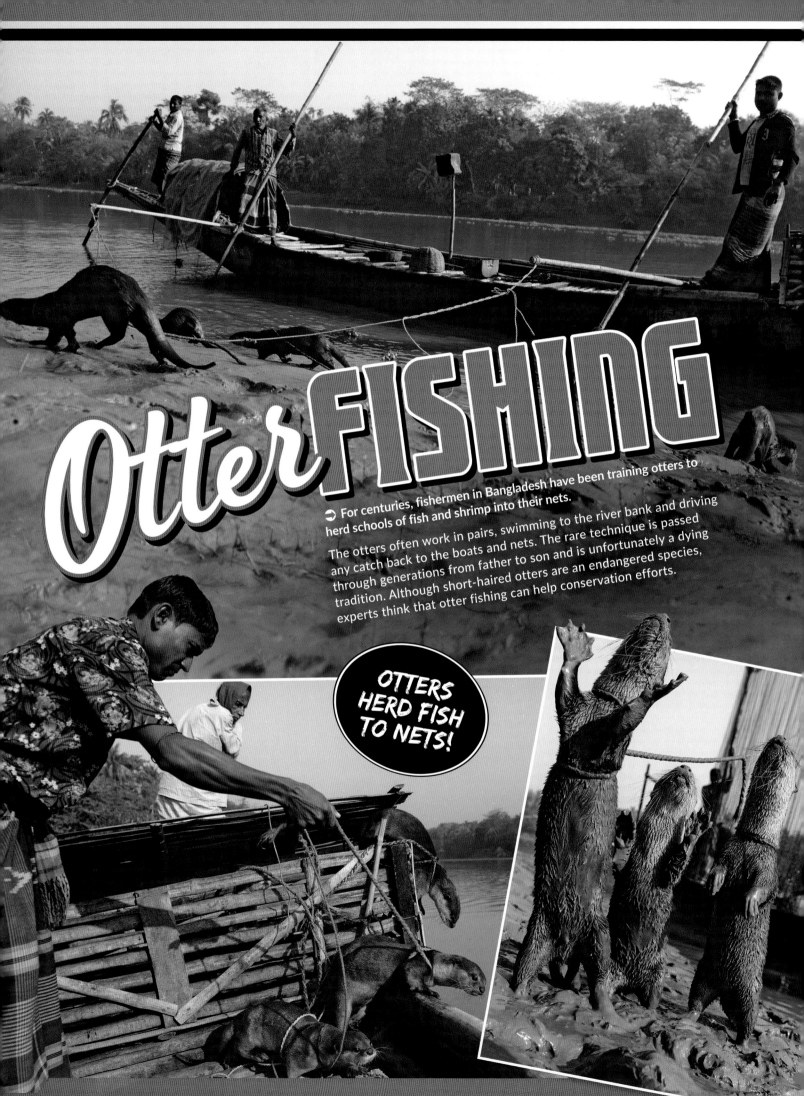

Otter FISHING

For centuries, fishermen in Bangladesh have been training otters to herd schools of fish and shrimp into their nets.

The otters often work in pairs, swimming to the river bank and driving any catch back to the boats and nets. The rare technique is passed through generations from father to son and is unfortunately a dying tradition. Although short-haired otters are an endangered species, experts think that otter fishing can help conservation efforts.

OTTERS HERD FISH TO NETS!

SOARING SQUID

⭕ Believe it or not, some squids can launch themselves out of the water and fly! Some squids go solo while others soar in large groups, using jet propulsion to get an astonishing amount of airtime, sometimes reaching speeds of 36 ft (11 m) per second—faster than Usain Bolt!

Some species can soar as far as 33 ft (10 m) before they dive back into the water!

DONKEY DROP > A wandering donkey fell through the roof of a hillside home in Cajazeiras, Brazil. It quickly wriggled free from the hole it had made, dropped to the floor, and walked off unhurt.

CHICKEN BOARDER > Karly Venezia takes Loretta, her pet Rhode Island Red hen, paddleboarding around the Florida Keys, and, unusual for a chicken, she is perfectly at home in the water.

The cuddly otters are like hunting dogs that flush out hidden prey.

SPECIAL CHAIR > Tink, a silver Labrador retriever owned by Tom Sullivan, of Grand Rapids, Michigan, has to eat standing up on her hind legs in a specially built high chair. She was born with a rare condition called megaesophagus, which prevents food eaten in a normal position from entering her stomach.

RANDOM FLUSH > When the toilet of a home in Doonan, Queensland, Australia, began flushing itself at random, the residents discovered the cause was a brown tree snake that was hiding in the wall and resting on the flush mechanism.

JUMPING FISH > The giant trevally fish (*Caranx ignobilis*) of the Indian and Pacific Oceans can pluck birds out of the sky. It grows up to 5.5 ft (1.7 m) long, weighs as much as 176 lb (80 kg), and by lurking near the surface, can jump up to catch and eat seabirds as they fly low across the water.

TORTOISE RIDE > While hiking through Pima County, Arizona, Mario El Pachuco saw a rattlesnake hitching a ride on the back of a desert tortoise.

DOLPHIN GIFT > Male humpback dolphins will sometimes present females with large sea sponges that they have torn from the ocean floor in the hope of creating a favorable impression and winning a mate.

SOFT SPOT > Visitors to a claw machine in Dubai found a real cat sleeping among the stuffed toys waiting to be picked up as prizes.

WEED CLEARING > A herd of 170 goats were used to remove weeds from Rundle Park in Edmonton, Alberta, Canada, in 2017, and now the city employs a human "goat coordinator" to oversee its use of goats for tidying up recreation areas.

EGG SURPRISE > Staff at Eagle Heights Wildlife Foundation in Kent, England, were shocked to discover that Harold the griffon vulture was actually a female when she laid an egg after 20 years in captivity.

DONKEYS JAILED > Eight donkeys were imprisoned for four days in November 2017 after eating over $6,000 worth of plants outside Urai Jail in Uttar Pradesh, India.

KISS OF LIFE > John Fletcher saved the life of his drowning pet tortoise Freda by giving her mouth-to-mouth resuscitation for an hour. He had found 45-year-old Freda at the bottom of his garden pond in Gloucester, England.

PLASTIC RING > Adam Turnbull, from Sarnia, Ontario, Canada, found a northern pike in the Saskatchewan River that had grown around a discarded plastic drink ring. The ring circled the middle of the pike's body, and after removing the plastic, Turnbull released the fish back into the river.

FAKE COYOTES > To scare sea lions away from the harbor at Newport Beach, California, officials spent $200 on a pack of eight plastic coyotes, which they moved to different locations each day.

EQUINE GUEST > Lindsey Partridge, a horse trainer from Pontypool, Ontario, Canada, paid $10 to check her five-year-old gray thoroughbred mare, Blizz, into a hotel room in Georgetown, Kentucky.

BUTTERFLY SWARM > A swarm of migrating painted lady butterflies over Denver, Colorado, in October 2017 measured around 70 mi (112 km) wide and was so large it showed up as a cloud pattern on weather radar imagery.

FROZEN IGUANAS > When temperatures in Florida dropped below 40°F (5°C) in January 2018, iguanas froze and even fell from trees. In extreme cold, their bodies stiffen up, leaving them unable to move in a state of suspended animation, but they usually recover when it gets warmer and they thaw out.

SMUSHED SMILE

SKULL SQUISHED IN THE WOMB!

Beaux Tox the dog has a face only his mother could love—well, his mother and about 140,000 Instagram followers!

Beaux Tox's (pronounced like "Botox") strange face is a result of him being squished in his mother's crowded womb. His skull shape doesn't affect his brain function in any way, but his unique appearance sadly kept him from being adopted, and he ended up with an owner who did not properly care for him. Thankfully, Jamie Hulit of Texas took him in and nursed him back to health before it was too late. Now he has a loving forever home and thousands of online admirers!

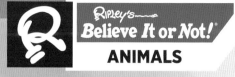
CELL YEAH! ⮕ Believe it or not, this blob is a single-celled organism! While most unicellular creatures are impossible to see with the naked eye, *Valonia ventricosa*—also known as "bubble algae" or "sailor's eyeball"—can grow more than 2 in (5 cm) wide.

SLINGSHOT JAW > The goblin shark (*Mitsukurina owstoni*) is the last remaining member of the 125-million-year-old *Mitsukurinidae* family and lives 4,000 ft (1,300 m) below the ocean surface. It catches prey with its slingshot jaw, which juts out at 10 ft (3 m) per second, making it faster than most cobra strikes. The shark's jaw mechanism allows it to attack without moving the rest of its body.

EAGLE SNATCH > Zoey the Bichon Frise was safely reunited with owner Monica Newhard after being snatched and carried off by an eagle that swooped down on the family's yard in Bowmanstown, Pennsylvania. The 8-lb (3.6-kg) dog was dropped on a road 4 mi (6.4 km) away, where a passing driver found it cold and bruised.

FACE RECOGNITION > As an alternative to installing a cat flap, Arkaitz Garro, a Dutch software engineer, built a face-recognition gadget for a friendly neighborhood cat so that it does not have to wait too long to be let into the house. The setup takes a picture when it detects movement, and if the image matches the cat's face, it sends a message to Garro's phone so he knows to open the door.

SNIFFER DOG > In her first five months at work as a sniffer dog at London's Heathrow Airport, Jessie, a Springer Spaniel, located more than $1.3 million of illegal bank bills that were being smuggled through the building.

DEADLY TINSEL > A 5-ft-long (1.5-m), venomous, red-bellied black snake wrapped itself around a family Christmas tree at a home in Melbourne, Australia, before being removed by snake catcher Raymond Hoser.

DEER RESCUE > Storm, a golden retriever owned by Mark Freeley, instinctively swam out into the Long Island Sound and dragged a struggling baby deer safely back to shore. After completing the rescue, Storm kept nudging the fawn to make sure it was okay. The deer was later transported to a local animal rescue center for a period of recovery.

SUGAR THIEF > An elephant with a sweet tusk was filmed wandering into a road in Chachoengsao, Thailand, and deliberately blocking traffic so that it could snatch sugar cane from the backs of trucks as they slowed down. The elephant tried to steal from more than a dozen trucks in two hours before wandering back into the jungle.

ARROW JUST MISSED VITAL ORGANS!

HEADSTRONG

⮕ A goose in Plymouth, Massachusetts, survived after being shot in the head with an arrow! Through pure luck, the arrow missed vital organs and the bird didn't even bleed when it was removed. Staff at the New England Wildlife Center were able to release the fortunate fowl back into the wild a month later.

CAT SCAN

⊃ In a quirky, ironic twist, a 14-year-old African lion named Tomo had a CAT scan at the Columbus Zoo and Aquarium! The big cat's home is one of just six zoos in the United States with the imaging machine on site, and with it, veterinarians determined that an infection within Tomo's gums was localized. The king of the jungle is expected to make a full recovery!

ZOO POO > The first 1,000 visitors to Detroit Zoo on April 14, 2018, were given free buckets of zoo poo—5 lb (2.3 kg) of animal manure that contain valuable nutrients for improving garden soil.

SLOW ESCAPE > A giant tortoise named Abu that escaped from Japan's Shibukawa Animal Park was found two weeks later, just 500 ft (150 m) away.

GRASSHOPPER PLAGUES > Thousands of grasshoppers were mixed into the concrete for the foundation of the First United Methodist Church in Hutchinson, Kansas, because it was built in 1874 during the time of severe grasshopper plagues.

DROWNING ELEPHANT > In a 12-hour operation, the Sri Lankan navy rescued a drowning elephant from the ocean 10 mi (16 km) offshore of Kokkilai. The elephant was thought to have been swept far out to sea by a strong current.

SYNCHRONIZED BIRTHS > Groups of mongooses sharing an underground den all give birth on the same day to reduce infanticide. Synchronized birthing prevents the older, dominant females from killing the offspring of younger females, because they cannot be sure which babies are theirs and do not want to risk accidentally killing their own.

> The tongue of a blue whale can weigh as much as an adult elephant and is so big an entire football team could stand on it.

USEFUL LEGS > Sea spiders not only breathe through their long legs, but also females store their eggs in their legs.

PIG TREASURE > Bo Chunlou, a farmer from Shandong Province, China, found a 4-in-long (10-cm) pig's gallstone (or bezoar)—a mass of hair and other indigestible materials—and then learned that it was worth $600,000. Known as "pig treasure," gallbladder bezoars are used in traditional Chinese medicine to remove toxins from the body.

AIRPORT DELAY > Passengers waiting to step off a Spirit Airlines flight from Baltimore, Maryland, that had just landed at Orlando International Airport, Florida, on June 11, 2018, were ordered to wait inside the plane for a few minutes because a huge alligator was crossing the runway.

PYTHON PREY > Although they typically eat rodents, birds, and lizards, African rock pythons will also devour antelopes and even crocodiles. A rock python was once found with a small leopard in its stomach.

LANDFILL HATCHERY > A landfill near Marneuli in the country of Georgia was overrun with hundreds of tiny chicks after the scorching heat caused spoiled eggs that had been disposed there by a local poultry farm to hatch.

SHOT BY PET > Richard Remme, of Fort Dodge, Iowa, was accidentally shot by his dog Balew, a pit bull–Labrador mix. He was playing with the dog at home when it stepped on the trigger of Remme's handgun and shot him in the leg.

HOT DRINK > Flamingos can drink near-boiling water. Most lakes where the birds live have high concentrations of salt, and often their only source of freshwater comes from boiling geysers.

Ripley's **Rarities**

Rarity Nº 171018

Soviet Medal

Aluminum medal released in 2007 to mark the 50th anniversary of Sputnik 2, which carried Laika, the first animal to orbit Earth. Made from metal flown in space.

ЛАЙКА 1957 – 2007

Monkeying AROUND

○ **Two-year-old Samarth Bangari has befriended a pack of 20 langur monkeys in his home village of Allapur, Karnataka, in India.**

No one is quite sure why these primates took such a liking to Samarth, but for months they have been practically inseparable. The langurs will sneak into the toddler's room in the early morning hours to wake him up to play, and Samarth will bring food from home to give to his primate friends. When this first began, the boy's parents worried the monkeys would hurt him, but so far there have been no incidents—in fact, the monkeys seem extremely protective, even possessive, of Samarth.

MISLEADING NAME > Although it is known as the Wolverine State, there are no longer any wolverines living in the wild in Michigan.

SPOILED MILK > By chewing through a piece of vital equipment, a squirrel caused a fire that knocked out power to 150 residents of Burnaby, British Columbia, Canada, and spoiled 21,662 gal (82,000 l) of milk at a local cheese factory.

POISON ARROWS > Jellyfish use stinging cells containing high-powered "syringes" to shoot venom into their prey at a speed of 50 million meters per second—100 times faster than the speed of a rifle bullet.

CALLING CARD > A great white shark that bit a large chunk out of an Australian man's surfboard while he was kiteboarding off Ballina, New South Wales, left behind a sinister calling card—a razor-sharp tooth.

WILD TIMELINE > Woolly mammoths existed for centuries after the Egyptian pyramids were built.

DUCK DELAY > The busy M25 motorway around London was closed for nearly an hour during rush hour on July 19, 2018, after 30 ducks waddled across the eight-lane highway in Hertfordshire. The government blocked the road in both directions while the ducks were escorted to safety.

CATERPILLAR WOE > After biting into a spiny caterpillar, eight-month-old Kenzie Pyne, from Nanaimo, British Columbia, Canada, was rushed to the hospital for surgery to remove its hairs and spines that had attached themselves to her mouth. Its feelers had fused to her cheek, and its hairs were stuck to her tongue.

PET SOUNDS > Police officers were called to investigate a domestic disturbance in Loerrach, Germany, after a neighbor was worried about hearing shouting from the next-door apartment—but when they arrived, they found it was a man arguing with his girlfriend's parrot, which was squawking back at him.

CROC FEST

➲ Nearly every summer, the Sheedi ethnic group in Pakistan celebrates Sheedi Mela, which ends with devotees decorating and feeding the wild crocodiles at a shrine in Manghopir.

The celebration honors the sacred crocodile—spiritually associated with the shrine's saint and a symbol of their past, as the four clans involved trace their lineage to Africa. Clan leaders entice the oldest and largest crocodile in the swamp, whom they call Mor Sahab or "chief of the crocodiles," out of the pond before applying saffron and other fragrances over it as well as decorating it with a garland of flowers. The believers also feed the hundreds of crocodiles in the pond with sacrificial meat from four goats, representing the four clans. The reptiles are so revered that when they die, they are buried near the shrine.

HAND FEEDING!

MAGIC CARPET > A Singapore pet food company created an art exhibit designed for dogs and cats. The event included a room designed to give dogs the illusion that they were floating on a magic carpet through a sky full of toys and tasty meat snacks, as well as a giant fake cat containing four themed rooms that cats could explore.

WILD SIDE > A cow abandoned its life as a domestic animal on a farm in Poland and escaped to join a herd of wild bison in the Bialowieza Forest near the border with Belarus.

HUGE EGG > A kiwi is the same size as a hen, but its egg is seven times larger than a hen's egg. When a kiwi lays an egg, it is the equivalent of a human mother giving birth to a four-year-old.

FUR INK > German model Kathrin Tölle loves her 10-year-old cat Gizmo so much that she has got a thigh tattoo of her pet made with ink from its own fur. Swiss company Skin46 specializes in creating tattoo inks from medically clean organic carbon that has been extracted from human or animal hair.

HAPPY REUNION > Perry Martin lost his pet cat Thomas Jr. (or T2 for short) after Hurricane Jeanne hit Stuart, Florida, in 2004—but 14 years later they were reunited when the cat was found as a stray and officials discovered he had a microchip containing his owner's details.

QUACK ATTACK

➲ Around 6,000 ducks brought traffic to a halt in Long Phú District, Sóc Trăng Province, Vietnam, as they waddled their way to a new field. Cars and motorbikes could do nothing but wait for the birds to finish crossing, quacking loudly as they went. In Vietnam, ducks can be used as a form of pesticide in rice fields, as they eat damaging weeds and bugs while also fertilizing the land. Ducks are also raised in fields and later eaten as a free-range delicacy.

CAT RESCUER > Since 2014, Randall Kolb, a retiree from Baton Rouge, Louisiana, has devoted his time to rescuing cats from trees. Also known as "Cat Rescue Guy," he has plucked more than 150 cats to safety—for free.

WARM SPOT > While clearing out some old stuffed toys and teddy bears from a garage in Surrey, England, a woman discovered a real, live ferret snuggled up among them. She thought something was strange when one of the bags moved.

PET CROC > Muhammad Iwan, of West Java, Indonesia, shares his home with an 8.66-ft-long (2.6-m), 440-lb (200-kg) saltwater crocodile named Kojek. He bought the croc as a newborn in 1997 and Kojek, who eats 3.3 lb (1.5 kg) of goldfish every day, has lived happily with the family ever since, interacting with the children and never hurting them. Iwan gives Kojek regular skin care and even brushes the huge reptile's teeth.

FISH BANDAGES > Two bears and a cougar that were burned in the 2017 California wildfire had their paw wounds healed with bandages made of fish skin. Veterinarians purchased live tilapia fish at a market, then skinned them and sterilized the skin for several days. Tilapia skin contains collagen proteins that accelerate the healing process.

SAME BEAR!

UNINVITED GUESTS > A mother raccoon and her four babies fell through the ceiling of a home in Sheridan Township, Michigan, and landed in a living room chair.

HIDDEN BLADE > In addition to being venomous, the stonefish conceals a switchblade in its face. It has a bony, spiky protuberance under each eye that can be popped out to scare off predators.

HIGH MORTALITY > Only about 1 percent of young crocodile eggs survive to 5 years old. Most are eaten by lizards, herons, fish, and other crocodiles.

DEMONIC GOAT > A stillborn goat on Gladys Oviedo's farm in San Luis, Argentina, had such a demonic face that terrified townspeople called the police.

BUSH ORDEAL > Max, a 17-year-old blue heeler dog, saved a three-year-old girl's life by keeping her safe for 15 hours overnight in the dense bush in Queensland, Australia, even though he is deaf and partially blind. After staying by her side through the rainy night, he led rescuers to the child the next day.

FAT BEAR WEEK ⟳ You've heard of Shark Week, but what about Fat Bear Week? Every year, Alaska's Katmai National Park holds a bracket-style competition to let the public vote on which bears they think have done the best job of gorging on salmon and putting on the pounds for hibernation. The 2018 winner was Beadnose, who stole the Internet's heart with her amazing transformation over just a few months.

STARMAGEDDON

⟳ Tens of thousands of dead starfish washed up on a beach in Ramsgate, England, in March 2018, probably as a result of sub-zero temperatures and stormy weather.

PRAIRIE HOME > A vast prairie dog settlement on the high plains of Texas in 1900 contained an estimated 400 million prairie dogs and measured 250 × 100 mi (400 × 160 km).

PLATYPUS POISON > The venom of a male Australian duck-billed platypus is potent enough to kill a small dog.

WALKING FISH > A member of the anglerfish family, the sea toad has lived in the deepest, darkest regions of the Gulf of Mexico for so long that its fins have evolved into feet, helping it to shuffle along the ocean floor.

SPONGE SURVIVORS > There are sea sponges alive today that were around when the first humans arrived in North America 15,000 years ago.

RACCOON DELAY > A raccoon caused a seven-hour flight delay after hiding in the duct system of an Air Canada jet airplane in Saskatoon, Saskatchewan.

CROC JAWS > Although a crocodile's jaws can apply 5,000 lb (2,268 kg) of pressure per square inch (6.5 sq cm)—giving them a bite that is over 30 times more powerful than that of a human—the muscles that open the jaws have very little strength, and its mouth can be held shut with a rubber band.

COLLIE TRICKS > Hero, a five-year-old rescue collie owned by Sara Carson of North Bay, Ontario, Canada, can perform 49 different tricks in 60 seconds, including walking on his front legs, dancing, spinning, and jumping onto Sara's back.

DESTRUCTIVE PETS > Nearly $2 million in loose cash has been eaten by pets in the United Kingdom since 2003.

DOG COLOGNE > Dan Capps, a veterinarian from Coolum, Queensland, created a range of dog toiletries and fragrancies, which he called Kevin because they were inspired by his miniature Australian bulldog, Kevin.

HONEY BEES > Around 80,000 bees were removed from the walls of Maude Mack's house in Houston, Texas—and the honey collected from inside the walls was sold at local stores, with the proceeds going toward relocating honey bees.

MONSTER DINOSAUR > The long-necked dinosaur *Patagotitan mayorum*, which lived more than 100 million years ago in modern-day Argentina, measured more than 120 ft (37 m) long and weighed 76 tons—the same as 12 adult African elephants.

HIGH JUMP > The southern cricket frog can jump to a height 60 times its body length—equivalent to a person jumping the height of the Statue of Liberty.

FIVE LEGS > A bull was born on a farm in Mudanjiang City, China, in October 2017 with an extra leg growing out of its back—but the calf was still able to run around normally and lead a healthy life.

HUGE HORNET

⟳ The Asian giant hornet (*Vespa mandarinia*) measures 2 in (5 cm) long with a wingspan of 3 in (7.5 cm), and its sting contains a venom so powerful it can damage human tissue and essentially melt flesh.

Found in Russia and throughout Southeast Asia, the world's largest hornet is both big and aggressive, launching coordinated attacks on unsuspecting honey bees. A group of just 30 hornets can kill a hive containing 30,000 bees in less than four hours. It's when the hornets interact with humans that things get even scarier. Every year in Japan, around 30 to 40 people are killed by Asian giant hornet stings. Unbelievably, in other parts of Asia, the fierce insect is sometimes used in alcoholic drinks.

FOX FUR > Arctic foxes are so well insulated by their thick fur that they don't begin to shiver from the cold until the temperature drops to –40°F (–40°C).

BABY FOOD > A blue whale calf drinks 50 gal (190 l) of its mother's milk—enough to fill a bath—and gains about 198 lb (90 kg) in weight every day for the first year of its life.

DOLLHOUSE > A hermit crab on uninhabited Henderson Island in the Pacific Ocean used a discarded doll's head as its shell home. The doll's head had been washed ashore with other debris.

LOYAL STORK > Every year for 16 years, a male stork, Klepetan, has flown 8,750 mi (14,000 km) from his winter home in South Africa to the Croatian village of Brodski Varoš to be with his mate, Malena, who cannot fly due to an old gunshot wound. Each year they mate and have chicks, which Klepetan teaches to fly before migrating with them to South Africa.

SINISTER HUNTER > A newly discovered yellow sea snake—*Hydrophis platurus xanthos*—from Costa Rica floats on the surface of the ocean at night and hangs down with its mouth open to catch small fish.

ZOMBIE VIRUS > In 2017, caterpillars of the oak eggar moth (*Lasiocampa quercus*) in Lancashire, England, were infected by a deadly virus that caused them to climb to the tops of trees and explode. The "zombie virus" brainwashes the bugs' natural instincts and drives them to get as close to the sun as possible. They then die and the virus liquefies their bodies, which burst open to infect more caterpillars.

KILLER SPIDER > The venom of the Australian funnel-web spider can kill a person in less than an hour, and its fangs can bite right through a shoe.

PARASITES?
(MORE LIKE PARA-YIKES!)

YIN MENG, of China's Yunnan Province, had a 4-IN-LONG (10-CM) PARASITE INSIDE HER HEAD for six years—from eating LIVE FROGS when she was a child!

Most ticks eat just THREE TIMES in their lives!

Over half of the human population has EYELASH MITES living undetected on their eyelids!

Rats infected by the TOXOPLASMA GONDII PARASITE lose their fear of cats, meaning they are more likely to BE EATEN and continue the life cycle of THE PARASITE INSIDE THE CAT.

HEDGEHOGS enjoy eating CREOSOTE AND DISCARDED CIGARETTES—substances toxic to humans—and also rub them on their spines, possibly to PROTECT THEM FROM PARASITES.

After a patient documented A LUMP MOVING AROUND HER FACE over 10 days with selfies, Dr. Vladimir Kartashev removed A PARASITIC WORM that had been living under her skin.

SIDE STABBER > The stiletto snake of the Middle East and East Africa does not even need to open its mouth to inject its venom. Instead, a ball-and-socket joint in its jaw allows a fang to swivel out sideways without the mouth being opened. For this reason, these reptiles are sometimes known as "side-stabbing snakes."

TANGLED TAILS > Staff at a wildlife rehab center helped rescue a group of six baby squirrels whose tails had become tangled together with sticky tree sap while they were playing in their nest at Elkhorn, Nebraska. The tangled tail phenomenon is known as a "squirrel king."

TOBACCO BREATH > The tobacco hornworm not only consumes doses of nicotine that would be deadly to most other creatures, but also utilizes the toxins in the tobacco plant as a defense mechanism. When threatened, it opens tiny pores in its skin and breathes out toxic puffs of nicotine to deter would-be predators.

SNAKE BITES > Joe Quililan, a snake catcher from the Philippines, builds up his immunity to venom by allowing deadly cobras to bite him every week. He also regularly injects himself with small quantities of snake venom, and the procedure is so effective that after being bitten twice by a northern Philippine cobra, he went to the hospital as a precaution but was released just an hour later in perfect physical condition.

WERECAT

↻ Lykoi cats look like little werewolves! The unique appearance of this breed is due to a naturally occurring genetic mutation that results in partial hairlessness. The hair that does appear has a "roan" pattern—a dark base color with light highlights. Appropriately enough, the name Lykoi is derived from the Greek word for wolf—*lýkos*.

Tied Up
TUMMY

⟳ The owners of Toby the Cavalier King Charles Spaniel were shocked when they found out why their dog wasn't eating much, despite always seeming hungry—his stomach was full of 205 elastic hair ties!

Over the course of a few months, Toby had stashed away and swallowed 1.7 lb (0.8 kg) worth of hair ties belonging to the mother and her two daughters of his human family. Worried for their pet, but not knowing the cause behind his symptoms, his owners took Toby to Heart River Animal Hospital in Mandan, North Dakota, where Dr. Elizabeth Kraft took an X-ray of the ailing dog and performed surgery to remove the obstructions. Toby fully recovered and no longer eats hair accessories.

The hair ties in Toby's tummy!

SCARE TACTICS > Denison University hung dead vultures in trees around its campus in Granville, Ohio, in an attempt to scare off live vultures and keep them from damaging buildings.

RAT CARERS > Two rats, Remy and Emile, helped look after the kittens at New York's Brooklyn Cat Café. Although in nature rats and cats are sworn enemies, these rats were raised around the kittens from a young age and slept with them and even groomed them.

CRAFTY CRAYFISH > A crayfish at a restaurant in China severed its own claw to stop itself from being boiled alive in a cooking pot. Finding that one of its claws was trapped in the water as it tried to climb out of the pot, the crustacean successfully detached the claw, which later regrew. The crayfish was rewarded for its enterprise by being adopted as a pet by the customer who had intended to eat it.

AVIAN ARSONISTS > Scientists believe that some Australian birds of prey deliberately start wildfires to flush out mice and frogs from the burning grasslands. Black kites, whistling kites, and brown falcons have all been known to spread fires by swooping to pick up burning sticks and then carrying them for distances of more than 150 ft (46 m) to unburned parts of the bush before dropping them onto dry grass.

LION AROUND

⊃ Of all the sideshow acts that have graced the pages of history, only this one served as the mane attraction—riding in a motor drome with a lion!

Here Ethel Purtle and her feline copilot King sped around the Wall of Death Motor Drome in 1949. Motor dromes involved vehicles driving around a 90-degree circular wall—talk about flirting with catastrophe.

DRIVING ON A VERTICAL WALL!

POOP CUBE > Wombat poop is cube-shaped, possibly so that the nocturnal Australian marsupial can mark its territory with droppings that won't roll away. Wombats can produce up to 100 of these fecal cubes every night.

WONDER WHIPPET > When Adele Schwartz fell down the basement stairs at her home in Saint-Laurent, Quebec, Canada, in the middle of the night, hitting her head and knocking herself unconscious, her 12-year-old whippet Sabrina saved her life. The dog woke Schwartz's sleeping husband Bill by nudging him repeatedly and pulling the comforter off his bed.

UNIQUE STRIPES > Every tiger in the world is unique because, like human fingerprints, no two tigers have the same pattern of stripes.

BEER-DRINKING DUCK > Star, a bow-tie-wearing Indian runner duck owned by Barrie Hayman, regularly drinks beer in pubs in North Devon, England, and even has his own stool in some bars.

ZOMBIE RACCOONS > In 2018, police in Youngstown, Ohio, received more than a dozen reports of zombie-like raccoons coming out by day, baring their teeth, and then mysteriously falling on their backs in a comatose-like state. The animals, which seemed to have lost their natural fear of humans, were believed to have been suffering from a disease called *distemper*.

RED-HANDED

➲ The red handfish, of Tasmania, Australia, has strange, hand-shaped fins, which it uses to crawl along the ocean floor. The fish is so rare that its total population is thought to be fewer than 80.

GREEN HAIR > The endangered Mary River turtle (*Elusor macrurus*), from Queensland, Australia, breathes through its anus—a function called *cloacal ventilation*, which allows it to stay underwater for days at a time. It is also known as the *green-haired turtle* because its head or shell is covered in what appears to be a shock of bright green hair, but is actually vertical strands of growing algae.

Amanda Friedrick found 19 rattlesnakes—one adult and 18 babies—inside of her children's plastic playhouse in the backyard of her home in Ridgecrest, California.

ENORMOUS TONGUE > Mochi, a St. Bernard dog owned by Carla Rickert of Sioux Falls, South Dakota, has a 7.3-in-long (18.6-cm) tongue—the world record holder for the longest tongue on a dog!

SEVERED HEAD > Milo Sutcliffe was bitten and almost killed by the severed head of a rattlesnake. Finding the 4-ft-long (1.2-m) reptile in the yard of his home near Lake Corpus Christi, Texas, he decapitated it with a shovel, but as he bent down to pick up the remains, the severed head bit him. Suffering seizures and internal bleeding, he was airlifted to a hospital, where he needed 26 doses of antivenom—13 times the amount an average snake-bite patient receives.

TO DIE FOR > During a three-week season, the male antechinus, a small Australian mouse-like marsupial, has sex with as many females as possible in vigorous mating sessions that can last for more than 14 hours at a time—but the exertion puts the male's body under such strain that it dies soon after.

HOMEWARD BOUND > After a North Carolina family decided they no longer wanted their pet cat, Toby, they gave him to another family, but he missed his old owners so much that he walked 12 mi (19 km) from his new home to be reunited with them.

POOP SNACK > Seagulls on Guafo Island in Chilean Patagonia feed on seal feces and even peck the butts of seal pups to get at their poop. The seal poop is laced with parasitic hookworms, which the gulls consider a tasty treat.

Food FIGHT

In May 2018, an epic tug-of-war took place in the skies above San Juan Island National Historical Park in Washington as a bald eagle snatched a rabbit from a fox.

When the eagle scooped up the bunny, it also caught hold of the fox, who was clinging to its meal relentlessly, and the troupe was lifted 20 ft (6 m) high before the fox had to let go. Nature photographer Kevin Ebi captured the close encounter and witnessed the bald eagle fly off into the sunset with its rabbit food.

MILITARY HERO > Mali, a Belgian Malinois dog, received the Dickin Medal, the United Kingdom's highest award for animal heroism, for saving the lives of Special Boat Service troops during a 2012 operation in Afghanistan. Although wounded by three grenade blasts, which left him with injuries to his chest, ear, and legs, Mali remained by his handler's side and helped pinpoint the exact locations of enemy Taliban fighters who were hiding in a multi-story building.

UNDERGROUND FROG > Bhupathy's purple frog (*Nasikabatrachus bhupathi*) from India spends almost its entire adult life underground and only surfaces to mate when it rains in the monsoon season. Its tadpoles have sucker-like mouths, which they use to latch on to rocks behind waterfalls created by the monsoons. They stay there for four months, feeding on algae, before going underground, where they use their long tongues to eat ants and termites.

RARE BREED > The Dandie Dinmont Terrier, a British breed of dog once popular with Queen Victoria and named after a character created by Sir Walter Scott in his 1815 novel *Guy Mannering*, is now considered to be rarer than the giant panda.

FOUR LEGS > A four-legged chicken was born in Rojhada, India, in December 2017, with its smaller, surplus limbs suspended behind it. Dozens of people visited Javed Ali's home to see the bizarre bird, which had polymelia, a condition that caused it to develop two extra legs inside the egg.

MILLION CATS > An estimated one million cats live on Alla and Sergey Lebedeva's farm in the village of Prigorodny, Siberia. The couple acquired their first cat in 2003, but there are now so many that their home is known as Koshlandia, or "land of the cats."

STRONG SMELL > While humans can just about smell a spoonful of sugar in a cup of tea, a dog's sense of smell is so powerful that it could smell the same amount of sugar in two Olympic swimming pools' worth of water.

CHEMICAL SPRAY > Even if it has just been eaten by a frog or a toad, a bombardier beetle can survive by emitting a hot jet of boiling chemicals from its rear end. It launches the attack from inside the predator's stomach, forcing it to vomit the beetle back up.

VENOMOUS PASSENGER > Hearing a strange sound coming from the engine of his car in Thailand, Thaichai Kongnimit looked under the hood of the vehicle and came face to face with a 15-ft-long (4.6-m) king cobra.

HUNGRY SEAL > Sammy the gray seal crosses the road almost every day to beg for scraps from The Lighthouse, a waterfront fish restaurant in Wicklow, Ireland.

WUNDERPUS

⮑ Scuba diver and photographer Wu Yung-sen found this see-through wunderpus octopus hatchling while diving in the ocean near Anilo, Philippines. When grown, this species is a rusty-orange color with white spots and has arms five-to-seven times longer than its head! Believe it or not, octopuses have blue blood and three hearts!

TONGUE REMOVED > Nyan htoo, a bear housed in a monastery in Myanmar, underwent a four-hour surgery to have his enormous 6.6-lb (3-kg) tongue removed so he would be able to eat and live more comfortably. Before the operation, his tongue was so long it dragged along the ground and was so heavy he used to rest his head against the cage to support his weight. The bear's condition was probably caused by elephantiasis, a mosquito-transmitted infection that makes body parts swell alarmingly.

TALKING WHALE > Wikie, an orca at Marineland Aquarium, Antibes, France, can mimic human speech by saying "hello," "bye-bye," and "one, two, three" through her blowhole. The whale copies its trainer and can even blow raspberries.

LIONESS MANE > In 2017, Bridget, a lioness at the Oklahoma City Zoo, suddenly grew a mane—at the age of 18. Tests showed that her body contained significantly raised levels of androstenedione, a hormone that can produce male traits in humans and animals.

GIRAFFE BED > Yellow-billed oxpeckers sometimes sleep on a giraffe's body, particularly in their "armpits," the areas at the top of the giraffe's legs. The birds roost there overnight to be close to their food supply, as they live off parasites in the animal's hair.

TWO HEARTS > A young boa constrictor that was brought to Coral Springs, Florida, veterinarian Dr. Susan Kelleher (celebrity vet Dr. K) not only had two heads but also, even more unusually, had two functioning hearts. Most two-headed animals share internal organs, but this was effectively two snakes in one skin.

CLEVER SHEEP > A study by scientists at Cambridge University, England, found that sheep can recognize different faces. Researchers tested the sheep with pictures of famous people, including Barack Obama and actors Jake Gyllenhaal and Emma Watson.

TERRIER STOWAWAY > Rusty, a three-year-old terrier, secretly hitched a 932-mi (1,500-km) ride from Goondiwindi, Queensland, to Snowtown, South Australia, aboard Paul McDowell's truck after his owners, the Scudamore family, had gone on vacation. They had left Rusty with relatives on a cattle farm, but the dog's sense of adventure got the better of him. Two years earlier, he had made a similar escape, traveling 125 mi (200 km) before being reunited with his family.

FEELING FLUSHED ⮑ A sneaky squirrel slipped into a London toilet and had to be saved when it got stuck! When an animal rescue officer offered the hapless rodent a mop handle, it quickly latched on, and the officer was able to clean, dry, and release it back into the wild.

Total TREE-CALL

⮥ A sculptor carved a life-size Arnold Schwarzenegger statue out of a single tree trunk.

Artist James O'Neal has carved other wood sculptures of athletes in the past, including Floyd Mayweather and Muhammad Ali, but his 2018 sculpture of the Austrian Oak is truly breathtaking. The Arnie sculpture is 6 ft 1 in (1.88 m) tall and sports the then-bodybuilder's seventies haircut and vacuum pose. Fans of O'Neal's work can view pictures of his progress on his Instagram page @jamesonealwoodart, where he has images of the tree-trunk-turned-Mr.-Olympia from start to finish.

⮥ A sculptor carved a life-size Arnold Schwarzenegger statue out of a single tree trunk.

SELFIE JET

↪ Have you ever wanted to take a selfie inside a private jet like all of your favorite Instafamous celebrities? Artist Matty Mo has made that dream a reality with his newest project "The Private Jet Experience." The installation is a small backdrop that looks exactly like a private jet, down to the color scheme and portal window, and those who want to take the fabled private jet selfie need only wait, as it will be transported to more than 30 locations across the U.S. during 2019—by van.

REALITY BITES >

A 2010 Australian election TV debate was hastily rescheduled so that it did not conflict with the final of the reality cooking show *Masterchef.*

PLASTER OSCARS >

Due to metal shortages during World War II, Oscar statuettes were instead made from painter's plaster for three years. When the war was over, the Academy invited recipients to exchange the plaster figures for gold-plated metal ones.

MOUTH PAINTER >

Even though he was born without arms or hands, Tom Yendell has been a successful professional artist for more than 30 years by holding the paintbrush in his mouth or between his toes. He uses different body parts, such as the teeth, tongue, and lips, to vary the intensity of the brush strokes. From his purpose-built studio in Hampshire, England, he has created hundreds of works that have appeared on greeting cards and wrapping paper.

SUPER POWER >

Superman couldn't always fly. In the beginning, he merely possessed the ability to jump great distances, but that power proved difficult to animate. Consequently, Fleischer Studios, which produced the 1941 series of short films, asked DC Comics to change Superman's powers so that he could fly.

SCIENCE DEGREE >

In real life, actress Pauley Perrette, who played forensic scientist Abby Sciuto in *NCIS*, has a master's degree in criminal science.

NUMBER ONES >

On August 4, 1984, Prince had the number one movie, album, and single in the United States at the same time—with *Purple Rain* and "When Doves Cry"—matching the Beatles' feat from 20 years earlier with *A Hard Day's Night.*

BRYANT RETWEET >

William Pate, a student at Ben Davis High School, Indianapolis, Indiana, won a bet with his teacher to call off a final exam by getting Kobe Bryant to give him a retweet. The retired NBA star tweeted back: "Hope you have an A in this class."

THE ONE AND ONLY POOP EMOJI

↪ Toronto artist Justin Poulsen celebrated the 10th anniversary of the infamous poop emoji with an art series named *Poo-moji.* Poulsen got creative depicting the well-known emoji's spiral shape 50 different ways, including as a disco ball, a cake, a candle, mashed potatoes, lights, and even ice cubes.

IF *Looks* COULD KILL

⟳ Designer Jess Eaton of Brighton, England, created runway fashion from the remains of dead animals—more specifically, roadkill.

The animals all died of natural causes, were hit by cars, or were killed for food. Eaton's Roadkill Couture collection includes necklaces made from 12 pheasant skulls, a bolero jacket made from the furs of 50 white rats (consumed by her friend's pet reptile), and a hat made from four magpie wings. Eaton skins the "fabric" herself, even using flesh-eating bugs to clean the accessories in her own home.

MADE FROM MUSSEL SHELLS!

WHITE RAT!

MADE FROM ANIMAL SKULLS!

DIGITAL *Ink*

Tattoo artist Andreas Vrontis of Limassol, Cyprus, inks portraits made out of letters, numbers, and symbols.

Similar to ASCII art from the early days of the internet, Vrontis's work appears to come to life the further away you view it. It is particularly impressive because of how notoriously difficult it is to tattoo small letters; if the tattoo needle goes too deep into the skin, the ink can spread and blur the lines. Because of this, Vrontis works with some of the smallest tattoo needles available.

AUTO VIOLIN > Israeli musician Adar Goldfarb used his car's windshield wipers to play the violin. He strapped a violin to the car's side-view mirror and used the motion of the wipers to operate the bow.

SUPERMAN'S NUMBER > Clark Kent's Social Security number, 092-09-6616, as revealed in a 1966 issue of Action Comics, once belonged to a New York man, Giobatta Balocchi, who had died a year earlier.

HIDDEN GRASSHOPPER > Vincent van Gogh accidentally painted a live grasshopper into his 1889 work *Olive Trees*, but the insect was only discovered embedded in the canvas 128 years later. The find happened while examining the painting under magnification. Van Gogh was known for painting outdoors.

JELL-O SHIRT > To create the sound of E.T.'s walk in the 1982 movie, foley artist John Roesch used a wet T-shirt filled with Jell-O.

NETFLIX PROPOSALS > People asked Netflix to marry them more than 1,000 times on social media in 2017—with 365 proposals coming from Brazil alone.

MINIATURE PAINTINGS > Jax Frey, an artist from New Orleans, has painted more than 20,000 "Little View" mini artworks—4-in (10-cm) square pictures showing Louisiana images and icons.

SUGAR KING > Chinese patissier Zhou Yi, known as the "Sugar King," molds edible fondant into incredible figurines that look just like human dolls. His handmade figurine of Wu Zetian, China's first and only female emperor, was so detailed that it was possible to count her eyelashes.

HAND SOAPS > Artist Suzanne Proulx, of Erie, Pennsylvania, uses molds to make soaps in the shape of her family's hands—including those of her aging parents and also her nieces and nephews soon after birth.

CROWDED PIANO > Eighteen children and two music teachers played the same piano simultaneously in Sarajevo, Bosnia. Although some of the 20 were on their knees and others were lying on top of the piano, they managed to perform "Galop-Marche," a piece by 19th-century French composer Albert Lavignac, which he wrote originally for eight hands.

KITTEN ACCOUNT > English singer Ed Sheeran once created a Twitter account for his kitten, Graham, who quickly notched up 66,000 followers just by posting a picture of himself sitting on a guitar.

FAMILY LINK > Actor Kit Harington (who plays Jon Snow in the TV series *Game of Thrones*) is a descendant of Robert Catesby, one of the Gunpowder Plot leaders who tried unsuccessfully to blow up the English Parliament in 1605. Harington actually played Catesby in the U.K. TV series *Gunpowder*.

Mary Shelley started writing *Frankenstein* in a villa on the shores of Lake Geneva, Switzerland, in the summer of 1816—when she was only 18.

FURBY KEYBOARD > Musician and inventor Sam Battle, from London, England, dissected 44 Furby toys and wired them into a keyboard to create a unique "Furby Organ." Under his control, the toys' artificial voices sing together to make music.

SOLD GRAVE > Although paintings by Dutch artist Rembrandt now sell for more than $20 million, he died penniless in 1669—and seven years earlier he had even been forced to sell his wife Saskia's grave.

CHANCE MEETING > Daryl Hall and John Oates (Hall & Oates) were brought together by a shoot-out between rival gangs. They were attending a band convention at the Adelphi Ballroom in Philadelphia, Pennsylvania, in 1967, and when shots rang out, they both ran to the same service elevator and found they shared similar musical tastes.

LOVE POEM > "Marína," a love poem written in 1844 by Slovak writer Andrej Sládkovič to his girlfriend Maria Pischlova, has 2,900 lines. A museum in Banska Stiavnica, where Andrej and Maria fell in love at age 14, celebrates the poem and contains a basement vault with exactly 100,000 tiny drawers, one for each letter, gap, and punctuation mark of the original manuscript.

DORAEMON HOUSE > Reghina Karwur is so obsessed with Doraemon, the time-traveling, blue-and-white robotic cat from the Japanese manga series, that the inside and outside of her house in Indonesia serve as a shrine to the popular character. In addition to Doraemon wallpaper, stickers, figurines, and hundreds of items of memorabilia, her pillows, bed covers, curtains, suitcases, clocks, tableware, floor tiles, and rice cooker are all Doraemon-themed. Naturally the exterior of the house is painted blue and white, and even the family car has Doraemon floor mats and a matching steering wheel cover.

HISTORIC BAND > Swedish power metal band Sabaton teach history through their music and in 2010 recorded an album, *Coat of Arms*, that was almost entirely devoted to World War II, with tracks about the Warsaw Uprising, the Holocaust, the Battle of Midway, and the Battle of Britain.

IRON GIANT

➔ Inspired by Japanese sci-fi anime, engineer Masaaki Nagumo spent six years building a 28-ft-tall (8.5-m), functional Gundam mecha robot. The metal robot, which weighs more than 7 tons, can move its arms and fingers, walk at 0.6 mph (1 kmph), and is equipped with a bazooka-like air gun that is able to fire sponge balls at 87 mph (140 kmph).

COMPUTER CITY > Zimbabwe-born artist Zayd Menk spent three months building an accurate scale model of midtown Manhattan out of discarded computer components and other old electronic items. He used 27 motherboards, 15 batteries, 13 floppy disk readers, 12 cell phones, 11 central processing units, seven power supplies, four watches, four audio cards, three hard drives, and 263 sticks of hot glue.

BANNED PLAY > Eugene O'Neill's play *Long Day's Journey into Night* was so closely based on his own family that he forbade any performance of it until 25 years after his death.

WORD PORTRAITS > Phil Vance, an artist from Sonora, California, spends hundreds of hours creating handwritten typography portraits of famous people out of the subject's quotes. To form the contours, shadows, and details of each word portrait, Vance writes sayings from the subject thousands of times in different sizes, layers, and colors. His "In Their Own Words" series includes Heath Ledger as the Joker from the movie *The Dark Knight*, Mark Twain, Albert Einstein, Audrey Hepburn, and Winston Churchill.

EIGHT-SECOND CONCERT > On June 29, 2017, Japanese band Golden Bomber gave an eight-second concert in Tokyo to promote their single, an eight-second song called "8-Second Encounter." Fans had waited in line for six hours for the free concert and were rewarded when the band did an encore, performing a different song in full, so the encore lasted longer than the concert.

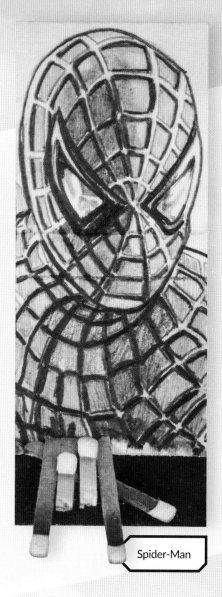

Spider-Man

Catwoman

Batman

Rarity № 169367, 169269, 169263

Matchbook Art
Artist Mike Bell collects matchbooks to turn them into unique miniature 3D portrait sculptures.

Ripley's Rarities

BAD DOG > An early draft of John Steinbeck's 1937 novel *Of Mice and Men* was eaten by his dog Max.

ROCK DRILL > Einstürzende Neubauten, an experimental rock band from Berlin, Germany, sometimes incorporate the sounds of a jackhammer into their stage performances.

RECYCLED DRESSES > Costume designer Olivia Mears, of Asheville, North Carolina, creates Disney-style fairy-tale dresses out of used Christmas wrapping paper.

HAIR PICTURES > Indian artist Midhun R. R. creates detailed pictures of people and animals using human hair. With a white sheet of paper for a canvas, he uses a long needle to arrange the individual hairs into portraits of the likes of Marilyn Monroe and Mahatma Gandhi.

BEE SHARP > Beekeeper and musician Bioni Samp, from London, England, combines his two passions to make electronic music with his bee colonies. He records the frequencies of bees communicating and uses them in his compositions. He always performs wearing a beekeeper's suit and spent 10 years building his own "hive synthesizer" that emulates bee sounds.

Loose LIPS

◯ Artist Alexis Fraser, who goes by the name Lipstick Lex, creates prints using nothing but lipstick and kisses.

Fraser hopes to spread the positive message of love through her unique pieces, which feature pop culture icons like Frida Kahlo, David Bowie, and Marilyn Monroe, as well as bright pineapples, turtles, bananas in heart shapes, and flamingoes.

Princess ETCH

➲ **Jane Labowitch of Chicago, Illinois, can create incredibly detailed drawings on Etch A Sketch toys!**

Jane, aka Princess Etch, started playing with an Etch A Sketch at the age of four and now in her late twenties is a full-time etching artist. Invented in France more than 60 years ago, the Etch A Sketch works by turning knobs connected to a pulley system that drags a stylus along a clear screen coated with aluminum powder. The stylus removes the powder, drawing a line that shows the dark-colored inside of the toy. Shake the toy and the powder recoats the screen. It's simple, but not easy, so we reached out to Jane to ask her some questions about creating Etch A Sketch art.

Q Why Etch A Sketch?

A I would visit my grandma on weekends growing up, and she wouldn't let me and my siblings watch much TV. I became obsessed with drawing on the toy, and over time my skills improved and things started to click. Once it became muscle memory, my etching skills grew hand in hand with my drawing skills. It wasn't until I was around 12 that I learned that other kids didn't play with an Etch A Sketch obsessively like I did.

Q How do you keep your art from disappearing if someone shakes it?

A I drill a hole in the back of the Etch A Sketch and remove the excess aluminum powder from the inside. That way, when you shake the Etch A Sketch, there is nothing left to recoat the screen, and the image that is etched on the screen will remain intact. I then glue down the knobs so that they cannot be turned anymore. I've shipped my art all over the world and every rendition has safely arrived at its destination!

Q What happens if you make a mistake while sketching?

A If it's a small mistake, I can usually cover it up with shading or layering lines on top. If it's a medium mistake, I can tilt the Etch A Sketch and tap it from beneath, causing powder inside to recoat a portion of the screen. It's not an exact science and can cause much of the image to erase, but it's a good way to only remove a part of an etching. If the mistake is really bad, the easiest thing to do is shake the Etch A Sketch and start over! I try to etch the most difficult things first for that reason.

Q How many Etch A Sketches do you own?

A The number fluctuates, but at any given time I typically have at least 300!

Q What are some of your other interests?

A I love roller coasters! I worked at Cedar Point one summer because it's known for having some of the best coasters in the world. I also enjoy traveling, playing Uno, watching *Frasier*, and trying out macaroni and cheese at different restaurants.

Q Do you make any other kind of art?

A I do! I draw, paint watercolors, create digital illustrations, and love experimenting with different kinds of markers and pens.

Q Who are some artists you look up to?

A Some of my favorite traditional artists are Van Gogh, M. C. Escher, and Keith Haring. I am continually inspired by the small but vibrant community of Etch A Sketch artists, many of which have become my friends through our shared love of the medium. I also look up to my professors from college and peers who have taken different artistic paths since graduation.

YELLOW PERIOD > Vincent van Gogh's "yellow period," during which he painted *The Starry Night*, was probably the result of doctors treating his epilepsy by giving him digitalis—a medicine extracted from the foxglove plant—a side effect of which adds a yellow tinge to everything the patient sees.

SOLD HANDLE > Fifteen-year-old Darian Lipscomb, of Prospect, Virginia, agreed to surrender his Snapchat handle, @CarnivalCruise, in exchange for a $5,000 cruise for himself and his family. He chose the handle after enjoying a cruise when he was nine, but Carnival wanted it for the company and thus made him an offer he could not refuse.

HOGWARTS CLASSROOM > Harry Potter fan Kyle Hubler, a teacher at Evergreen Middle School in Hillsboro, Oregon, spent 70 hours transforming his classroom into a real-life version of Hogwarts, complete with stone-brick wallpaper, costumes, wands, quill pens, ornamental owls, and a full set of quidditch balls.

Fittingly, this scene from *Alice in Wonderland* was painted on a pressed penny from Disneyland.

Q What inspired you to paint on coins?

A Originally my inspiration came from the challenge of painting on a surface smaller than the average postage stamp. Now it is more of the concentration I crave. Every brush stroke has to be made with equal importance as the previous, which keeps me in the moment. I can paint for hours and not realize how much time has passed.

Q What's been the hardest thing to paint?

A I painted a portrait of a young woman, and I can easily say it was my most difficult painting to date. The eyes were so unbelievably small, I had to use a single whisker for the highlights.

Q Do you need to use a special type of paint on pennies?

A I paint with traditional oils, but I do use a thinning medium to make the paint easier to use on such a small scale.

Penny Painter

➲ With a steady hand and small brushes, Bry Marie of Tucson, Arizona, turns ordinary pennies into works of art.

She paints a variety of subjects, including clouds, insects, and landscapes, but much of her portfolio is filled with pieces from pop culture that she loves—Harry Potter, Lord of the Rings, and Disney films, to name a few. We caught up with Bry and asked her some of our most burning questions about her artwork.

WHOA! 23 FT (7 M) LONG!

LIFE FINDS A WAY ➲ In July 2018, to celebrate the 25th anniversary of Jurassic Park, UK streaming service NOW TV unveiled a statue of actor Jeff Goldblum as his character Dr. Ian Malcolm in his iconic pose. The statue, which weighs 331 lb (150 kg) and lounges 23 ft (7 m) long, thrilled visitors to Potters Field, London, England, in front of Tower Bridge. The scene with Ian Malcolm's shirt unbuttoned has spawned countless "Sexy Jeff Goldblum" memes, as well as a Funko action figure.

NUMBER PHOBIA > Horror writer Stephen King has triskaidekaphobia, a phobia of the number 13, that extends not only to the number itself but also to multiples of 13. He will not ascend or descend a staircase that has 13 steps, and if writing or reading a book, he will not stop until he has reached a page that is a nonmultiple of 13. Similarly, he will not stop reading a book on pages where the sums of the numbers add up to 13—such as 76 or 355.

COFFEE PORTRAITS > Allan Pachino Wallace, an artist from Nassau in the Bahamas, creates celebrity portraits—including Barack Obama and rapper Drake—using such unconventional items as salt, coffee, baking soda, cereal, and leaves.

BEADED ART > Ab Majid Ab Rahman, from Pahang, Malaysia, made a beaded artwork (held together by string) that measured 3.3 ft (1 m) wide and 58 ft (17.8 m) long—more than half the length of a basketball court.

TEXT ART > A program launched by the San Francisco Museum of Modern Art allows people to text a number for art on demand. By texting the phrase "send me" along with a key word or color, they are sent an image of the closest match from the museum's 34,678 artworks. The museum's collection is so vast that only about 5 percent is displayed in galleries at any given time— because to view every item would require a walk of 121.3 mi (194 km).

PLASTER SPHINX > In 2017, archaeologists working in the Guadalupe-Nipomo Dunes on the central California coast dug up an intact, 300-lb (136-kg) plaster sphinx that was part of an Egyptian movie set built more than 90 years ago for Cecil B. DeMille's Biblical epic *The Ten Commandments*. The set of the 1923 movie included more than 20 sphinxes, which DeMille ordered to be buried in the dunes when filming was finished.

INK DOTS > David Bayo, an artist from Strasbourg, France, creates amazing portraits by painstakingly hand-placing ink dots on a white canvas. Each portrait can take him up to 300 hours and may consist of more than three million dots.

YELLOW BRICK ROAD

➲ The Land of Oz is real—and it's in Beech Mountain, North Carolina. An abandoned theme park based on the classic *The Wizard of Oz* film, complete with a yellow brick road, reopened for just six days in June 2018. Visitors were taken on guided tours through the 1970s-era park, which also featured the Wicked Witch of the West's Castle and a miniature Emerald City.

WHAT NOT TO WEAR

⮑ For an operating room-themed show at Milan's Fashion Week in February 2018, Gucci models walked the catwalk carrying life-size replicas of their own heads. According to Gucci's creative director Alessandro Michele, the eerily-realistic noggins represent the struggle of self-identity.

FAKE HEADS

TIDE CHANGES > Hawaiian street artist Sean Yoro (aka Hula) created a waterfront mural at Canada's Bay of Fundy that disappeared below the surface of the ocean and then re-emerged hours later with the changing of the tide. Using non-toxic paint to avoid harming the water, he spent nine days making the 30 ft x 45 ft (9 m x 14 m) mural that showed a woman reaching toward the sky. He had to paint quickly because the tide in Saint John, New Brunswick, rises by more than 1 ft (0.3 m) every 15 minutes and in total rises and falls by an incredible 28 ft (8.5 m) every six hours.

FREE DRINKS > To celebrate St. Patrick's Day in 2018, Irish rock band The Script bought 8,000 of their fans a drink at their concert in Brussels, Belgium.

YOUNG TATTOOIST > At age 12, Ezrah Dormon was working as a tattoo artist at a shop in Panama City and was already one of the most in-demand tattooists in the whole of Panama.

VAN GOGH MURAL > Nancy Nemhauser and Ludomir Jastrzebski had the exterior of their home in Mount Dora, Florida, painted with a huge mural of Vincent van Gogh's *Starry Night*.

CLUMSY HANDS > Actor Peter Weller's suit for the movie *RoboCop* had hands made of foam rubber, which meant that whenever he tried to catch car keys in one scene, they bounced off his hand. In the end, it took more than 50 takes and an entire day of filming just for the shot of him catching the keys.

BARNEY TROUBLE > Mel Blanc voiced up to 65 episodes of Barney Rubble in *The Flintstones* from his own bed. Blanc spent 70 days bedridden in 1961 following a serious car crash, but even though he was so badly injured he was wearing a full-body cast and was unable to sit up, the TV show's crew managed to record episodes by arranging microphones around his bed.

FAKE NEWS > The Musée Terrus in Elne, France—a museum dedicated to the works of local 19th-century artist Étienne Terrus—discovered recently that 82 out of the 140 paintings in its collection were fakes.

PIANO ARC
⮑ Brockett Parsons is a musician and currently Lady Gaga's keyboard player. He is also the inventor of the PianoArc, a wraparound keyboard that has three 88-note keyboards fused together to create a 360-degree music experience. Sometimes called the Brockettship, the PianoArc took a group of designers, engineers, and musicians to bring it to life and is often enjoyed for its incredible stage presence.

RUBIK'S CUBISM

➲ Most people can't even solve a Rubik's cube, but Italian artist Giovanni Contardi actually uses them to create giant portraits of his favorite celebrities.

While Contardi says he's been solving Rubik's cubes for years, he only recently became a full-time artist and started collaborating with a gallery in order to create his astounding visual pieces. He prefers to make portraits of pop culture icons who inspire him and has already captured several famous faces, including Bob Marley, Will Smith, Robert Downey Jr., and Justin Timberlake. Contardi's portraits usually measure about 5 ft (1.5 m) on all sides and require about 700 cubes shaped to create a specific design.

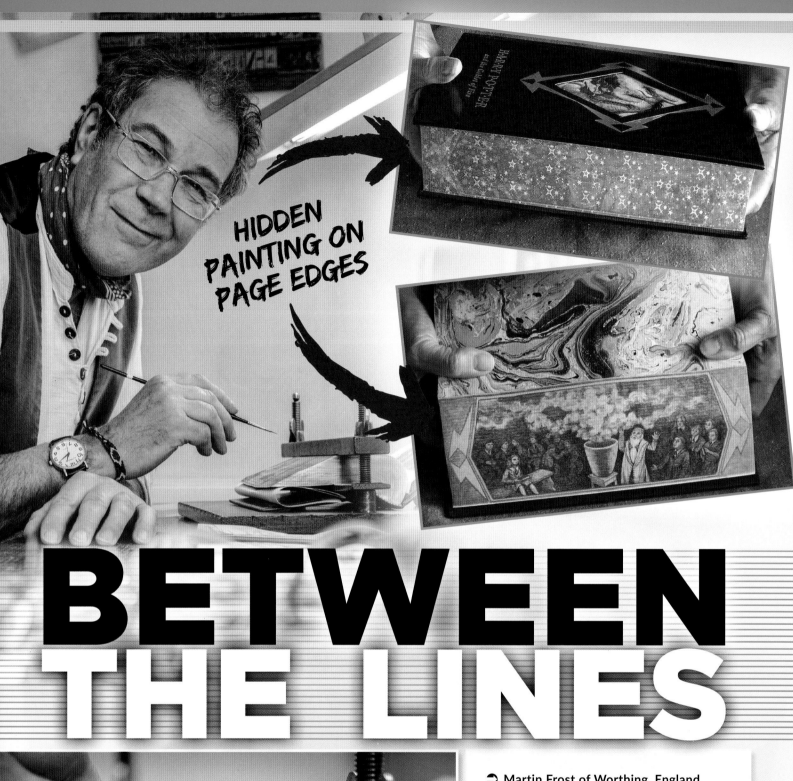

HIDDEN PAINTING ON PAGE EDGES

BETWEEN THE LINES

⊃ **Martin Frost of Worthing, England, paints pictures that disappear!**

When shut, the books Frost paints appear normal, but fan the pages out just right and a hidden painting along the gilt edges emerges. The art of vanishing fore-edge painting goes back to 17th-century Britain, but Frost has brought the curiosity into the modern age by painting books like Harry Potter and *Alice's Adventures in Wonderland*. Believe it or not, he can add multiple paintings to one book by flipping the direction the pages are spread or by splitting the book in two, so that when it is laid open at the middle, there is a different painting on the left and right sides.

2 HIDDEN PAINTINGS ON ONE BOOK!

BEAUTIFUL PAINTED EDGES!

UNCOMMON Threads

Arun Kumar Bajaj of Patiala, India, paints portraits with a sewing machine!

Also known as "Needleman," Bajaj has been stitching since he was 12 years old. At age 16, he took over the family tailor shop when his father passed away and decided to combine his talent for sketching with his family's business. Bajaj creates his paintings in one layer and doesn't overstitch in order to give them a smooth, neat appearance. Using a sewing machine rather than embroidering by hand means the stitched strokes can't be undone if he makes a mistake.

HOLY STITCH!

The largest piece he's ever done is a 4 × 6 ft (1.2 × 1.8 m) painting of Krishna, created with 1,762 mi (2,836 km) of thread!

CURSED RING > A ring owned by silent movie star Rudolph Valentino was said to have been cursed, resulting in a series of deaths of people who wore it. Ignoring stories about its dark history, Valentino bought the ring in 1920 from a San Francisco jeweler and died six years later at age 31. The ring was passed to actor Russ Colombo, who was killed a few days later in an accidental shooting, and then to entertainer Joe Casino, who was run over by a truck just days after finally being brave enough to put on the ring for the first time. It was then stolen by burglar James Willis, who was shot dead by police officers with the ring in his pocket. The ring was subsequently borrowed for a screen test by a young actor, Jack Dunn, who died 10 days later of a rare disease.

SECRET IMAGE > A self portrait of Michelangelo was discovered, disguised in the artist's sketch of his friend Vittoria Colonna, after being hidden for 500 years. The small likeness, which blends in perfectly with the drawing, was spotted by Brazilian researcher Dr. Deivis de Campos, tucked away between the lines that form part of the subject's dress.

SILENT HERO > Jimmy Chitwood, the hero of the 1986 basketball film *Hoosiers*, has only four lines in the entire movie.

LOST MANUSCRIPT > T. E. Lawrence (better known as Lawrence of Arabia) had to rewrite his classic book *Seven Pillars of Wisdom* in full after leaving his only manuscript in the refreshment room at Reading station, England, while changing trains in 1919. The rewrite took him three months.

VERBLESS NOVEL > *The Train from Nowhere*, a 233-page novel written in 2004 by French author Michel Dansel under the pen name Michel Thaler, contains no verbs.

FROZEN CANVAS > In January 2018, a group of artists created a 23,895-sq-ft (2,220-sq-m) snow painting on the frozen surface of the Hunjiang River in Tonghua, China.

ELEVATOR BIRTH > Academy Award–winning actor Jack Lemmon was born in an elevator at Newton-Wellesley Hospital, in Newton, Massachusetts, on February 8, 1925.

TINY JESUS > Surendra Acharya, from Karkala, India, has sculpted a 0.08-in-tall (2-mm) statue of Jesus into the lead of a pencil. His other micro pencil lead artworks include a 0.12-in (3-mm) horse.

STOLEN PAINTING > A $1 million painting by French impressionist artist Edgar Degas was found on a bus outside Paris in 2018—nine years after being stolen from a museum in Marseille. His 1877 work *Les Choristes* (The Chorus Singers) was feared lost until being discovered inside a suitcase in the bus luggage compartment during a routine check at a gas station by French customs agents. None of the passengers admitted to owning it.

THE FUTURE & THE SIMPSONS

The American sitcom THE SIMPSONS has been on air since 1989, making it the LONGEST-RUNNING scripted primetime TV series in U.S. history. But did you know that the show has also made some WILDLY ACCURATE PREDICTIONS about the future?

In 1991, Homer dreams of the Land of Chocolate... In 2011, a CHOCOLATE THEME PARK opened in Shanghai, complete with edible attractions! (Episode: "Burns Verkaufen der Kraftwerk")

In 1995, a SMARTWATCH is depicted, with Lisa's husband speaking into a phone on his wrist... almost 20 YEARS BEFORE the first smartwatches. (Episode: "Lisa's Wedding")

In 2000, the character Lisa becomes president after Donald Trump... 16 YEARS BEFORE Donald Trump actually became PRESIDENT OF UNITED STATES. (Episode: "Bart to the Future")

In 1998, a sign at the 20th Century Fox studio revealed it was now "A Division of Walt Disney Co."—NEARLY 20 YEARS BEFORE Disney reached a deal to acquire Fox for $66.1 billion. (Episode: "When You Dish Upon A Star")

In 1990, Bart catches a THREE-EYED FISH in the river near a power plant... More than 20 YEARS LATER, a three-eyed fish was caught in Argentina in water that came from a nuclear power plant. (Episode: "Two Cars in Every Garage and Three Eyes on Every Fish")

The show PREDICTED THE NFL SUPER BOWL champions in 1992, 1993, AND 1994.

PAPER WATCHES > Manabu Kosaka, an artist from Saitama, Japan, makes perfectly detailed replicas of wristwatches out of paper. He uses a sharp knife to cut pieces of paper as small as 0.04 in (1 mm) and then delicately puts each part in the correct place with tweezers. He even manages to make the internal mechanism of a watch with its tiny gears.

REPLICA WALKER > Nick Meyer spent six months building a 19-ft-tall (5.8-m) replica AT-AT walker from Star Wars as a Halloween decoration in the front yard of his house in Parma, Ohio. The four-legged All Terrain Armored Transport vehicle was almost as tall as his house and was made from wood, hard foam, and plastic barrels.

PERSIAN DESIGNS > Even though he is colorblind, Miami-based artist Jason Seife hand-paints the colorful patterns of Persian carpets onto canvas. He uses a mixture of ink and acrylic to recreate the intricate designs, each one taking him up to three months.

ALTOGETHER OOKY
⮑ Callie Scardina of Albuquerque, New Mexico, created an eerily lifelike lamp-version of Uncle Fester from *The Addams Family*. The character has an uncanny ability to generate electricity, which he demonstrates by lighting a bulb in his mouth. Callie's artwork is based on the 1964 television series, where Uncle Fester is played by Jackie Coogan.

⮑ In 2018, José Maurício dos Anjos of Brazil unveiled a masterpiece—a tattoo of his favorite team's entire soccer jersey on his torso.

The Flamengo soccer club fan had dreamt of inking 40 percent of his body with the black and red uniform, finishing out a year of visits to the tattoo parlor—the equivalent of 32 sessions and more than 90 hours of work. The jersey is a replica of the 2015 home shirt (minus the sponsors' logos, of course).

JERSEY BOY

REN RIDE

➲ Renowned inventor and viral YouTuber Colin Furze built a life-size model of Kylo-Ren's TIE Silencer from *Star Wars: The Last Jedi*. Furze, of Lincolnshire, England, was challenged by the online auction site eBay to create the model out of parts found only on their website. The project took Furze and his team members seven weeks to complete, and it ended up weighing more than 7 tons! The model includes a cockpit with targeting screens, a chair, flight controls, and lighting.

MATCHBOX INSPIRATION > Matt Garrick and Mark Roy, from Darwin, Australia, drew their inspiration for their 10-minute short film *Sumatra* from 400 vintage matchboxes that they found at a thrift shop at Shoal Bay. They studied the images on the matchboxes and used them as a basis for the film's characters and settings.

FIRESIDE VIEWING > Around 40,000 people watched an online livestream of American video game designer Jeff Kaplan spending 10 hours sitting in front of a fire. He sat in complete silence for most of the time, apart from answering a phone call and eating a cookie.

SWORD THRONE > A team of artisans from Blagoveshchensk, Russia, spent three months recreating the iconic Iron Throne from the TV series *Game of Thrones* by welding 387 iron swords together. Around half a ton of metal went into the construction of the life-size throne.

CAT CHASE > A December 2017 Broadway performance of the musical *Cats* was briefly halted after an audience member's service dog chased one of the feline characters, Bombalurina (actress Mackenzie Warren in a cat costume), during the show's opening number.

FAVORITE FILM > Gemma Chalmers, from Peterhead, Scotland, watched the 2007 film *Bee Movie* 357 times in 2017—because it is her young son Jaxson's favorite. Sometimes she would put it on four times a day to keep him happy.

AVOCADO FIGURINES > Irish artist Jan Campbell makes detailed carvings of miniature figures from avocado pits. She carves the fruit's hard internal seed into molds for silver sculptures of mythical beings, and each figurine can sell for $180.

WARCRAFT DIORAMA > Video game developer Blizzard Entertainment created a 1,300-sq-ft (121-sq-m) *World of Warcraft* diorama featuring more than 10,000 unique, 3D-printed characters.

Costume designers for *The Lord of the Rings* trilogy of films pieced together so much chainmail armor that it rubbed away their fingerprints.

CARPET IMAGES > Japanese Twitter user @agito0219, who likes to remain anonymous, uses her carpets as a canvas for her artworks. With simple tools such as credit cards, she carefully brushes the carpet fibers to form temporary images of people and animals.

DIAGON ALLEY > Jon Chambers drew trick-or-treaters to his Seattle, Washington, home on Halloween 2017 by building a replica of Diagon Alley from the Harry Potter books on his driveway. He used 3D printing to recreate the secret London shopping district for wizards.

MULTITASKING > Jackie Chan had 15 different credits in the 2012 movie *Chinese Zodiac*, including actor, writer, director, cinematographer, art director, and catering coordinator.

LONG SONG > "Apparente Liberta," a 2005 pop song composed by Italy's Giancarlo Ferrari, is 76 minutes 44 seconds long.

SYRINGE ARTIST > Kimberly Joy Magbanua, a nurse from the Philippines, paints pictures with syringes instead of brushes. Having come up with the idea as she was preparing to inject a patient, she fills syringes with different colored paints and uses the tips to scribble the paint onto the canvas. It takes her up to five hours to finish a painting, and she has to replace the needles several times because they become clogged with paint.

WRONG BAND > Duncan Robb, of Chesterfield, England, flew his girlfriend to Belfast, Northern Ireland, for what he thought was a concert by the Red Hot Chili Peppers, only to discover that it was a bagpipe cover band, the Red Hot Chilli Pipers.

FANTASY CAKE > The Broadway Bakery in Dubai spent $27,000 creating a 4-ft-tall (1.2-m), 70-lb (32-kg) *Game of Thrones* cake featuring character Tyrion Lannister sitting on the Iron Throne. All of the edible swords that made up the throne were individually shaped and coated with colored fondant icing, and the likeness of Tyrion was detailed right down to his stubble and facial scars. The cake was large enough to feed more than 100 people.

ALL *Dolled* UP

CHER

Original factory paint

↻ Filipino-American artist Noel Cruz repaints mass-produced celebrity dolls to make them look like realistic models of their subjects and sells them at auction for up to $3,500 each.

Cruz caught the artistic bug after he saw a repainted doll on eBay (his wife is a doll collector), and decided he should stretch his creative muscles. Today he's one of the best in the niche doll-painting community. Among the dolls he has treated are Emma Watson as Belle in *Beauty and the Beast*, Jim Parsons as Sheldon Cooper in *The Big Bang Theory*, Daniel Radcliffe as Harry Potter, and even Beyoncé.

DANIEL RADCLIFFE AS HARRY POTTER

MICHAEL
JACKSON

Original factory paint

Original factory paint

GLENN CLOSE AS
CRUELLA DE VIL

BEYONCÉ
KNOWLES

JENNIFER LAWRENCE
AS KATNISS EVERDEEN

Original factory paint

HORSE *Vs.* HORSEPOWER

⟳ **In 2017, a Ferrari 458 Italia faced off against two thoroughbred horses pulling a Roman-style chariot in a bizarre matchup.**

Taking place just south of Rome in a venue that was the movie set for the 2016 *Ben-Hur* remake, driver Fabio Barone was given a few handicaps to make the contest fair. He drove along the longer outside lane and over extra sand on the course. In addition, he drove an extra half lap and could not use electronic steering. Barone commented that he basically had no brakes, since the sand clogged up the circuit. Despite all this, the horses still lost to the sports car by a handful of seconds.

FLORAL STATUE > A 2018 statue of Mickey Mouse in Dubai was made from 100,000 plants and flowers. It stood 60 ft (18 m) tall and weighed almost 35 tons.

PRICE INCREASE > *Salvator Mundi*, a painting of Jesus Christ by Leonardo da Vinci, sold for $450.3 million at auction in New York in 2017 after selling for just $60 in 1958. Sixty years ago, it was thought to have been the work of da Vinci's pupil, Giovanni Antonio Boltraffio, and was not attributed to Leonardo until 2011.

EAGER READER > At age four, Caleb Green, from Chicago, Illinois, read 100 books in just one day.

KLINGON CUISINE > A Klingon tourist center opened in Stockholm, Sweden, in 2018, where fans can learn the history of the fictional alien race, study their language, train in their deadly martial art Mok'bara, and sample Klingon cuisine, including gagh (a delicacy made from serpent worms) and blood wine.

VAST DRAPE > *The Horse Trotted Another Couple of Meters, Then It Stopped*, a drapery installation by German artist Katharina Grosse, covers an area of more than 86,100 sq ft (8,000 sq m)—nearly the size of two football fields. She spent 10 days applying vibrant colors to the cloth with an industrial spray gun.

HOTEL CARPETS > Bill Young, an airplane pilot from Texas, has an Instagram account, @myhotelcarpet, that features pictures of dozens of unusual carpets from hotels around the world where he stays on stopovers—and the account has more than 450,000 followers.

BLURRED VISION > French artist Claude Monet's distinctive, blurry painting style was the result of cataracts restricting his vision.

WIRE SNAKE > Japanese artist Tsutamoto Dawiki twisted copper and brass wire into an incredible sculpture of a large snake, which is so flexible it can coil around itself and its mouth can be opened and closed.

MONSTER DRINK ➲ Drink combinations are nothing new, but when Sobelman's Pub and Grill in Milwaukee, Wisconsin, garnished their Bloody Mary with an entire fried chicken, they created art. Named the Chicken Fried Bloody Beast, the drink (or meal, depending on how you look at it) includes cheese, sausage, pickles, olives, onions, mushrooms, asparagus, scallions, shrimp, lemons, brussels sprouts, tomatoes, celery, skewers of bacon-wrapped jalapeño cheese balls, and one whole fried chicken—a $50 monster drink that really clucked with their patrons.

ZELDA COLLECTION > Anne Martha Harnes, from Molde, Norway, has a collection of more than 2,000 items of memorabilia from Nintendo's *The Legend of Zelda* series of video games, including costumes, life-size statues, and life-size inflatables.

FIRST DUEL > Frenchman Alexandre Dumas, who would later write *The Three Musketeers*, fought his first duel in 1825 at age 23. He did not sustain any serious injury, but his pants fell down in the course of the duel!

SILVER GOWN > The portrait of the Silver Queen that hangs in the Silver Queen Saloon in Virginia City, Nevada, is 15 ft (4.6 m) tall, 8 ft (2.4 m) wide, and has an evening gown made from 3,261 silver dollar coins and a belt made from twenty-eight 20-dollar gold pieces.

CROCHET DOLLS > Mother India's Crochet Queens, a group of around 2,000 people from all over the world, made 58,917 individual crochet doll sculptures for an environmental project in Chennai.

TINY PENCIL > Prakash Chandra Upadhyay, a micro-sculptor from Uttarakhand, India, created a working pencil measuring just 0.2 in (5 mm) long. He drilled a tiny hole into a piece of wood and inserted graphite to make a pencil that could write with the help of tweezers.

BLOOD PAINT > Instead of conventional tools, Kel Cruz, from Quezon City, the Philippines, creates pixelated portraits using a range of unusual mediums, including duct tape, lipstick, matchsticks, fingerprints, rubber stamps, and even blood stains.

TRACTOR TREE

➲ In October 2018, the Big Fresno Fair in California unveiled a 33-ton, 32-ft-high (9.8-m) "Tractor Tree." A team of welders and structural engineers installed the new permanent exhibit, which is made of 23 tractors of all sizes with some parts being 110 years old! The installation celebrates Fresno County's agricultural history in response to the Smithsonian's National Museum of American History pronouncing 2018 the Year of the Tractor.

As Sweet as PIE

➲ Self-taught confectionery artist Jessica Leigh Clark-Bojin, of Vancouver, British Columbia, Canada, learned to bake in six months—and now she makes pies with incredible decorations, arranging toppings to create amazing pop culture portraits.

Using intricately cut layers, edible paint, and glitter, plus lots of patience, Jessica is able to recreate instantly recognizable characters such as Harry Potter, Lando Calrissian, and Jigglypuff. Some of her more impressive creations are her "Piescrapers," which are towering three-dimensional scenes. She posts her pies on Instagram, where her sweet skills have earned her more than 50,000 followers.

The Nightmare Before Christmas–themed double-pie carousel!

The Hogwarts crest with a different flavor for each house!

A fashionable Lando Calrissian created using edible glitter.

Crochet COSTUMES

➲ **Every year, Stephanie Pokorny of Mentor, Ohio, crochets elaborate pop culture–inspired costumes for her children.**

Believe it or not, all of these outfits were created freehand, meaning Pokorny used no guide or pattern. She makes sure to craft the costumes in such a way so that the wearer can see out of them but their face is hidden when viewed from above or when they look down.

E.T.

PENNYWISE THE CLOWN

PAPA SMURF

SPANIEL SKIN > Gilbert White's book, *The Natural History and Antiquities of Selborne* (about a village in Hampshire, England), has never been out of print in more than 220 years. White's own copy of the book was bound in the skin of his pet spaniel, Fairey Queen.

BALLOON FLIGHT > Overcoming her fear of flying, Austrian Noëmi Lakmaier, who has been in a wheelchair all her life, floated for nine hours strapped to 20,000 helium balloons inside Australia's Sydney Opera House as a temporary art installation.

EYE MAKEUP > After applying mascara to the actress' eyes, Audrey Hepburn's Italian makeup artist, Alberto De Rossi, would separate each eyelash—one by one—with a safety pin.

TURTLE SCULPTURE > Artist Curt Halvorsen made a turtle sculpture in Dunseith, North Dakota, from 2,000 old car rims that had been collected by local thrift store owner George Gottbreht over a period of 16 years. Halvorsen welded the rims together to form a 40-ft-long (12-m), 18-ft-tall (5.5-m) turtle whose head alone weighed a ton.

BUTTERFLY WINGS > Li Zheng, an art student from Quanzhou, China, recreated some of Vincent van Gogh's most famous paintings—including his self-portrait—using more than 500 colorful butterfly wings.

CARTOON STRIP > Unaiza Ali Barlas, a 20-year-old from Lahore, Pakistan, created a cartoon strip measuring 877 ft (267 m) long—more than the length of 11 tennis courts. It took her a year to draw, working day and night.

GLOWS IN THE DARK!

SLIMER

THE PREDATOR

Harley Quinn from DC Comics' Batman universe.

Marvel's new female Thor character.

ACTUAL PHOTOGRAPHY!

Watery COSPLAY

➲ Teaming up with some of the world's best cosplay stars, photographer Brett Stanley has unlocked a dreamlike new universe of surreal underwater images.

Submerged beneath the waves, the pop culture legends of cosplay come to otherworldly life, complemented by eerie underwater lighting and gravity-defying poses. A typical shoot lasts about an hour, although Stanley once spent more than 10 hours in the water to get the

Sailor Neptune (left) and Sailor Uranus (right) from the popular Sailor Moon

NDCASTLE > Artists in Duisberg, used 3,500 tons of sand to build a ll (16.7-m) sandcastle—the height tory building. The structure was with sand models of European s, including Barcelona's Sagrada mple, Athens' Acropolis, and Italy's ower of Pisa.

ALLERGY > Actor and Bill Hader, the voice of Planters' g mascot Mr. Peanut, has a severe ergy.

WOOL GARDEN > Clare Young, from Gloucester, England, knitted an entire garden, featuring flowers, grass, flower pots, and walls—all made from wool. The garden, created in memory of her late husband Ken, also contained 40,000 woolen hearts sent in by 450 knitters from around the world.

SELFIE PROJECT > Starting in 2008, Hugo Cornellier, from Montreal, Canada, took a selfie every day for nine years from age 12 right up to his wedding day—more than 3,000 in total—so that he could document how much his appearance changed throughout his teens.

CROWE AUCTION > On April 7, 2018, on his 54th birthday and his 15th wedding anniversary (although he was about to be divorced from singer Danielle Spencer), actor Russell Crowe held an "Art of Divorce" auction of personal belongings in Sydney, Australia. His torso armor from *Gladiator* fetched $95,000, and the 128-year-old Italian violin that he learned to play in just a few months for his starring role in *Master and Commander* sold for more than $103,000.

PARTY CLOWN > Australian actor Hugh Jackman used to work as a clown at children's birthday parties.

DUCKOMENTA

➲ DUCKOMENTA is a touring art exhibition created by a group of artists working in the conceptual and pop art spheres. The collection features iconic images from the Western tradition recreated with human-like ducks as subjects. From "webbed" impressionist works to quacky Egyptian tombs, guests to the exhibit are both delighted and confounded by the sight of human history whimsically retooled from the perspective of ducks.

Barbie COUTURE

➲ Jian Yang, a businessman from Singapore, has quite the fashionable hobby: he not only owns more than 9,000 Barbies, but also outfits them in glamorous wedding gowns made of tissue paper, toilet paper, and tape.

Yang has been collecting the iconic doll since he was a child. Now 38, his collection includes dolls from more than 50 countries, and the gowns he makes for them are stunning. Despite liking movies and pop culture, the business director insists there was really no inspiration behind the dresses, which take as little as 10 minutes to create. If he gets the sniffles, not to worry—he photographs his designs and then disposes of them.

TOILET PAPER DRESS!

MUNSTER MANSION > Charles and Sandra McKee, of Waxahachie, Texas, have spent hundreds of thousands of dollars renovating their house room by room to create a replica of 1313 Mockingbird Lane, the ramshackle home of the Munsters. They watched all 70 episodes of the 1960s sitcom and drew up plans based on what they saw on TV. When the McKees eventually moved into the 10-room house, former cast members of *The Munsters* attended.

MULTILINGUAL > During a six-hour concert in Dubai on January 25, 2018, Suchetha Satish, a 12-year-old Indian girl, sang songs in 102 different languages, including English, Japanese, French, Hindi, German, and Armenian.

SCARY STATUE > Diver Curtis Lahr created a life-size statue of Jason Voorhees, the murderous villain from the *Friday the 13th* series of movies, and installed it 110 ft (34 m) below the surface at the bottom of Crystal Lake, near Crosby, Minnesota. The scary statue is fitted with Voorhees's trademark hockey mask and machete.

FAN SEARCH > When the superhero movie *Black Panther* was released in 2018, fans searching for the fictional kingdom of Wakanda began bombarding the villagers of Wauconda, Illinois, with phone calls. There were even requests to change the mascot of the local high school from a bulldog to a black panther.

BIEBER BOOST > Luis Fonsi's 2017 "Despacito" remix hit with Justin Bieber led to a 45 percent increase in tourists wanting to visit Puerto Rico in the three months following its release. The song has lyrics about the Caribbean island and its video features Puerto Rican landmarks.

SALTWATER PAINTINGS > Japanese artist Mai Hirashima uses saltwater as paint. She first paints the outline of her composition onto a black canvas before brushing on the saltwater in the desired shape and then adding heat so the water evaporates, leaving the salt to crystallize. She also uses a thin bamboo skewer to apply thicker layers and create different shades of white.

READY, SET, LEGO!

➲ In 2018, a team of 16 specialists built a life-size Bugatti Chiron made almost entirely of LEGO parts! The seats, the dashboard, the removable steering wheel, and even the engine is made of the tiny Technic bricks, wheels, and cross axles. It took more than 13,400 hours to develop and complete, using more than a million pieces and no glue whatsoever. Fitted with real Bugatti wheels, the car is fully drivable and can seat two people. Those looking for a fast ride might have to settle—the LEGO vehicle has a top speed of about 18 mph (29 kmph), while a real Bugatti can reach 261 mph (420 kmph)!

BEER SHAMPOO > For her role as U.S. ice skater Tonya Harding in the 2017 movie *I, Tonya*, Australian actress Margot Robbie had stale, sticky beer poured over her blonde hair to recreate Harding's frizzy fringe.

MOVIE LOCATIONS > For her 21st birthday, *Lord of the Rings* fan Bry Voydatch traveled from Worcester, Massachusetts, to New Zealand to photograph herself in the exact locations and poses from the fantasy trilogy.

GREEK DEGREE > Chris Martin, the lead singer of U.K. rock band Coldplay, studied ancient world studies and graduated with a first-class honors degree in Greek and Latin from a U.K. university.

DUBBING QUEEN > Irina Margareta Nistor of Romania dubbed as many as 5,000 movies into Romanian between 1985 and the collapse of the Communist regime three years later. Most were Hollywood films, which were banned in Romania at the time and had to be smuggled into the country. She voiced everyone from Bruce Lee to Baloo in *The Jungle Book*.

LANDFILL LIBRARY > Garbage collectors in Ankara, Turkey, have opened a public library filled with 6,000 discarded books that were otherwise destined for landfills.

LEAF GOWN > Four science students at the University of Hefei, China, spent nearly six months creating a gown by threading together 6,000 plant leaves. To ensure that the foliage they collected did not shrivel or rot, the students removed the leaves' flesh by boiling them in an alkali and sodium carbonate solution. This left just the "skeleton" of each leaf to be used in making the gown.

FOR THE BIRDS

⮌ Santa Claus usually flies with his eight reindeer, but this time he opted for a flock of 14 geese! Christian Moullec of Cantal in France has been flying with birds for more than 20 years, helping guide them to well-protected areas during their migrations. This time, Moullec's friend Jacky Herbert joined him dressed as jolly old Saint Nick to help spread some Christmas cheer.

FREE SHOES > Sarah Agee and all of her female classmates were supplied with 124 pairs of free Croc shoes to wear to their 2018 graduation at Seminole High School, Florida, after her online request to the company attracted 2,018 retweets.

MAFIA THREAT > Nintendo was forced to ship its Super Nintendo video game consoles by night because the company was worried that they might be stolen by the Yakuza, Japan's violent mafia.

STRAIGHT LINES > Slovenian artist Sašo Krajnc makes portraits that consist of several thousand crisscrossing straight lines. He uses a circular wooden frame lined with metal nails and tightly winds a single sewing thread around the nails to form an image. By overlapping more lines, he is able to create darker shades in his picture.

HIDDEN LANDSCAPE > Pablo Picasso painted over the work of another artist to create his 1902 masterpiece *La Misereuse Accroupie* ("The Crouching Beggar"). Recent X-rays revealed the presence of a mystery landscape underneath Picasso's oil painting.

NAME CHANGE > WPMT-TV Fox 43 weatherman Drew Anderson, from West Chester, Pennsylvania, legally changed his name to Meteorologist Drew Anderson.

MICKEY ARTIST > Staffer Floyd Gottfredson was chosen by Walt Disney in 1930 to draw the artwork for Mickey Mouse. Gottfredson was not keen on the assignment at first and was assured that it was only temporary—but he ended up doing it for 45 years, right up until 1975.

EERIE COINCIDENCE > A performance of *Titanic* the musical at the Mayflower Theatre in Southampton, England, to mark the 106th anniversary of the doomed liner's only voyage, was abandoned on its opening night in April 2018 when lumps of debris from a wall fell onto the stage shortly after the scene where the ship hits the iceberg.

CLAY CAFÉ > Customers have decorated the walls and ceiling of the Didu Café in Moscow, Russia, with more than 140,000 colorful clay figures. The owner places boxes of modeling clay on every table and invites customers to create their own artworks. Behind the bar is a 64-in-tall (160-cm), 41-in-wide (103-cm) Mona Lisa portrait that was made from 264 lb (120 kg) of modeling clay by visitors under the guidance of artist Nikas Safronov.

WAKE UP AND SMELL THE SELFIE

⮌ In a rare case of "have your cake and eat it, too," a London café now offers what they've coined the "Selfieccino." For just £5.75 ($7.60), the Tea Terrace in House of Fraser department store will apply your image to the foam of a caffeinated beverage using edible food dye and a fine art printer. The custom drink only takes 4 minutes to create and tastes no different than a regular coffee sans selfie.

A BUTTER *Idea*

➲ For the 2017 Canadian National Exhibition (CNE) in Toronto, David Salazar and his team created a butter sculpture of Canadian Prime Minister Justin Trudeau cuddling Toronto Zoo panda cubs Jia Panpan and Jia Yueyue.

Butter sculpting has only grown in popularity at state fairs and exhibitions, and it has been a feature at the CNE—which uses 2,700 lb (1,225 kg) of butter every year—since the 1950s. Celebrities and pop culture figures are always a crowd pleaser, so Trudeau's buttery likeness was also joined by the famous Ikea Monkey.

SCULPTING BUTTER!

The sculpture is based on an actual 2016 photo shoot where Trudeau revealed the baby pandas' names.

SHOE SHACK

An Airbnb in Nelson, New Zealand, is channeling major fairy-tale vibes. Based on the nursery rhyme "There Was an Old Woman Who Lived in a Shoe," the house is shaped just like a boot and appropriately named The Boot. The private cottage comes complete with a spiral staircase and sits on the Tasman Coast.

FAST FILM > Indian director Vijeesh Mani's film *Vishwaguru* was completed from script to screen in just two days. Scripting began on December 27, 2017; it was shot in a day and then screened at a movie theater in Thiruvananthapuram at 11:30 p.m. on December 29.

DIRTY WORK > James Gibson, an engineer from Essex, England, uses the corner of a cardboard cereal box as a tool to create amazing pictures in dirt on a white van. Nicknamed "Van Gogh," his artworks include images of the Battle of the Somme from World War I, musician Stormzy, and boxers Anthony Joshua and David Haye.

SILO MURAL > Cam Scale, from Melbourne, South Australia, painted a 200-ft-wide (60-m), 98-ft-tall (30-m) mural on round grain silos in the small farming town of Kimba. The mural, which took a month to complete, depicted a young child in a wheat field at sunset.

MUSICAL MIXER > Jean-Hervé Péron, from German experimental band Faust, uses a cement mixer as a musical instrument and has even composed a symphony for orchestra and cement mixer.

BUTT BOARD > As a protest against beach pollution, surfer Taylor Lane, from Santa Cruz, California, made a surfboard covered with 10,000 discarded cigarette butts.

YOUNG AUTHOR > Thanuwana Serasinghe, a Sri Lankan boy living in the Seychelles, had his first book published at age four. The book, which is titled *Junk Food*, took three days to write and warns of the dangers of unhealthy eating.

REAL SKELETONS > During a scene in the 1982 film *Poltergeist*, actress JoBeth Williams swam with real skeletons because it was cheaper to buy them from a medical company than to create replicas.

BEETHOVEN MARATHON > On November 26, 2017, Russia's St. Petersburg Symphony Orchestra, conducted by Sergei Stadler, played all nine Beethoven symphonies in one eight-hour concert.

BABY ACCOUNT > Calihan Gee had 109,000 Instagram followers before he was even born. His parents, Garrett and Jessica Gee, from Provo, Utah, revealed the gender and name of their unborn child on their Instagram account and then set up an account for him 37 weeks into the pregnancy.

CITY SKETCHES > Using photos that he takes while walking for weeks around cities, as well as aerial footage from books and Google Maps, English artist Carl Lavia is on a mission to draw detailed, large-scale sketches of all 69 U.K. cities. His 10-ft (3-m) sketch of Dundee, Scotland, took him more than three months, and he used more than 100 pens.

SOLE SCOOP

MOONSHINERS in 1920s Prohibition-era America wore shoes that left **FOOTPRINTS LIKE COWS,** in an attempt to throw off police when they were followed to their illegal stills.

In 1978, German filmmaker **WERNER HERZOG COOKED AND ATE HIS SHOE** on film after losing a bet!

Originating in the late 1800s, the term **"SNEAKER"** referred to the near silent sound of **WALKING IN RUBBER SOLES.**

After the criminal **GEORGE "BIG NOSE" PARROTT** was hung by an angry mob in Carbon County, Wyoming, a local doctor had his **SKIN MADE INTO A PAIR OF SHOES!**

Women require a license to wear **HIGH-HEELED SHOES** more than 2 in (5 cm) tall in the Californian town of **CARMEL-BY-THE-SEA!**

The **FOUNDERS OF ADIDAS AND PUMA** shoes were estranged German brothers, **ADOLF AND RUDOLF DASSLER,** who fell out with each other in 1948!

BAD TIMING > Actor Tony Randall, who had been appointed spokesperson for U.S. National Sleep Disorder Month, overslept on May 9, 1995, and missed a guest spot on the TV show *Wake Up America.*

BLIND ORCHESTRA > Egypt's Al Nour wal Amal orchestra is made up of 48 blind women from Cairo who rely solely on their memory to play classical pieces.

STAGE ATTACK > A Brazilian man was arrested on Easter 2018 after jumping on stage during a *Passion of the Christ* theater production in Nova Hartz and hitting an actor playing a Roman soldier over the head with a motorcycle helmet in an attempt to save Jesus from being crucified.

UNSUITABLE VIEWING > An episode of the children's cartoon show *Peppa Pig* was pulled from Australian TV because it taught viewers not to fear spiders.

MUSICAL PRINTER > Pavlos Georgiadis from Greece designed and built his own 3D printer from scratch—and he even made a file so that the machine's movements and software bleeps can play Beethoven's "Für Elise."

TRASH EXHIBITION > A 2017 art exhibition in Melbourne, Australia, celebrated a local garbage dump, the Werribee tip.

MANHOLE DESIGNS > Founded by Emma-France Raff, Berlin-based art collective Raubdruckerin (German for "pirate painters") tour European cities turning street utility hole covers into fashion designs. The artists apply ink to the manhole covers and then transfer the patterns on the spot to T-shirts and gym bags.

BATHROOM MASTERPIECE > After Leonardo da Vinci's death, King Francis I of France hung the *Mona Lisa* in the bathroom of his palace at Fontainebleau.

BAMBOO INSECTS > Japanese artist Noriyuki Saitoh creates life-size sculptures of insects out of bamboo—and they are detailed down to the tiny whiskers of grasshoppers and the veins on the wings of dragonflies.

ELVIS IMPERSONATOR > Four years before writing and directing the movie *Reservoir Dogs*, a 25-year-old Quentin Tarantino played an Elvis impersonator in a 1988 episode of the TV comedy *The Golden Girls.*

Mini Minty MASTERPIECES

⊃ **Steve Casino of New York has spent hundreds of hours painting tiny portraits and scenes onto itty bitty Tic Tac mints!**

This isn't Steve's first miniature mission—for years he has been painting peanut shells, turning them into celebrities, pop culture characters, and even the queen of England! He turned to painting Tic Tacs when he noticed a red mint had somehow gotten into his pack of white mints, reminding him of the red balloon from the movie It. He turned one of the white mints into Pennywise the clown to go with the balloon and has since gone on to turn these little breath fresheners into a miniature Van Gogh, the Incredible Hulk, and even a burger with a can of soda!

Spider-Man SKYDIVER

◗ **A skydiver made a death-defying video of himself flying through the air while dressed as Spider-Man!**

Adam Myers dressed as the popular webslinger to jump out of a plane, taking the "friendly neighborhood" thousands of feet above the ground. To capture some truly epic poses in his Spidey suit, Myers had his friend Brad North take a video of his stunt. Myers wore everything down to the full mask for most of the dive, although he did need to remove the mask for safety once he deployed his parachute. Myers hopes to create a routine for future Spider-Man jumps, even though he already was able to pull a few of the character's classic moves on the way down.

HIGH-FLYING WEBSLINGER!

LIP ART > Australian makeup artist Jazmina Daniel painted the image of Prince Harry and Meghan Markle's first kiss at their wedding onto her own lips using different-colored lipsticks and liners. Her artwork was amazingly detailed, right down to Meghan's sprig of myrtle and Harry's beard. In the past, she has created lip art featuring portraits of musicians such as Beyoncé and Tupac, as well as scenes from *The Wizard of Oz* and *The Little Mermaid*.

BOND SUIT > Eighty-five different versions of James Bond's Tom Ford suit were tailor-made for the spectacular opening chase sequence in the movie *Skyfall*—30 for actor Daniel Craig and similar numbers for his double and stunt double. Each version of the suit was made for a particular scene in the sequence. For example, when Craig was riding a motorcycle, he wore a suit with longer sleeves so that it wouldn't raise up over his forearms.

ANCIENT HARP > An ancient mouth harp discovered recently in the Altai Mountains region of Russia still makes music even though it is 1,700 years old.

FIVE ENDINGS > U.S. filmmaker Armen Perian made a short film, *The Angry River*, that has five different endings, depending on the viewer's preferences. It uses high-tech eye-tracking technology and artificial intelligence to determine which character the viewer looks at most on screen and then, armed with that information, it edits itself into one of five possible storylines.

COMIC TATTOOS > Rick Scolamiero, from Edmonton, Alberta, Canada, has 31 Marvel comic book characters tattooed on his body. His first Marvel tattoo was Spider-Man in 2011, and with the help of artist Tony Sklepic, he has since added 30 others, including Mystique (neck), Galactus (left shoulder), Wolverine (left inner forearm), Captain America (right inside calf), and Ultron (right hip).

PRO GAMER > Kyle Jackson, from Kent, England, is a professional gamer at age 13. He plays the survival shooting game *Fortnite* as part of a four-person team.

WOODEN SCAFFOLDS > Michelangelo painted the fresco ceiling of the Sistine Chapel in Rome while standing up the whole time—a total of four years. He invented a series of wooden scaffolds designed to be fixed to the chapel walls with brackets so that he and his assistants could be close enough to the ceiling to reach above their heads and paint.

GRAMMY DOORSTOP > For a while, Foo Fighters' Dave Grohl used his Grammy Award for Best Rock Album as a doorstop. It held his bedroom door open because otherwise it kept creaking shut.

SHARED BIRTHDAY > Israeli actress Gal Gadot, who played Diana Prince in the 2017 film *Wonder Woman*, and British actress Emily Carey, who played the 12-year-old Diana, share the same birthday, April 30, having been born in 1985 and 2003, respectively.

FAKE GERMANS > Bruce Willis played an all-American cop facing off against "German" terrorists in *Die Hard*, when in reality Willis was born in West Germany to an American father and a German mother. Alan Rickman, who played Hans Gruber, was English, and Alexander Godunov, who played Gruber's main henchman Karl, was Russian.

IT'S NINJA TIME!

MICHELANGELO 2X

The Metropolitan Museum of Modern Art got an unexpected visitor during its Michelangelo exhibition: the Teenage Mutant Ninja Turtle named for the great master himself! TMNT Michelangelo, who was actually at the museum as an ambassador for NYC's official tourism group, visited some of his namesake's most famous pieces, as well as a few other well-known exhibitions like the Temple of Dendur.

Clover Lover

Eighty-two-year-old Barbara Nieman of San Diego, California, wrote to Ripley's about her "unusual hobby"— she has collected four- and five-leaf clovers every day for more than a decade. She preserves them by sticking them to a calendar on the day she found the clover.

GLOBAL FLIGHT > Using four scheduled commercial flights, New Zealander Andrew Fisher flew around the world in only 52 hours 34 minutes. His 25,859-mi (41,375-km) journey took him from Shanghai, China, to Auckland, New Zealand, then on to Buenos Aires, Argentina, and Amsterdam, Netherlands, before returning to Shanghai.

SCAVENGER HUNT > September 10, 2017, saw 2,733 people—many wearing costumes—successfully complete a mass scavenger hunt in Ottawa, Ontario, Canada. Challenges included answering trivia and taking pictures of specific items or scenarios throughout the city.

120-FOOT PUTT > Corporate pilot Paul Shadle, from Rosemount, Minnesota, won a $100,000 prize at the Minnesota Golf Show in February 2018 by sinking a 120-ft (37-m) putt—a distance equal to one-third the length of a football field.

FIRST POINT > On December 3, 2017, Italian soccer team Benevento earned their first Serie A point in the club's 88-year history thanks to a goal by their goalkeeper Alberto Brignoli, who headed a 95th-minute equalizer against AC Milan.

STICKER BALL > In Longmont, Colorado, Sticker Giant CEO John Fischer and his team made the world's largest sticker ball using around 200,000 stickers and labels. It weighs more than 230 lb (104 kg) and has to be moved with a forklift and a wheeled wagon.

SPEED TYPIST > Shaik Ashraf, from Falaknuma, India, typed the entire alphabet from A to Z—with spaces between each letter—in only 3.37 seconds. He also did it blindfolded in 4.13 seconds.

ANIMAL IMITATOR > Ghanaian teen Justice Osei can imitate the sounds of more than 50 different local animals, including crocodiles, tortoises, and even mosquitoes.

STEADY HANDS > In Abensberg, Germany, barman Oliver Strumpfel carried 29 one-liter glasses of beer, weighing a total of 154 lb (70 kg), in his arms for a distance of 130 ft (40 m).

DINER CHALLENGE > Ray and Wilma Yoder, of Goshen, Indiana, have eaten at all 645 Cracker Barrel Old Country Store locations in 44 states across the United States. The challenge took them more than 50 years, beginning in the 1960s, and they dined at their final restaurant—in Tualatin, Oregon—in August 2017, on Ray's 81st birthday.

BLIND ADVENTURER > Although he is blind and almost completely deaf, Tony Giles, from Devon, England, has traveled solo to 127 different countries, all seven continents, and every U.S. state. During his travels, he has bungee jumped 16 times, skydived three times, and gone white water rafting everywhere from Costa Rica to New Zealand.

4.12 LB (1.873 KG) REMOVED!

1.873

CT SCAN SHOWS TUMOR!

DOUBLE HEADER

⮑ **In February 2018, doctors in Mumbai, India, removed the heaviest recorded brain tumor from 31-year-old Santlal Pal in a marathon seven-hour procedure.**

Weighing in at 4.12 lb (1.87 kg), the tumor was protruding from Pal's scalp, causing swelling, headaches, and blindness in both eyes, as well as making it seem like he had two heads on top of each other. Scans determined that the growth was not just inside the brain but also outside, between the skull and scalp. The patient has made progress on his recovery, although his vision has yet to return.

177

Mr. Sand Man

➲ Marcio Mizael Matolias has been living in a huge sand castle on the beach of Barra da Tijuca in Rio de Janeiro, Brazil, for more than 20 years!

Known locally as "The King," Matolias, who built and maintains the castle, often sits inside it in a small room surrounded by books, golf clubs, and fishing poles, and sleeps there unless the sand is too hot. To keep his fortress from collapsing, he has to water it regularly.

MARCIO IS KING OF HIS CASTLE!

YOUR UPLOADS

Breastmilk Jewelry

Designer Tiffany Villarreal of Oklahoma owns The Milky Way Breastmilk Jewelry—yes, it's exactly what it sounds like. Along with her two young daughters, Villarreal creates personalized rings, necklaces, earrings, and bracelets out of mothers' breastmilk. Mothers all over the world mail in their milk, and she sterilizes, preserves, and mixes the liquid in a resin to form a solid breastmilk stone. Villarreal tells Ripley's, "I am able to incorporate hair, placenta, birthstones, or umbilical cords to personalize these keepsakes even more."

CHILD STAR > Anna Hursey, from Cardiff, Wales, represented her country in ping pong at the 2018 Commonwealth Games in Australia at age 11. She needed just 17 minutes to win her first game in straight sets against a Ugandan opponent who was eight years older.

POGO STUNT > Russian Xpogo athlete Dmitry Arsenyev can do eight consecutive no-handed backflips on his pogo stick, a stunt he performs by releasing his hands from the handlebars while upside-down without falling off or losing control. He has also pogo-jumped over a bar more than 11 ft (3.4 m) high.

GETTING UP THERE > Sam Westwood, from Trunkey Creek, New South Wales, Australia, celebrated his 100th birthday with a skydive from 15,000 ft (4,570 m). He has traveled around Australia twice on his own and at age 80 climbed the 1,142-ft-high (348-m) sacred rock Uluru.

WHEELCHAIR FLIP > Lily Rice, a 13-year-old former Paralympic swimmer from Pembrokeshire, Wales, can do a backflip off a ramp in her wheelchair.

STROLLER PUSH > Ann Marie Cody, of Sunnyvale, California, pushed her 15-month-old triplets in a stroller along the full 26.2-mi (42-km) course of the 2018 Modesto Marathon in 4 hours 6 minutes 33 seconds. The 4-ft-wide (1.2-m) stroller weighed 120 lb (54 kg) when loaded with the children. A month later, she ran in the inaugural Silicon Valley Half-Marathon in San Jose, and, despite again pushing her children in the triple stroller, she completed the course in 1 hour 46 minutes 13 seconds, placing her 49th out of 753 women and 153rd overall out of 1,474 entrants.

RED HOT > When 17-year-old Red Gerard won the men's slopestyle snowboarding at the 2018 Winter Olympics, he became the United States' youngest men's Winter Olympics gold medalist in 90 years. Gerard practiced routines in his own miniature snowboarding park that he and his brothers constructed in the backyard of their home in Silverthorne, Colorado. It has hand-built jumps, rails, and even a rope tow.

PASTA RACER > Michelle Lesco, a math teacher from Tucson, Arizona, ate an entire bowl of pasta—containing 3.5 oz (100 g) of pasta and 1.75 oz (50 g) of sauce—in only 26.7 seconds at a restaurant in Scottsdale. She has also consumed 227 oysters in three minutes at a competitive eating competition in Ireland.

MOUNTAIN CHALLENGE > In a single push in February 2018, German-born trail runner Sunny Stroeer circumnavigated and reached the summit of the 22,841-ft-high (6,962-m) Aconcagua mountain in Argentina—a 64-mi (103-km) endurance challenge known as the "Full 360"—in only 47 hours 30 minutes.

REGULAR VISITOR > Muriel Thatcher has visited Dudley Zoo, near Birmingham, England, at least twice every month since the zoo opened in 1937. She made her first visit at age 10 and has since been more than 2,000 times.

TURN THE TABLES

➲ Most recreational activities happen on land or on water, but a fashion show in February 1947 took the runway underwater. In an impressive display at Marineland in Miami, Florida, a few models played ping pong underwater as a sandbar shark cruised on by.

SIDESHOW *Opera*

⮑ Classically trained musicians Nick and Lindsay Williams of New Orleans, Louisiana, combine their musical talents with dramatic acts such as glass-walking, eating razor blades, and throwing knives—with their feet!

Nick first combined singing and sideshow in 2014, when he sang opera while laying on a bed of nails. Lindsay would accompany him on the violin, but she wanted a circus talent of her own. In 2016, she found her calling in knife throwing and soon became so proficient that she could throw with her feet! The couple has taken their musical sideshow act across the country, having found a way to combine their love of music, each other, and history into one-of-a-kind performance art.

Lindsay was inspired by armless knife thrower Judge Desmuke, who was featured in Ripley Odditoriums in the 1940s!

Believe It or Not!
by Ripley

JUDGE
DESMUKE
**ARMLESS
KNIFE
THROWER**

THROWS
10 BUTCHER KNIVES
WITHIN ONE INCH OF
HIS WIFE STANDING **7** FEET AWAY

NOW APPEARING IN THE *ODDITORIUM*

Lindsay putting a cinderblock on Nick

Q How has your classical training led you to Sideshow Opera?

A Nick's intense vocal training included his teacher stacking heavy books on his diaphragm to build breath support, which has led to Nick being able to sing opera while Lindsay uses a sledgehammer to smash a cinderblock on his chest while he's lying on a bed of nails!

Q What inspired you to combine sideshow acts with opera and classical music?

A We both find that the dramatics of classical music go very well theatrically with the dramatics and emotions that sideshow and circus acts create. We wanted to make classical music and opera more accessible to all ages and walks of life. Going to the opera or experiencing "high art" has always been an expensive experience, which can alienate some social classes. There has also been a lack of interest in going to the opera recently, so we wanted to make something that could resonate with anyone by making opera and classical music more interesting, edgy, and fun.

Q Are there any limitations when combining sideshow and opera?

A Nick feels that his voice comes first before trying to attempt types of sideshow acts such as sword swallowing or glass eating. He refuses to do anything that may potentially damage his vocal cords.

Nick, aka Guglielmo "The Opera Singing Daredevil," swallows razor blades on a chain!

Lindsay, aka Madame Daggers "The Dangerous Dame of Daggers."

WOEFUL WHISKERS

⮕ When Valentine Tapley died in 1910, he had not shaved for 50 years and had a beard 12.5 ft (3.8 m) long!

When Abraham Lincoln ran for U.S. president, Democrat Valentine Tapley, from Pike County, Missouri, vowed that if Lincoln was successful, he would never shave again for the rest of his life. On November 6, 1860, Lincoln was elected the 16th president of the United States, and the rest is history.

TRICK SHOT > Bowler McKinley Knopp, from Campbellsville, Kentucky, achieved a strike using two bowling balls. He put extreme spin on one and sent it slowly toward the pins, then bowled the second ball at normal speed. The fast ball crashed into the pins, knocking them all over except for one, which was taken down by the slow ball.

RIVER RIDE > Dan Bolwell, from Melbourne, Australia, and a group of fellow cycling enthusiasts pedaled penny-farthings for 875 mi (1,400 km) along roads and tracks running next to the Murray River. They set off from Khancoban, New South Wales, on April 22, 2018, and arrived in Goolwa, South Australia, 16 days later.

YOUNG CLIMBER > At age 8, Edward Mills, from Dunnet, Scotland, climbed the Old Man of Hoy, a 450-ft-high (137-m) column of rock off the coast of Orkney, whose vertical face makes it one of Britain's toughest climbing challenges.

VINTAGE ELECTRICS > John Scott, of Maffra, Victoria, Australia, has a large collection of vintage electrical goods, including dozens of old TVs and radios and more than 1,500 electric jugs used to boil water for cups of tea, the oldest dating back to 1928.

BALL CONTROL > Without using his hands, Khris Njokwana successfully controlled a soccer ball that had been dropped by crane from a height of 123 ft (37.4 m) in Johannesburg, South Africa. He brought the ball under control with his thigh and made more than 30 touches with his feet, knees, and head before finally allowing the ball to hit the ground.

HEART SWAP > Randy Foye has enjoyed a distinguished NBA career despite suffering from a rare condition called *situs inversus*, where his internal organs are mirror images of a normal body—so his heart is on the right side of his body instead of the left, and his liver is on the left, not the right. Foye is the only player in major American sports with the condition, which affects about one in 10,000 people.

ALPINE SPECIALISTS > Liechtenstein has competed in 17 Summer Olympics without winning a single medal, but the country has won 10 medals at Winter Olympics—all in alpine skiing.

GRETZKY RECORD > If you removed all of Wayne Gretzky's goals from record, he would still be the NHL's all-time leader in points.

VINTAGE CAR > Since 2012, Dirk and Trudy Regter, from the Netherlands, have been driving around the world in a 100-year-old car—a 1915 Ford Model T. They have visited more than 50 countries and driven more than 50,000 mi (80,000 km)—even though the car had to be rebuilt after being hit by a truck in Belgium in 2014.

TWO WHEELS > At the 2018 Goodwood Festival of Speed in West Sussex, England, stunt driver Terry Grant drove a 2-ton Range Rover Sport SVR on only two wheels along an uphill, winding course without mishap for 1 mi (1.6 km), covering the distance in just 2 minutes 24.5 seconds.

This photograph was taken in 1896, so his beard was even longer than this by the time he died!

HAIR-RAISING FACTS

In the early 20th century, **X-RAYS** were used to remove excess body hair in clinics and salons.

Tiny **MUSCLES** attached to each and every hair follicle on your skin cause *goosebumps!*

The Hair Museum in Cappadocia, Turkey, has walls lined with more than **16,000 LOCKS OF HAIR.**

An ancient Roman hair dye formula included **LEECHES** pickled in vinegar.

Your hair contains traces of **GOLD!**

Men with **LONG HAIR** were not allowed to enter **DISNEYLAND** until the late 1960s!

EYE DICTATION > Born with severe cerebral palsy that has left him with locked-in syndrome, a rare brain disorder that causes complete paralysis of muscles and means that he cannot speak or move, 12-year-old Jonathan Bryan, from Wiltshire, England, wrote his autobiography with his eyes. His mother Chantal taught him to communicate his thoughts by flicking his eyes toward letters on a board. It takes him around 30 hours to "write" 500 words.

KITE CROSSING > At age 14, Adam Farrington kite-surfed 69 mi (110 km) across the English Channel from his home county of Dorset to Cherbourg, France. The crossing took him 5 hours 19 minutes, and he endured more than a dozen wipeouts in the face of 25 mph (40 kmph) winds and rough seas. He also had to avoid huge container ships while negotiating one of the world's busiest shipping lanes.

HIGH-HEELED HIGHLINER > French slackliner Mimi Guesdon won a three-nation contest in China's Hunan Province by walking across a 230-ft-long (70-m) line with a 4,200-ft (1,300-m) drop to the ground below in 9 minutes 24 seconds... while wearing high-heeled shoes. High-heeled slacklining is an extreme version of an already dangerous sport and involves walking across a loose line high above the ground while wearing 2-in (5-cm) heeled shoes and without using a pole for balance.

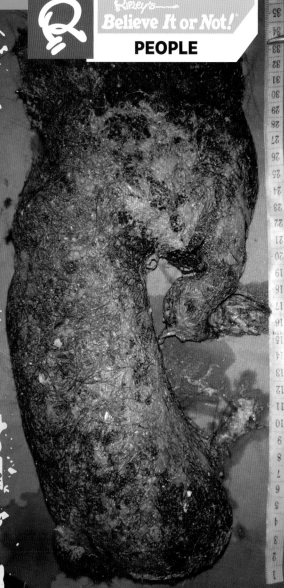

ONE-HANDED > Krishna Sai, of Chennai, India, solved 2,474 Rubik's Cube puzzles in 24 hours using only one hand.

HER OWN HAIR!

HAIRY PILLOWS

◑ Ezzeya Daraghmeh, from Tubas, Palestine, has stuffed three pillows with 67 years' worth of clippings of her own hair. She started collecting her hair when she was 15, and whenever she combs or washes it, she keeps any that falls out.

RAPUNZEL MOM ➲ Suman Prasad of India was rushed to the hospital complaining of stomach pains after giving birth. However, doctors soon found that she had a massive hairball lodged in her stomach weighing more than 3.3 lb (1.5 kg)! It turns out Prasad was suffering from trichotillomania, or Rapunzel syndrome, an extremely rare condition that causes people to compulsively chew on and swallow their own hair. The hairball (aka a bezoar) was successfully removed in a three-hour surgery.

BIG HEARTED > American middle-distance runner Mel Sheppard won a total of four gold medals at the 1908 and 1912 Olympics, despite having previously been rejected for a job as an officer with the New York City Police Department due to a weak heart.

FAST FINGERS > Rosie Baldwin of the United Kingdom typed the entire alphabet on a touchscreen cell phone in only 7.44 seconds at a festival in Cannes, France.

FOILED
Again

⬤ You've heard of surfboards and paddleboards, but what in the world are foilboards?

Foilboards use the same basic principles as airplanes to allow riders to glide several feet above the water. When the board and rider are pulled through the water, usually by a kite or boat, the wings below the board push water down and force the board up, in the same way an aircraft's wings push air down to make the plane fly. The result is a super-smooth and fast ride. Some professionals can even surf on their foilboards, using the water pressure from waves to propel themselves.

KEY TO SURVIVAL

A 19-year-old in Maharashtra, India, was hospitalized when he got into a fight and ended up with a motorcycle key lodged in his skull! Doctors successfully performed a craniotomy surgery, removing a flap of skull in order to access the key stuck 2 in (5 cm) deep into the patient's head. The procedure took about 3.5 hours, and the victim was able to leave the hospital just three days later. No word on if the owner got his key back.

WEDGED INTO SKULL!

WATER WINGS!

HUMAN CANNONBALL >
On March 12, 2018, in Tampa, Florida, human cannonball David Smith Jr. ("The Bullet") was launched 194.7 ft (59.3 m) through the air by a massive, 34-ft-long (10.3-m) cannon modeled after a weapon from the pirate-themed Xbox game *Sea of Thieves*. He hit a speed of 60 mph (96 kmph) in just 0.2 seconds. He has been fired from a cannon more than 5,000 times in his career.

BOTTLE COLLECTOR >
Beachcomber Wim Kruiswijk has collected more than 1,200 messages in bottles since 1983 and has replied to most of them. He can sometimes find 50 bottles a year washed up near his home at Zandvoort on the Dutch coast.

HEARSE PULL >
Stuntman Ian Brown, from Hampshire, England, pulled a 4,400-lb (2,000-kg) funeral hearse, which had people sitting on it, for a distance of 180 ft (55 m) with a sword that was plunged 15 in (38 cm) down his throat.

BLIMP TOW >
Water skier Kari McCollum, from San Diego, California, traveled 6.9 mi (11.1 km) across Lake Elsinore while being towed by a blimp.

BACKYARD RIDE >
Sixteen-year-old Logan Moore spent two months hand-building a wooden roller coaster that rises to a height of 8.5 ft (2.6 m) in the backyard of his home in Knox County, Kentucky.

POGO JUMPS >
Dalton Smith, an Xpogo athlete from Franklin, Tennessee, can jump on a pogo stick over the roofs of three cars in succession, taking only one bounce in between each car.

SLACKLINE ACROBATS >
German highliner Lukas Irmler and Frenchman Pablo Signoret carried out daring acrobatic feats on a slackline stretched 500 ft (152 m) above ground between two frozen waterfalls in the French Alps in freezing temperatures of 5°F (–15°C). Irmler performed a handstand, and both men also stopped to lie down on the line. To anchor the 1,400-ft-long (427-m) line, they first had to climb the waterfalls while carrying 440 lb (200 kg) of equipment.

Living on the EDGE

At 36 years old, Karina Oliani has already become a two-time Brazilian wakeboard champion, a doctor, a helicopter pilot, climbed Mount Everest (twice), free-dived with great white sharks, and hosted numerous adventure and nature TV programs—and she's just getting started.

The TV personality and extreme-sports enthusiast from São Paulo, Brazil, spoke with Ripley's about her adventures. When asked *What is your ultimate goal?* Oliani had just one thing to say: "I want to have an outstanding life, to inspire people to be their best, to search for their dreams; I want to bring light to those who need it and to make people happy."

Q Can you tell us about your volcano ziplining?

A It was a childhood dream. I was always very fascinated by fire and especially lava. I had to wait to meet the right person, Frederick Schuett, to be able to pull this off. He is from Canada, and without him, this would not have been possible.

Q What's the most scared you've ever been?

A I hate cockroaches. Once I had to sleep in a cave full of them. I hated it so much.

Q How, when, and why did you start your adventurous lifestyle?

A Since I was a little kid, my mum noticed I was "different." While my younger sisters were always playing with their dolls, I was climbing roofs and trees, or jumping into the pool from a balcony. As I became a teenager, that passion for outdoor sports became very clear. By the age of 18, I was a two-time Brazilian wakeboard champion, and I hold a free-diving national record.

Q What has been your favorite experience so far?

A It's impossible to pick just one. I loved climbing Everest (from both sides), and I also had a blast when I became the first person ever to traverse the largest lava lake in the world.

In December 2017, Oliani became the first person ever to zipline over the world's largest permanent lava lake in Ethiopia's Erta Ale volcano. Preparing for the feat took around six months, from getting government permissions to creating the necessary gear. She ziplined—braving acidic winds from the active volcano—almost 328 ft (100 m), limited by the length of heatproof rope (since it's not manufactured in long lengths and used almost exclusively by firefighters). The heat suit, which looked like something out of a sci-fi movie, even needed special thread that wouldn't melt at the high temperature.

GIANT ANACONDA!

Q What do you hope to teach people?

A To be the difference they want to see in the world. I know this is very cliché, but if we treat each other the way we want to be treated, the entire world will be such a better place to live in.

Q Can you tell us about your experience with a giant anaconda underwater?

A That was so cool. I will never forget it. At first, I have to say it was a little breathtaking, but after 5–10 minutes of hanging around it, I could notice it was totally fine with our presence. I was able to dive with this anaconda for more than an hour, and we both got along really well. It was magical.

Oliani has even dived with and petted a 26-ft-long (8-m) wild anaconda in Brazil while filming her TV series *Wild Ocean with Karina Oliani*. It took her four days just to find the sizable snake. Oliani became a certified open water scuba diver when she was only 12 years old.

In December 2015, Oliani posed for an underwater photoshoot—without any breathing equipment—in the Bahamas, complete with sharks circling around her. Oliani hopes that the shoot will bring attention to the conservation issues surrounding sharks.

ARMED AND ARMLESS

Matt Stutzman of Iowa is one of the best archers in the world, and he does it all with no arms!

Stutzman has never let his lack of limbs hold him back from experiencing the world. He uses his feet for everything, including archery and driving an unmodified car! In 2010, he entered his first archery tournament, and just two years later, he represented the United States at the Paralympics, earning the silver medal. In 2015, he set the world record for the farthest accurate shot in archery—he hit a 4 ft (1.2 m) diameter target from more than 930 ft (283.5 m) away!

Matt uses a special belt around his chest to hold the arrow until he's ready to release it.

LINCOLN GATHERING > On February 14, 2018, at Lincoln Elementary School in Louisville, Kentucky, 556 people—including students and faculty members—dressed as Abraham Lincoln, donning stovepipe hats and fake chinstrap beards.

NATIVITY SCENES > Shirley Squires, of Guilford, Vermont, displays more than 1,400 miniature nativity scenes in her home each Christmas. She started collecting them more than 20 years ago and has since acquired scenes from more than 55 countries. Some of them are as small as a thimble, one is made out of beeswax, and another is in a sandwich bun.

145 DEGREES > Professor V. N. Parthiban, who teaches in Chennai, India, has obtained 145 academic degrees in 30 years.

SEATED BACKFLIP > Brandon Burns, a 20-year-old student at the University of Michigan, can perform a seated backflip without using his hands for liftoff. He is one of only two people in the world known to accomplish the acrobatic feat.

QUAD POWER > German racing cyclist Robert Förstemann has 34-in (85-cm) quads—larger than some people's waists. He is nicknamed "Quadzilla," and his thighs are so strong that when pedaling they can generate enough electricity to power a 700W toaster and toast a slice of bread.

LOVE SEARCH > Over a period of eight years, 31-year-old Niu Xiangfeng from China has been rejected for a date by 80,000 women.

FIVE-MILE DRESS > Volunteers in Caudry, France, made a wedding dress train that was more than 5 mi (8 km) long. They spent two months stitching individual pieces of the train before sewing them together to create the 26,559-ft-long (8,095-m) garment

To promote reading, father-of-three Boyade Treasures-Oluwunmi read aloud for 122 hours—more than five days—in Lagos, Nigeria.

NEW SPORT > Nick Druce went water-skiing on top of an iPad on a lake in Hampshire, England. Druce, who calls his new sport iPadding, wore a special water-skiing shoe that was attached to the screen of the tablet. He has also skied with PC keyboards duct-taped to his feet.

JET SUIT > Wearing a jet engine power suit fitted with six kerosene thrusters, real-life Iron Man Richard Browning reached a speed of 32 mph (51 kmph) while flying several feet above a lake at Reading, England, on November 8, 2017.

TINY WAIST > By wearing a corset for 23 hours a day, 39-year-old Diana Ringo, from San Diego, California, has been able to maintain a tiny, 18-inch waist. She only removes the corset when she showers or works out.

RUBIK'S ROBOT > Ben Katz, a student at the Massachusetts Institute of Technology, and software developer Jared Di Carlo constructed a robot that can solve a Rubik's Cube puzzle in only 0.38 seconds.

SURE SHOTS > Six members of the Harlem Globetrotters basketball team made 348 half-court shots in one hour while appearing live on *Good Morning America* in New York City.

LOWEST SCORE > At the 2017 Open Championship at Birkdale, England, South African Branden Grace became the first golfer to shoot a round of 62 in a men's major championship. Only 29 players had previously carded a 63 in 442 majors dating back to 1860.

YOUNG RUNNERS > In December 2017, 11-year-old Zara Rahim and her nine-year-old brother Mekaal completed a full 26.2-mi (42-km) marathon in Antarctica, braving temperatures of 14°F (−10°C) and a running track covered by 12 in (30 cm) of snow. In the space of nine months, the Canadian siblings traveled more than 156,000 mi (250,000 km) around the world to take part in and finish marathons on all seven continents.

FRECKLES BE GONE

⟳ This nightmarish contraption was actually used in the 1930s to try removing freckles. Italian physician Dr. Matarasso came up with the method: he compressed carbon dioxide snow (aka "dry ice") into sharp points, like lead pencils, and then pressed it against each freckle for up to three seconds to freeze off the colored skin. The patient had to breathe through a special tube, while their eyes were covered with air-tight pieces and their nostrils were plugged.

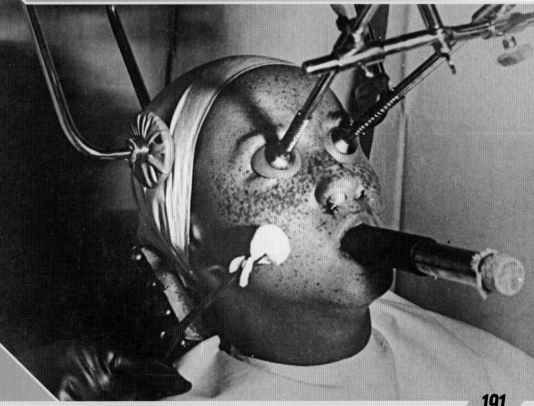

➲ David Phillips of Claverdon, Warwickshire, England, has been running all his life—and the 74-year-old is aiming to run his 500th marathon in 2019! Running more than 13,000 mi (20,921.5 km) and raising more than £100,000 (about $129,720) for charity in the process, the racing granddad stretches his legs every day and runs long distances every weekend.

STICK BOMB > Students at Natick High School, Massachusetts, set off a "stick bomb" with 68,480 sticks in the school's gym. The bomb was made by interlocking tongue depressors in such a way that removing one caused a chain reaction that sent the sticks flying into the air. It took more than 20 students nearly 24 hours to build the structure, but it "detonated" in less than 30 seconds.

TATTOOED COUPLE > At age 69, Charlotte Guttenberg, from Melbourne, Florida, has nearly 99 percent of her body covered in tattoos, including 216 tattoos of feathers. She received her first inking at age 50. Her partner, 76-year-old Chuck Helmke, has 376 skulls tattooed on his body.

TONS of TUMORS

➲ K. Palanisami of Tamil Nadu, India, has five tumors that weigh a total of more than 40 lb (18 kg).

The growths first appeared when he was 12 years old. Now there are five—two on each of his arms and one on his neck that affects his speech. Even after X-rays and blood tests, doctors are mystified by the lumps and hesitate to remove them out of fear that the operation could be fatal to Palanisami. In the meantime, he lives with his brothers and sisters-in-law who care for him.

TURBAN DAY > To celebrate Turban Day, a Sikh organization in New York City tied more than 9,000 turbans in Times Square in eight hours on April 7, 2018.

STUNT RIDE > Lee Musselwhite, of Somerset, England, rode 100 ft (30 m) on a BMX bike without using his hands or his feet. After building up speed with a run up, he sat on the handlebars with his chest on the seat of the bike and rode on one wheel.

HORSE LIFT > Ukrainian strongman Dmytro Khaladzhi can lift and carry a live horse on his back. He can also bend steel rods with his teeth and drive nails through wood using the palm of his hand.

LONG SERVICE > American Airlines' Bette Nash has worked as a flight attendant for more than 60 years, chiefly on the route from Washington, D.C., to Boston, Massachusetts, which she has been flying since 1961. The 81-year-old from Manassas, Virginia, began her career with Eastern Airlines when Dwight D. Eisenhower was U.S. president and tickets cost only $12.

ELASTIC MAN

⮩ Possessing double cartilage and extra tissue in his knee joints, hips, and ankles, 57-year-old Moses Lanham (aka Mr. Elastic) can turn his feet completely backward 180 degrees and walk! He attributes his abnormal agility to a rope-climbing accident he had when he was 14 years old.

FIVE TUMORS WEIGH A TOTAL OF 40 LB (18 KG)

Martin Joe Laurello, aka "The Human Owl," could twist his head 180 degrees. He turned heads in Ripley's Odditoriums throughout the 1930s. Here "The Human Owl" performs at a wild party hosted by Robert Ripley.

HIS FEET ARE COMPLETELY BACKWARD!

CYCLING PUZZLER > P. K. Arumugam, a 17-year-old student from Chennai, India, solved a Rubik's Cube 1,010 times in 6 hours 7 minutes 44 seconds—while riding a bicycle, his feet never once touching the ground.

NO HANDS > Mahdi Gilbert, from Toronto, Ontario, Canada, performs sleight-of-hand magic tricks even though he has no hands! He was born without hands and feet, so he had to spend nine years creating all of his own techniques for illusions. He has become so skilled with playing cards that he was able to trick famous magicians Penn & Teller on their show *Fool Us*.

HAIR SNAKE > Trinh Thi Nghien, an 81-year-old woman from Vietnam, has a 10-ft-long (3-m) mass of thick hair growing from her head like a snake. Her hair was normal until 1995, when she noticed a bun of tangled hair on the back of her head. She cut it off, but it soon grew again and has become longer and thicker over the years, taking an entire day to dry after washing. It is now so big that when she goes out she has to coil it around on her head and cover it up because people always want to touch it. Although the rest of her hair is dark and turning gray, the long "snake" is light brown and shows no sign of graying.

GIANT PUZZLE > Working up to eight hours straight at a time, Jack Brait, from Marshfield, Massachusetts, spent 80 days completing an enormous, 40,320-piece Disney-themed jigsaw puzzle that measured 6 ft (1.8 m) long and 22 ft (6.7 m) wide. He has autism, which he says helps him understand how to put the pieces together.

Rarity Nº 7599

Tattooed Human Skin

Removed from the arm of sailor Duane Katz, who gifted the framed skin to his wife.

Ripley's **Rarities**

CHOPPED OFF!

BABY BOARDER > Cash Rowley, of Boise, Idaho, could ride a snowboard before her first birthday. She comes from a snowboarding family, and her parents, Nick and Whitney Rowley, bought her a board when she was just a few weeks old and started practicing with her in the house on the carpet.

TOY SHIP > A year after being launched from Aberdeenshire, Scotland, in May 2017 by young brothers Ollie and Harry Ferguson, a small, plastic toy pirate ship passed Guyana in South America—more than 4,500 mi (7,200 km) away. The boat had a counterweight added to help it stay afloat, and its hull was padded with polystyrene to improve buoyancy. Named *Adventure*, it has sailed via Denmark, Sweden, and Norway and carries a written note asking anyone who finds it to launch it back into the ocean.

SMASHED BLOCKS > Turkish martial artist Ali Bahçetepe had 16 concrete blocks smashed on his body by an assistant with a 14-lb (6.4-kg) sledgehammer in only 4.75 seconds. Bahçetepe can also use his bare hands to smash 1,175 concrete blocks in a minute.

PROUD PARENTS > Guido Huwiler and Rita Ruttimann, the father and stepmother of Swiss freestyle skier Mischa Gasser, cycled 10,500 mi (17,000 km) from Olten, Switzerland, to Pyeongchang, South Korea, to see him compete in the 2018 Winter Olympics. The ride across Europe and Asia took them a year and through 20 countries.

PINKY NECKLACE

◗ Torz Reynolds, from Essex, England, chopped off her own finger with bolt cutters in 2017, simply because she thought it would look good. The 30-year-old originally kept the severed finger in her freezer and then celebrated the one-year anniversary of the detachment by turning the pinky into a pendant necklace. Reynolds proudly displays her digit in a glass vial filled with alcohol.

BREAKING
TATTOO TABOO

⟳ Inking the skin has been an art largely reserved for male artists. It wasn't until the early 1900s that Maud Wagner became the first bona fide female tattoo artist in the United States.

In 1907, she traded a date with her eventual husband, Gus, for tattoo lessons in traditional hand-poking. Both she and Gus were circus performers—Maud a contortionist and aerialist. Her husband inked her skin extensively; she sported tattoos of monkeys, butterflies, lions, horses, snakes, trees, an American flag, and even her own name. Lotteva Wagner followed in her parents' footsteps, also becoming a tattooist. Interestingly, Lotteva never actually had any tattoos because her mother Maud wouldn't allow it.

UP UP, UP, and Away!

⟳ **Tom Morgan of Bristol, England, flew 15.5 mi (25 km) over South Africa in a camping chair attached to 100 helium balloons!**

Over the course of two hours, Morgan reached a height of more than 8,000 ft (2,488 m) before having to pop his balloons to hurriedly land after receiving a radio alert of imminent strong winds. Part of The Adventurist, a company that organizes extreme adventure events, he hopes the successful stunt will give way to a wacky air race.

15 MI (25 KM) IN THE AIR!

BACK AND FORTH > On August 8, 2017, the Lady Patriots, the volleyball team from Lincoln County High School in Stanford, Kentucky, completed 1,027 consecutive volleyball passes, passing the ball for 23 minutes straight.

BEE BEARD > On August 30, 2017, in a public square in Toronto, Ontario, Canadian beekeeper Juan Carlos Noguez Ortiz allowed 100,000 live bees to rest or crawl on his face for more than one hour—and was only stung twice during the challenge.

LEMONADE CUP > In Cape Girardeau, Missouri, convenience store Rhodes 101 Stops built a 4,730-gal (17,905-l) soft drink cup filled with lemonade to celebrate National Lemonade Day. The 13.7-ft-tall (4.2-m) cup weighed 3,200 lb (1,452 kg).

SCUBA DIVE > Ray Woolley, from Cheshire, England, spent his 94th birthday scuba diving 125 ft (38 m) underwater on the wreck of the *Zenobia*, a cargo ship that sank on its maiden voyage in 1980 off the coast of the Mediterranean island of Cyprus.

HOME RUN > In 1952, in his very first bat as a 29-year-old rookie pitcher, the New York Giants' Hoyt Wilhelm hit a home run against the Boston Braves. His career lasted for 21 more years and 493 plate appearances, but he never hit another home run.

SNOOKBALL

➡ A new sport has emerged that combines the best of billiards and the best of soccer—Snookball. The Frankenstein sport takes its name from the popular billiard game snooker and football (aka soccer). Played on a pool table about four times the usual size, two to four players try to kick numbered and colored soccer balls into the pockets around the table. The first player or team to sink all their balls, as well as the 8-ball last, wins.

LONG SNAP > On January 27, 2018, during practices for the Pro Bowl in Orlando, Florida, Cincinnati Bengals football player Clark Harris snapped a ball 36.66 yards (33.5 m). At the time, he had delivered 1,284 consecutive playable snaps over a period of nine years.

WAKEBOARDING TOUR > Becca Stuck, a student at Mount Pleasant High School, North Carolina, went wakeboarding on lakes in all 50 U.S. states in 23 days 6 hours 5 minutes.

SKATING MARATHON > Rudra Chaitanya Dalal, 12, roller-skated nonstop for 51 hours—more than two days—in Karnataka, India, covering a distance of 507 mi (816 km).

THREE-DAY GAME > Military veterans from around the U.S. played baseball nonstop for 74 hours 26 minutes 52 seconds at the GCS Ballpark in Sauget, Illinois. The marathon game was contested by two teams of 28 players, and ended with the blue team beating the gray team in the 292nd inning, 396 to 255.

EXTRA WORKOUT > In December 2017, body builder Michael Danforth, 52, from Orlando, Florida, lifted over 1,000,000 lb (454,000 kg) in a single 18.5-hour workout at a local gym. He trained for eight months beforehand, working on different muscle groups more than five hours a day.

It has no bottom jaw, which means the owner was cannibalized! The bottom jaw was broken off, and the brain removed from within and then eaten.

Rarity Nº 169328

Engraved Skull

Extremely rare carved trophy skull once worn as a necklace by Dayak headhunters in Borneo.

Ripley's *Rarities*

Flying WALLENDAS

SEVEN-PERSON CHAIR PYRAMID

◗ The Wallenda family has been shocking audiences with their high-wire acts since the early 1920s!

Perhaps their most famous—and dangerous—stunt is the seven-person chair pyramid, which in 1962 sadly resulted in the death of two performers and left a third paralyzed from the waist down. Despite this, the Wallendas continued to perform, eventually branching off into several different troupes as the family grew larger. In 2012, Nik Wallenda helped Ripley's celebrate the opening of our Baltimore, Maryland, Odditorium by crossing the 300-ft-wide (91-m) harbor 100 ft (30 m) above the water.

BAREFOOT SKIERS > A total of 32 barefoot water skiers were towed simultaneously along the Wolf River in Shawano, Wisconsin, by a single boat.

HAND WALKER > Dirar Abohoy, from Tigray, Ethiopia, can climb mountains by walking on his hands. Abohoy, who practices hand-walking for six hours every day, can also pull cars and even carry people on his back while doing handstands.

BLIND SURFER > Despite being born blind due to glaucoma, Derek Rabelo, from Guarapari, Brazil, is a professional surfer—and has conquered Hawaii's Pipeline big wave break, one of the most difficult surfing challenges in the world. To compensate for his lack of vision, he uses other senses—touch and hearing—to help him navigate the ocean as well as be able to stand up and duck dive at the right time to ride big waves.

TOY BUSES > Geoff Price, of Walsall, England, has traveled around the world to build up his collection of more than 14,000 toy buses. He has been collecting toy buses of all sizes for more than 60 years and has models dating back to 1903, from countries such as Japan, Tunisia, and Sri Lanka.

BOTTLE FLIPPER > In one minute, Ohio State University student Drue Chrisman flipped 63 partially filled plastic water bottles lined up on a counter top so that each one landed upright.

ICE CAROUSEL > About 100 residents of Sinclair, Maine, created a 427-ft-diameter (130-m) ice carousel on a frozen lake. To cut the huge circle, they bored more than 1,300 holes into the 32-in-thick (90-cm) ice on Long Lake. They then sliced through it with chainsaws and other equipment to form a circular chunk of ice that was estimated to weigh more than 11 tons. Once the circle was cut, they waited for the weather to warm up a little before using four outboard boat motors to get it rotating.

CAR FLIP > With the help of a ramp, Pete Racine performed a perfect barrel roll to flip a car at Bear Ridge Speedway in Bradford, Vermont—at the ripe age of 92, even though he is blind in his right eye and has restricted vision in his left eye.

FULL MOUTH > Manoj Kumar Maharana, of Odisha, India, can stuff 459 drinking straws into his mouth at once.

POLAR CONQUEST > By age 16, skier Jade Hameister, from Melbourne, Australia, had reached the North and South Poles and traversed the Greenland ice sheet. Skiing unsupported and unassisted, she took 37 days to reach the South Pole in January 2018—a 373-mi (597-km) journey dragging a 220-lb (100-kg) sled across the Antarctic in the face of a wind chill temperature of −58°F (−50°C).

WHAT'S IN A NAME?

WINNER Lane of New York has been ARRESTED more than 30 times. Meanwhile, his younger brother, LOSER Lane, earned a prep school SCHOLARSHIP, graduated from COLLEGE, and joined the New York POLICE Department.

James M. FAIL was a SUCCESSFUL businessman who never named anything after himself... until he helped fund the building of the University of Alabama's visitors' locker room, now officially known as THE FAIL ROOM.

National Hockey League player Larry PLAYFAIR was well-known for getting into FIGHTS in the rink.

On October 2, 2017, Chief Danielle OUTLAW was sworn in as CHIEF OF POLICE in Portland, Oregon!

When ARCHBISHOP Jaime L. Sin was appointed as head of the Catholic Church in the Philippines, he became known as CARDINAL SIN.

The only member of the famously bearded band ZZ TOP to not sport facial hair is their drummer—Frank BEARD.

AIR SUDS

⊃ Brothers Johannes and Philipp Mickenbecker successfully built a flying bathtub! Built like a drone and boasting 120-horsepower, a pilot was able to ride in the remote-controlled contraption around Herzberg, Germany. The pair are known as "The Real Life Guys" online and post their wild builds to YouTube.

FLYING BATHTUB!

The REAL LIFE GUYS

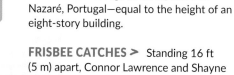

Road to Odd
Jeff Hanson
Cincinnati, Ohio, USA
Acrylic paint on heavily textured canvas featuring canvas knots, woven strips of canvas, and sisal rope.

Jeff's vision is impaired from an optic nerve tumor related to neurofibromatosis. He still creates works of art despite his visual impairment.

HIGH HEELS > Irene Sewell, a former professional ballroom dancer from Blacksburg, Virginia, ran an entire 26.2-mi (42-km) marathon in high heels. Running in 3-in (7.5-cm) stiletto heels, she finished the Seven Bridges Marathon in Chattanooga, Tennessee, in 7 hours 27 minutes 53 seconds.

MONSTER WAVE > On November 8, 2017, Brazilian surfer Rodrigo Koxa rode a colossal 80-ft-high (24.4-m) wave at Nazaré, Portugal—equal to the height of an eight-story building.

FRISBEE CATCHES > Standing 16 ft (5 m) apart, Connor Lawrence and Shayne Pheifer, two students from Winnipeg, Manitoba, Canada, completed 34 behind-the-back Frisbee catches in one minute on September 12, 2017.

POLICE ARTIST > Since starting her job as a forensic artist for the Houston Police Department in Texas in 1989, Lois Gibson has helped solve more than 1,200 crimes. She sits down with witnesses or victims to draw sketch likenesses of suspects for detectives.

SKATING FIRST > Skating nine hours a day for three days in February 2018, Jim Mee, from York, England, made history by becoming the first person to skate the entire 85-mi (136-km) length of the frozen Khovsgol Nuur Lake in Mongolia—despite not having skated for 20 years and facing temperatures that plunged to a bone-chilling −53°F (−47°C).

CONSECUTIVE ACES > With consecutive shots, two amateur players from the same golf group—friends Jayne Mattey and Clair Shine—hit holes-in-one on the same hole at East Berkshire Golf Club in England, beating odds of 17 million to one.

GREAT MEMORY > Santhi Sathyan, from Kerala, India, can memorize 45 random objects in 60 seconds and, after reshuffling, can arrange them back in the exact same order in less than three minutes.

SPLIT ENDS

➲ Kajol Deb of Agartala, Tripura, India, is a table tennis coach with no hands! The 51-year-old lost his hands in a bomb explosion in 1992, and after his arms were modified to allow him to hold objects, he found he could hold a table tennis paddle just fine. He slides the paddle in between the split parts on each forearm and then wraps it with rubber bands. Deb now trains eight students at his own school.

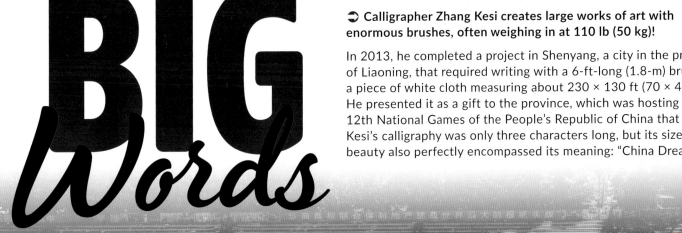

BIG
Words

⤷ Calligrapher Zhang Kesi creates large works of art with enormous brushes, often weighing in at 110 lb (50 kg)!

In 2013, he completed a project in Shenyang, a city in the province of Liaoning, that required writing with a 6-ft-long (1.8-m) brush on a piece of white cloth measuring about 230 × 130 ft (70 × 40 m). He presented it as a gift to the province, which was hosting the 12th National Games of the People's Republic of China that year. Kesi's calligraphy was only three characters long, but its size and beauty also perfectly encompassed its meaning: "China Dream."

DOWNHILL
From Here

⟳ **Speedy skaters tackle slippery ice, steep slopes, and sudden drops during the heart-pounding sport of downhill ice cross racing.**

On a course built out of steel scaffolding, wood, flexible mats, and 4 in (10 cm) of ice, athletes reach speeds of up to 50 mph (80 kmph) as they try to be the first to cross the finish line. Racers must be able to react fast and keep a sharp eye out for their fellow competitors, as crashing is frequent and expected.

WARNING!
CRASHES ARE
COMMON

BLIND RUNNER > Blind runner Sinead Kane ran 81 mi (130 km) on a treadmill in 12 hours—further than three marathons—at a gym in Dublin, Ireland.

NUT CRACKER > Kung fu expert Li Weijun used his bare hands to smash 302 walnuts in 55 seconds in Foshan City, China.

THREE-LEGGED WALK > Ryan Ramsay and Lexi Ligeti strolled 72 mi (116 km) in 24 hours while walking three-legged around a parking lot in Arbroath, Scotland. They completed 582 laps of the 200-meter circuit.

WORLD RIDE > Starting and finishing in Paris, France, and riding for 16 hours a day, Mark Beaumont, of Edinburgh, Scotland, cycled 18,000 mi (29,000 km) around the world in 78 days 14 hours 40 minutes. During his epic journey, he fractured an elbow in a fall and had to contend with subzero temperatures in New Zealand and forest fires.

BUZZER BEATER > On January 26, 2018, Blake Peters, a freshman at Evanston Township High School, Illinois, landed a one-handed, buzzer-beater basket from 80 ft (24 m)—almost the full length of the court—to win a basketball game against Maine South by one point, 45 to 44.

HUGE HOOP > Yuya Yamada, from Tokyo, Japan, can spin a 16.8-ft-wide (5.1-m) aluminum hula hoop around his waist using only his torso.

MOD MAN ⟳ Russ Foxx of Vancouver, British Columbia, Canada, has silicone horns and an intricate ultraviolet tattoo all over his head! The 36-year-old has had more than 100 body modifications—such as electrical key fobs fitted into his hand and numerous piercings and tattoos—since the age of five, and he's now a licensed body modification artist himself.

STRETCH NOODLE > A team of chefs in Nanyang, China, spent 17 hours rolling out a single noodle that was nearly 2 mi (3.2 km) long. The noodle, which was handmade from 97 lb (40 kg) of bread flour and 7 gal (26.8 l) of water, measured 10,119 ft (3,084 m) long.

MUCH TRAVELED > Don Parrish, of Chicago, Illinois, has visited all 193 member states of the United Nations and been to such remote spots as Easter Island, Conway Reef (located 280 mi [450 km] off the coast of Fiji), the South Pole, and North Korea. He has used 13 passports, visited more than 60 islands by ship, and has flown five million air miles. One trip alone required 73 flights.

TORTILLA TOWER > Joy Ehsan, from Rochdale, England, built a tortilla tower that measured 27 in (69 cm) tall and was made up of 389 individual tortillas.

FEWEST TRIPLES > The Toronto Blue Jays baseball team recorded only five triples in MLB in 2017—the lowest single-season total by any team on record since 1913.

Hardman's prosthetic nose is magnetic!

NOSE GOES

⟳ Jayne Hardman, from Reddich, England, has a magnetic nose! The 48-year-old had her nose removed after developing a rare autoimmune disease (Wegener's granulomatosis) that ate away the flesh of her nose. She says before she was fitted with a prosthetic sniffer, she was unable to hear without hearing aids and couldn't taste or smell anything, as her nasal receptors were damaged. The new nose clips onto her face with magnets, and after more procedures, all of her senses have returned and she's looking on the bright side of her "nose job."

LORD OF THE *Rings*

⮕ A Canadian artist living in Fukuoka, Japan, Sofia Molnar creates realistic miniature meals meant to be worn as jewelry.

The tiny treasures were inspired by the *kawaii* movement, a culture of cuteness that started in Japan and has since spread worldwide. Despite their tasty appearance, it is not recommended that wearers eat the rings, as they are made completely out of plastic and glue.

FAKE FOOD!

BABY *Blues*

↻ **No, these are not contacts. This Ethiopian boy has Waardenburg syndrome.**

The genetic condition causes changes in pigmentation (or color) of the hair, skin, and of course, eyes. There are four types of Waardenburg syndrome, and the differences have to do with gene mutation and the physical characteristics manifested from it, the most common being hearing loss. One in 40,000 people have Waardenburg syndrome.

MONKEY MISCHIEF > A driver was rear-ended in Zunyi City, China, when she slammed on her brakes because she mistook the red butt of an escaped circus monkey, which was perched on the pole above an intersection, for a stop light.

TEA DRINKER > Nathan Derek Garner, of England, changed his name to Nathan Yorkshire Tea because he drinks 20 cups of tea every day.

PHOTOGRAPHIC MEMORY > Mongolia-born Yanjaa Wintersoul, who lives in Sweden, can memorize the contents of a 328-page shopping catalogue in only a week. The 2018 IKEA catalogue contained 4,818 products, and not only did she remember all the products and what pages they were on, but she was even able to recall their special individual features.

10,000 RIDES > John Hale, of Brea, California, has ridden on Disney California Adventure's Radiator Springs Races more than 10,000 times. It took him five years, five months, and three days to reach the 10,000 milestone, visiting the theme park 760 times and averaging 13 rides per visit. He once managed 47 rides in a single day.

DRIVEN TO DRINK > Over a period of seven months, Ben Coombs, from Plymouth, England, drove a car 20,000 mi (32,000 km) across three continents and 21 countries, starting at the most northerly bar in the world—on the Norwegian island of Svalbard inside the Arctic Circle—and finishing at the most southerly bar, in Tierra Del Fuego, Chile.

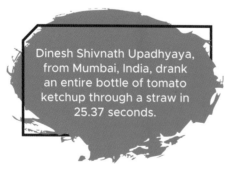

Dinesh Shivnath Upadhyaya, from Mumbai, India, drank an entire bottle of tomato ketchup through a straw in 25.37 seconds.

SUNDAE BEST > Thousands of volunteers at the Spirit of Texas Festival in Wolf Pen Creek teamed up to make an ice cream sundae that measured nearly a mile long. The ingredients for the 4,549-ft-long (1,387-m) sundae included 500 gal (1,892 l) of ice cream, 2,000 cans of whipped cream, 300 gal (1,364 l) of chocolate and strawberry syrup, 25 lb (11 kg) of sprinkles, and 20,000 cherries.

CURLING MARATHON > Ten curlers—divided into two five-person teams—played the sport for more than four days at Coldwater, Ontario, Canada. They eventually finished after spending 105 hours 6 minutes 51 seconds on the ice.

BUSY BIKE > In November 2017, 58 men from the Indian army climbed onto a single 500cc Royal Enfield motorcycle and rode together for 3,937 ft (1,200 m) in Bangalore.

MONSTER CATCH > After a two-hour struggle, fishermen Eddy Lawler and Clay Hilbert successfully caught a 1,089-lb (494-kg) blue marlin off the coast of Exmouth, Western Australia, on January 1, 2018—the heaviest blue marlin ever landed in Australian waters.

THUMBS UP > Wearing a 40-lb (18-kg) rucksack on his back, Irfan Mehsood, from Dera Ismail Khan, Pakistan, completed 22 push-ups in one minute, using just his two thumbs.

INCREDIBLE SHOT > Derek Herron, a member of Australian trick-shot basketball team How Ridiculous, successfully landed a throw from the top of the Maletsunyane Falls in Lesotho, Africa, through a hoop positioned 661 ft (201 m) below.

YOUR UPLOADS

Toe Claw

Natasha Soyini of Chesapeake, Virginia, shared with us the story and photos of her "bird claw pinky toe." According to family legend, when Natasha's grandmother was pregnant and working as a maid, she had to wash her female employer's feet, which she hated doing. Because of that hatred, her unborn child (Natasha's mother) was cursed with the "bird claw," which has also been passed down to Natasha and her siblings.

CHILI CHAMP > Competitive eater Carmen Cincotti, from Newark, New Jersey, consumed 2.438 gal (9.2 l) of chili in six minutes at the Orlando Chili Cookoff in Florida on February 17, 2018. He managed to devour nearly 10, 32-oz (0.95-l) bowls of chili. He has also eaten 101 bratwursts in 10 minutes, 61.75 ears of corn in 12 minutes, and 158 croquetas in eight minutes.

ATLANTIC CROSSING > Without any support craft and despite capsizing at one point, half-brothers Greg Bailey and Jude Massey, from Hampshire, England, rowed 3,000 mi (4,800 km) across the Atlantic Ocean in 53 days. They set off in their 24-ft-long (7.3-m) boat from Gran Canaria on January 15, 2018, and reached Barbados in early March.

INTERNATIONAL PLAYER > When former Uruguay soccer international Sebastián Abreu signed for Chilean club Audax Italiano in December 2017, it was the 26th team he had played for in a professional career that had taken him to 11 different countries, including Brazil, Mexico, Greece, Israel, and Spain.

DOUBLE ASCENT > Spanish mountain runner Kilian Jornet scaled the summit of Mount Everest twice in five days—both times solo and without extra oxygen or fixed ropes.

FAST CLAP > Seven Wade, aged 9, clapped his hands 1,080 times in one minute in Miami, Florida. He practiced daily by timing himself against the family's kitchen microwave.

EIGHT-HOUR DRIFT > On a skid pad in Greer, South Carolina, Johan Schwartz drove a BMW car in a continual drift for eight hours, covering 232.5 mi (374 km). The car had to be refueled with the help of a support vehicle five times while in mid-drift.

TOP SALESMAN > Auto salesman Ali Reda sold 1,582 cars (1,530 new and 52 used) at a dealership in Dearborn, Michigan, in 2017—the most cars sold by an individual in one year since 1973.

CINNAMON ROLL > At Wolferman's Gourmet Baked Foods, of Medford, Oregon, 100 workers spent 11 hours cooking up a massive cinnamon roll that weighed 1,149 lb (522 kg)—heavier than an adult moose. The 9-ft-long (2.5-m) sweet treat had to be baked in a custom-made stainless steel pan.

PENCIL STACK > Tayleigh Ward, Lily Brammer, and Lily Larsen, three middle school students from West Jordan, Utah, built a 419-layers-high stack of 6,765 pencils.

BROKEN NECK > Austrian snowboarder Markus Schairer got up and finished his heat at the 2018 Winter Olympics, despite breaking his neck in a fall partway around the course.

FRUIT NINJA

➲ In July 2018, 64-year-old Ashrita Furman, of New York, set a new world record for slicing the most watermelons in half on his own stomach in one minute. The veritable watermelon ninja sliced through 26 melons, which were donated to a local restaurant to make special juice drinks.

Dearly DEPARTED

→ An electronics repair company in Japan offers a Buddhist funeral service for robot dogs in a temple.

AIBOs (artificial intelligence robots) are sophisticated robot dogs that were released by Sony in 1999. Sony only sold 150,000 of these expensive pets before they decided to stop making them—and updating them—in 2006. However, many people had become attached to their AIBO pets, so former Sony employee Nobuyki Norimatsu opened a repair company where he eventually started fixing them when he could. Sadly, these repairs often require the use of parts from unfixable AIBOs, and to honor these pups, Buddhist priest Bugen Oi agreed to perform funeral ceremonies for the deceased pets that were sacrificing their parts so others could live on. The services themselves are catered to the occasion: robots recite Buddhist scriptures known as sutras, and instead of fruits, which are often given as offerings during Buddhist funeral services, pairs of pliers are placed before the deceased robodogs.

ROBOT DOG!

EMERGENCY LANDING > A Chinese copilot survived after being sucked halfway out of his airplane's cockpit window when its right windshield blew out at an altitude of 32,000 ft (9,800 m). After the copilot, who was wearing a seat belt, was pulled back into the cabin, Captain Liu Chuanjian managed to bring the Sichuan Airlines plane with 119 passengers down safely in an emergency landing.

SHORT SHOOTOUT > The gunfight at the O.K. Corral in Tombstone, Arizona, on October 26, 1881—the most famous shootout in the American Old West—lasted only 30 seconds.

BODY TREMORS > Georgie Weatherley, from Gloucestershire, England, suffers from Stiff Person Syndrome—a one-in-a-million disease of the nervous system where her body is engulfed by violent tremors that turn her into a human statue. Triggered by anything from noise to stress, the tremors occur up to 20 times a day and cause her muscles to spasm, then stiffen, holding her in a vice-like grip.

BURIED TREASURE > When Matthew Emanuel had some landscaping done in the backyard of his Staten Island, New York, home, the workers discovered a buried safe filled with gold, diamonds, and $16,300 in cash. The safe had been stolen seven years earlier from neighbors who had given up hope of ever seeing their belongings again.

WALMART WEDDING > Worried that some of their coworkers at the West Manchester Township Walmart in Pennsylvania would have to miss their wedding because the store is open 24 hours, Chrissy Slonaker Torres and Leida Torres decided to hold the ceremony in the store's garden center.

POSTCARD PICTURE > When Jim Wilson's father died in Natal, South Africa, in 1967, Jim informed his sister Muriel, who was living in Holland. Muriel contacted her husband, who was working in Portugal, and on hearing the news he flew to South Africa. Changing planes at Las Palmas airport in the Canary Islands, he bought a postcard showing Margate Beach, Natal, and sent it to Muriel. To her amazement, the photograph on the postcard showed her father walking along the beach with other vacationers.

CHRISTMAS SONS > Jacki and Josh Grossman, of Stony Brook, New York, have two sons born on Christmas Eve—Oliver (in 2013) and Elliott (in 2017).

GALLSTONE HAUL > In a two-and-a-half-hour operation, surgeons in Nashik, India, removed a staggering 4,100 gallstones, measuring between 2 mm and 4 mm, from the gallbladder of Yogesh Yeole. Even though Yeole had reported severe abdominal pain, the medics were not expecting to find more than 20 stones.

SHOE LOVER > German international soccer player Jerome Boateng owns more than 650 pairs of shoes.

BABY DISGUISE > Two men who stole a 1.5-ft-long (0.5-m) gray horn shark from a petting tank at the San Antonio Aquarium in Texas escaped by wrapping it in a wet blanket like a baby and then wheeling it out of the building in a stroller.

STOLEN BRAIN > On June 3, 2017, brain fragments of a relic of St. John Bosco were stolen from the Basilica of Castelnuovo in northern Italy. Police traced the thief to his home and discovered the brains hidden in his teapot.

TIGHTROPE VOWS

More than 3,000 people in Stassfurt, Germany, watched Nicole Backhaus marry Jens Knorr while the couple were sitting in a swing dangling from a motorcycle that was being ridden along a tightrope 46 ft (14 m) above the ground. Pastor Stefan Gierung conducted the ceremony while standing in a cage atop a fire ladder. The couple exchanged rings in the air but waited until they were safely on the ground before kissing. The bike was ridden by famous German high-wire artist Falko Traber.

EL OSO

➥ In Spain, the first carnival of the new year is *La Vijanera*—a festival of pre-Roman origins that celebrates the triumph of good over evil.

The spectacle features crowds of people wearing different masks, animal skins, and brightly colored clothing representing different characters: the *Zarramacos* (revelers wearing enormous cowbells) and *El Oso* (a young man dressed in sheepskins to look like a bear and simultaneously symbolize winter).

Other notorious characters in the festival include *Trapajeros* (scavengers), *Trapajones* (ragpickers), and *Danzarines Blancos y Negros* (black and white dancers). The festival concludes with the unorthodox appearance of *La Preñá* (the child-bearer), who goes into labor while the sheep-skin-covered bear dies—all meant to ward off evil spirits and bring in the new year with good vibes.

MASQUERADE

COWBELLS

ESSENTIAL INGREDIENT > Organizers of the 2018 Big Cheese Festival in Brighton, England, apologized to attendees after the event ran out of cheese.

ABANDONED HOUSE > On June 26, 2018, traffic was blocked in Dover, Delaware, by a large, prefabricated house that had been abandoned and dumped on the two-lane road.

STREET DANCE > Tutu-clad dancers from theater company Ardentia staged colorful shows for drivers waiting at traffic light stops at busy intersections in Mexico City. Dancing to music provided by a boombox plugged into an iPod, they did seven quickfire routines, ranging from ballet to Michael Jackson, with each performance lasting a total of just 58 seconds—the time it takes a Mexico City traffic light to turn from red to green.

EXCESS PACKAGING > Online retailer Amazon sent Nick Taylor, from Bath, England, a bag of dog food that was wrapped in 62 ft (19 m) of paper for protection.

DOUGHNUT APOLOGY > One of three armed robbers who held up a doughnut store in Houston, Texas, apologized to customers by handing them some stolen pastries.

FLUSH WITH CASH > Toilets in a bank and three nearby restaurants in Geneva, Switzerland, were temporarily blocked by $100,000 in high-denomination euro bank bills.

POTHOLE BREAKFAST > A 22-year-old Eastern Michigan University student drew attention to a large street pothole in Trenton by filling it with an entire box of cereal and milk and eating his breakfast from it.

BEAN MISSILES > A robber who held up a food store in Youngstown, Florida, was arrested when Bay County Sheriff's Major Jimmy Stanford snuck behind the suspect in a grocery aisle and took him down by throwing two cans of beans at him, scoring direct hits both times.

OUIJA BOARD GRAVE

What better way to commemorate the final resting place of Elijah Bond, creator of the Ouija board, than with a tombstone featuring a Ouija board? At least that's what noted paranormal enthusiast, Robert Murch, reasoned after locating Bond's grave in 2007. Prior to this, Bond was relegated to an unmarked grave in the Green Mount Cemetery in Baltimore, and believe it or not, it took Murch 15 years to accurately locate him!

213

DECK THE HALLS

➲ Sylvia Pope, a 76-year-old grandmother living in Swansea, Wales, hangs more than 2,000 ornaments from her ceiling every year in celebration of Christmas. She has to start in the summer to ensure that all the ornaments are ready in time for the holiday—something she does all on her own. While some are mere trinkets, a handful of the baubles are quite expensive. The entire display costs more than $19,000 (£15,000).

GETAWAY WOE > Bank robber Mark Brown was arrested in Manchester, England, while waiting for a taxi after his getaway vehicle had broken down.

HOPES DASHED > In the hope of buying 200 discounted Apple gadgets, 11,000 people lined up for up to 19 hours outside the Switch store in Kuala Lumpur, Malaysia, but when the doors finally opened, so many people stampeded through them that the sale was cancelled.

TWO-MILE CAKE > In China's Jiangxi Province, 210 cakemakers spent five hours baking a 10,457-ft-long (3,188-m) fruit sponge cake at Zixi County's Bread Tourism Festival. The nearly 2-mi-long (3.2-km) cake was made from 45,600 eggs and weighed more than 8 tons.

MAC MILESTONE

➲ On May 4, 2018, Don Gorske, a 64-year-old retired prison guard, ate his 30,000th Big Mac at his local McDonald's restaurant in Fond du Lac, Wisconsin. He has been eating Big Macs almost every day since 1972, missing only eight days in that time, and aims to make it to 40,000, which, at his current average of two Big Macs a day, would take him until 2032.

GORSKE PHOTO IN HOMETOWN MCDONALD'S

HEAVY METAL > Two elderly men in Germany escaped from a nursing home in August 2018 to attend Wacken Open Air, the world's largest heavy metal music festival.

FAMILY DISPUTE > The body of a Ghanaian chief who died in 2012 was kept frozen in a morgue for more than six years because his extended family could not decide who should be the head mourner at his funeral.

SELF-SERVICE > Finding that the entire staff of a Waffle House in West Columbia, South Carolina, were asleep, customer Alex Bowen walked into the kitchen, cooked his own meal, and even cleaned up after himself.

SALAD COMPLAINT > A 12-year-old boy from Halifax, Nova Scotia, Canada, called 911 twice to complain after one of his parents had served him a salad.

FLYING FISH > At the annual World Chabudai Gaeshi Tournament in Japan, competitors flip a small wooden table to send the plastic fish on top of it flying as far as possible—achieving distances of more than 26 ft (8 m).

CLOUD THEFT > In 2018, Iranian General Gholam Rexa Jalali blamed the country's summer drought on Israel, whom he accused of stealing Iran's clouds. He also accused Israel of working to ensure that any clouds that did reach Iranian air space were unable to release rain.

ABSENT FRIEND > A group of four friends from Durango, Mexico, traveled to the 2018 World Cup in Russia with a full-sized cardboard cutout of their friend Javier, whose wife had refused to let him join them. The cutout depicted Javier wearing a T-shirt saying "My wife didn't let me."

AVATAR

A still from the movie *Avatar*.

Acrobats

⮑ During a contest, adrenaline seekers raced along slacklines between cliffs in Zhangjiajie, China, dressed as characters from the movie *Avatar*!

The mountains actually served as inspiration for the movie's alien landscape, where mountains float in midair. Since the movie's release in 2009, they have taken on the nickname "Avatar Mountains," and it's easy to see why—when clouds roll in, these massive rocks also appear to hover above the earth.

SUPER MONSTER WOLF

➲ Farmers in Japan in need of a helping hand have turned to Super Monster Wolf—a robotic creature used to scare wild animals and keep them away from crops. The abnormal animatronic is just under 2 ft (60 cm) tall, is covered in realistic fur, has flashing red eyes, and is able to detect approaching animals from about 0.6 mi (1 km) away. When this happens, Super Monster Wolf lets out one of its many battle cries, ranging from a wolf's howl to human voices, to scare away any hungry creatures intent on eating crops.

FETAL ATTRACTION > Canadian music researchers Aura Pon, from the University of Calgary, and Johnty Wang, from McGill University, Montreal, have created what they call the world's first prenatal musical instrument. Called the Womba, the device is strapped across a pregnant woman's stomach to translate the kicks and other movements of her fetus into music.

BILL BLUNDER > Marty Boyer was puzzled why the energy bills for his Covington, Kentucky, business were so high—until he discovered that a mix-up by his energy supplier meant that for five months he had also been paying the electric bills to light the nearby Clay Wade Bailey Bridge, which spans the Ohio River.

PUPPY SURPRISE > Su Yun's family from Kunming, China, bought what they thought was a Tibetan mastiff puppy in 2016, but gave up the pet two years later when it turned out to be an Asiatic black bear. The family wondered why it ate a box of fruit and two buckets of noodles a day and why it kept growing to the extent that it soon weighed 250 lb (114 kg). But what really made them suspicious was when it started walking on its two hind legs.

BURIED ALIVE > As part of the 2018 Dark Mofo Festival, Mike Parr, a 73-year-old Australian performance artist, was buried alive in a steel container under a busy road in Hobart, Tasmania, for 72 hours. Oxygen was pumped into the container, where Parr also had access to water, a heater, reading and writing material, and a distress button in case anything went wrong. Parr's previous stunts have included wrapping himself in fuse wire before setting it alight and sewing his lips shut.

PUBLIC APOLOGY > In June 2018, managers of the public service waterworks bureau in Kobe, Japan, held a televised press conference at which they apologized to the Japanese people for the "deeply regrettable" behavior of a 64-year-old employee who had been caught starting his lunch break three minutes early on more than one occasion.

BUCKET HEADS

➲ Nearly every civilian in Britain during World War II had a gas mask—even the babies.

Since a baby's lungs are not strong enough to breathe through standard gas masks, these "baby helmets" were developed to encase the entire infant, and an adult would manually pump air into the rubber fabric sack. Thankfully, the gas masks were never needed.

TIMEWARP

FROM GAS MASKS FOR BABIES TO ROBOT WOLVES, INVENTIONS HAVE A SPECIAL PLACE IN THE TIMELINE OF HISTORY, BUT SOME CREATIONS CAN MAKE YOU FEEL LIKE YOU'RE IN A TIME WARP!

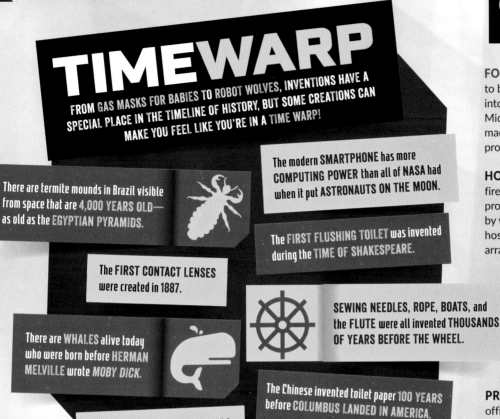

There are termite mounds in Brazil visible from space that are 4,000 YEARS OLD— as old as the EGYPTIAN PYRAMIDS.

The modern SMARTPHONE has more COMPUTING POWER than all of NASA had when it put ASTRONAUTS ON THE MOON.

The FIRST CONTACT LENSES were created in 1887.

The FIRST FLUSHING TOILET was invented during the TIME OF SHAKESPEARE.

There are WHALES alive today who were born before HERMAN MELVILLE wrote *MOBY DICK*.

SEWING NEEDLES, ROPE, BOATS, and the FLUTE were all invented THOUSANDS OF YEARS BEFORE THE WHEEL.

The Chinese invented toilet paper 100 YEARS before COLUMBUS LANDED IN AMERICA.

The TIN CAN was invented 48 YEARS BEFORE the can opener.

FLYING FRANKFURTER > Philadelphia Phillies baseball fan Kathy McVay ended up in a hospital emergency room with a black eye after being hit in the face by a hot dog wrapped in duct tape that had been launched at a game by the team mascot, the Phillie Phanatic.

TOE THEFT > Joshua Williams, 28, was charged with stealing human toes from a dead body exhibit in Auckland, New Zealand. The toes, which were valued at nearly $4,000 and were part of the Body Worlds Vital exhibition, were later returned to the museum.

FOOL'S GOLD > Spotting what appeared to be a stack of gold bars, a burglar broke into a flooring store in Grand Rapids, Michigan, only to find that they were made of foam rubber and were used for promotional purposes.

HOSE PROPOSAL > Ashton Hanway, a firefighter from Fayetteville, North Carolina, proposed to Lauren Wood at the fire station by writing "Will you marry me?" with a fire hose on the floor. It took him several hours to arrange the hose to spell out the words.

BATHROOM BIRTH > After Falon Griffin gave birth to daughter Gracelyn in a Chick-fil-A bathroom in San Antonio, Texas, the fast-food restaurant promised Gracelyn free food for life and a job when she turns 14.

PRESIDENTIAL PAPER > In 2018, police officers in Turkmenistan inspected public and private bathrooms across the country to warn anyone who might be disrespectfully using newspaper photos of President Gurbanguly Berdymukhammedov as toilet paper. Staff at landfills were also instructed to look out for soiled pictures of the controversial president. The crackdown was implemented after a school in Dashoguz had been found using strips of newspaper bearing the president's face as paper in the school bathroom.

This photo from 1938 shows a woman in Kent, England, pushing a gas-proof baby carriage. Featuring an air-tight lid, a tiny window, and a gas filter, the baby would presumably be kept safe during an air raid.

A group of nurses testing gas masks on babies at an English hospital in 1940.

PREMATURE AGING > Xiao Cui, an 18-year-old student in Harbin, China, has a rare skin condition that causes his facial muscles and skin to droop, making him look at least 60 years older than his classmates.

EAR OBSTRUCTION > A doctor in Leicester, England, removed a cotton swab that was lodged in a man's ear for two years. The patient only realized the swab was there when it swelled up after he went swimming.

SCREEN SHAMED > In what has become known as the "Reel of Shame," before the main movie starts in theaters in Hejiang County, Sichuan Province, China, the faces and names of local debtors are shown on the screen to humiliate them.

GOLDFISH BAN > British children can be held responsible for crimes from the age of 10, but they are not legally permitted to own a goldfish until they are 16.

SENSITIVE LIPS > Human lips have more than 1 million nerve endings and are 1,000 times more sensitive than fingertips. Like fingerprints, lips are unique; no two individuals make identical lip impressions.

SWOLLEN LEG > Before undergoing treatment, Janice Greene, of Jackson, Georgia, had a right leg that weighed 150 lb (68 kg) and measured 69 in (1.72 m) in circumference. She suffers from severe lymphoedema, which causes a blockage in the body's lymphatic system, resulting in excess fluid collecting under the skin.

FLAVOR GRAVEYARD

In Waterbury, Vermont, there exists one of the sweetest cemeteries in the world memorializing ice cream flavors that have come and, sadly, gone. Opened in 1997, Ben & Jerry's Flavor Graveyard is filled with nostalgic headstones for "dearly de-pinted" flavors, like Wavy Gravy, Turtle Soup, and Urban Jumble, and features pun-filled epitaphs, or inscriptions.

DASTARDLY MASH
Here the brazen
DASTARDLY lies.
Some say that raisin,
Caused its demise.
1979-1991

CHOCOLATE PEANUT BUTTER COOKIE DOUGH
1993-1997

HOLY CANNOLI
Now in front of the pearly gates,
Holy Cannoli sits and waits.
What brought its ruin no one knows,
Must have been the pistachios.
1997-1998

DOUBLE EXECUTION > On February 13, 1746, a Frenchman named Jean Marie Dubarry was executed for murdering his father. Exactly 100 years later, on February 13, 1846, another Frenchman named Jean Marie Dubarry was executed, also for patricide.

KILLER COSTUME

The 2013 B-rated classic *Sharknado* chronicles an improbable, unstoppable storm of man-eating sharks raining terror down on Los Angeles. The implausible plotline and bad acting, naturally, inspired somebody to translate the film into a cosplay look, although no one thought it would turn out so. . . elegant? Instagram's @beebinch appears red carpet–worthy in a gorgeous gray ballroom gown complete with stuffed animal sharks swimming in the folds of her dress. She accessorized the look with yellow theatrical eye contacts and shark puppets for each hand.

WISH GRANTED > A few hours after giving a speech where she said she would like to win the lottery to wipe out her student loan debt, Amanda Dietz, of Vicksburg, Michigan, bought a scratch-off ticket and won $300,000.

FRAGILE BONES > By the age of 21, Marie Holm Laursen, from Aarhus, Denmark, had broken over 500 bones in her body due to a rare genetic disease called *osteogenesis imperfecta*. Even a cough, a hug, or a sneeze can cause her to break multiple bones because they are so brittle, and she once shattered a rib after getting hiccups.

OLD FACE > From a CT scan of a human skull found in a Greek cave, scientists used a 3D printer to create a silicone reconstruction of the face of Avgi, a 9,000-year-old teenage girl, to show what people looked like in the Mesolithic period.

FACIAL GROWTH > Jaroon Suanmali, from Lopburi, Thailand, had a 4.4-lb (2-kg) facial tumor removed from the side of his head. The tumor was almost as big as his head, and because it covered his right ear, it affected his hearing and made it difficult for him to sleep.

STAND OUT

⮑ **Russia built a 125-ft-tall (38-m) power tower in the shape of Zabivaka the Wolf, the 2018 FIFA World Cup mascot.**

Zabivaka translates to "the one who scores" in Russian, and at night the structure would shine brightly from the side of the Primorskoye Koltso motorway near Kaliningrad, exciting soccer fans who drove by.

GOAL!

125 FT (38 M) TALL

SPORTS COINCIDENCE > In 1965, when golfer Jack Nicklaus won his second Masters title, jockey Willie Shoemaker won the Kentucky Derby, the Boston Celtics won the NBA championship, and the Montreal Canadiens won hockey's Stanley Cup. In 1986, Nicklaus won his final Masters—and the other three events happened again, too.

SIX-DAY ORDEAL > Joohee Han, a 25-year-old Korean tourist, survived for six days without food in the Australian wilderness after falling into a deep ravine while climbing Mount Tyson in Queensland. She was initially knocked unconscious but managed to crawl to a waterfall, where the running water kept her alive until she was rescued.

BALCONY RESCUE > Mamoudou Gassama, a 22-year-old man from Mali, scaled four floors of the outside of a tower block in Paris, France, to save a child who was dangling from a balcony. Heroically pulling himself up balcony to balcony with his bare hands, he was able to reach and rescue the boy in only 30 seconds.

PLAN BACKFIRED > After holding up a restaurant in Anchorage, Alaska, in February 2018, a robber tried to avoid being identified by burying his distinctive coat in snow three blocks away. He was quickly arrested when police officers followed tracks in the snow and spotted a man who stood out because he was the only person not dressed appropriately for the freezing temperatures.

PIANO BED

➲ In 1935—well before the invention of the laptop—bedridden patients in Great Britain enjoyed the modern convenience of a piano bed built to accommodate play while lying down.

Unfortunately, little is known about how prevalent these convenient contraptions actually were during the interwar years in the United Kingdom. But one photo, now housed at the National Archive of the Netherlands, does specify they were constructed for bedridden patients (as opposed to lazy pianists).

YOUR UPLOADS

Itty Bitty Tees

Devin Smith of Wisconsin sent us photos of his incredible handmade mini silk screen printing press. He prints teeny tiny T-shirts with the fully functioning machine and claims it's the smallest silk screen press in the world!

SIPHONED WATER > Angela Hernandez, from Portland, Oregon, survived in the wild for a week after her jeep plunged over a 200-ft-high (60-m) cliff in Big Sur, California, by using the hose from the vehicle's radiator to siphon water from a nearby creek. She told rescuers she had swerved to avoid hitting an animal.

TWIN CANDIDATES > Twin sisters ran for county commissioner seats in western Michigan in 2018—but on opposite sides politically. Monica Sparks ran as a Democrat for Kent County's 12th district while her twin Jessica Ann Tyson ran as a Republican in the 13th district.

SPINNING TOP > LIMBO, a smart, self-balancing, electric gyroscope spinning top made by Fearless Toys and Breaking Toys, spun nonstop for 27 hours 9 minutes 24 seconds on a single spin. The metal top contains a hidden motor that creates angular momentum that keeps it spinning for hours at a time.

FAJITA THEFTS > Gilberto Escamilla, from Cameron County, Texas, was sentenced to 50 years in prison for stealing $1.2 million worth of fajitas over a nine-year period.

TRAIN BIRTH > A baby boy born unexpectedly on an RER train in Paris, France, in June 2018 was granted free rides on the network until his 25th birthday.

WASHINGTON'S HAIR >
A lock of what is believed to be George Washington's hair was discovered recently inside a library book by an archivist working at Union College in Schenectady, New York. Neatly tied in a bow, the strands of gray hair were found in a yellowed envelope tucked inside a leather book titled *Gaines Universal Register* or *Columbian Kalendar for the Year of Our Lord 1793*. Written on the envelope were the words "Washington's hair." The lock is thought to have been a gift to the book's owner from James Alexander Hamilton, son of the first U.S. Treasury secretary, whose family was close to the Washingtons.

FLYING TEETH >
When former British prime minister Winston Churchill lost his temper, he would throw his false teeth across the room.

ROBOT RELAY > At a torch relay two months before the 2018 Winter Olympics, the Olympic torch was carried for 500 ft (150 m) in South Korea by a humanoid robot called Hubo.

GIANT STROLLER

➲ Kolcraft, creator of the Contours infant stroller, wanted to give parents a chance to experience life from a baby's perspective, so they built an adult-sized stroller that's an exact replica of their Contours Bliss model and more than 7 ft (2 m) tall!

Sky Art

● Some artists go to great lengths to capture a universal concept, and that's exactly what Michelle Nirumandrad, the skydiving painter, does.

Nirumandrad, self-proclaimed "art enthusiast and avid skydiver," creates one-of-a-kind images by painting canvases strapped to her arms and legs as she freefalls from more than 13,000 ft (3,960 m) in the air. As she descends above Skydive Spaceland Dallas, she lets the wind control the patterns the paints make on the canvases. In her words, "these paintings are a testament to the human desire to experience and take ownership of a piece of the heavens for themselves." Her project is aptly titled "Captured Sky."

Q How did you start painting while skydiving? What inspired you?

A I started jumping in 2008, and I longed for some sort of keepsake from the Sky. I obsessed about finding a way to bottle a cloud or color a piece of the wind so it could be caught and brought down, but none of my ideas were functional. I had nearly given up when it occurred to me: "I may not be able to color the wind, but I can give the wind something to color with."

Q *What kind of materials do you use?*

A I use non-toxic, water-based acrylics. The type of paint I use is very important and specific, both in regard to the safety of my skydiving gear but also to the safety of the environment. Because the paints are water-based, they don't degrade or compromise the safety of my gear in any way, and because they are non-toxic, they are not harmful to flora or fauna when they are released into the wind. I release very little paint (less than 5 oz [148 ml] in a jump), which gets carried over great distances by the winds.

Q *How high up in the air are you when you start painting?*

A My typical exit altitude is 13,500 ft (4.1 km)—the highest you can go without supplemental oxygen. This is roughly 2.5 vertical mi (3.4 km) above the Earth. I deploy my parachute around 5,000 ft (1.5 km), so I typically spend a little less than 60 seconds in freefall and about 4–5 minutes under canopy before landing back on the ground.

Q *Are there certain conditions that make the painting turn out better?*

A We need favorable weather to jump. We are not allowed to jump through clouds for lack of visibility, and we cannot jump in high or gusty winds for safety. For this reason, most of my Captured Sky collection is produced during the late spring to early fall months when the weather is usually the mildest.

Q *Was there some trial and error to get your method right?*

A Oh yeah, absolutely! I had to do a decent amount of research on materials and gear collecting before my first attempt. Even then, I had to start very small: tiny 3 × 3 in (7.6 × 7.6 cm) canvases held to my arms by torn up T-shirts. They moved around a lot, and it took several jumps before I even started to get paint to actually meet canvas!

Nirumandrad warns "I have been in the sport for over 10 years and have completed more than 3,000 skydives. This activity is not for the novice jumper."

HOW DOES IT WORK?

PREFLIGHT: I rig canvases and paint in such a way so that they can endure and be safely transported through the winds of **terminal velocity**, which is roughly 130 mph (209 kmph) because of my flight orientation. (I fly on my back.) Industrial-strength Velcro straps allow me to wear the canvases on my body, usually attached to my legs and arms. I wear all of your typical skydiving gear—rig, helmet, goggles, altimeter—plus a hook knife to cut away canvases if I have any sort of issue, and a camera to catch the action!

1. I experiment with different colors and consistency of paint in a sketchbook on the ground to get an idea of how the paints may interact together in the wind.

2. The paints are mixed and placed in flip-top containers that I wear in a vest across my chest; I memorize their placement so I can grab specific colors quickly mid-air.

3. The moment we leave the plane I begin releasing paint into the wind, allowing the sky to manipulate the colors on the canvas. I fly on my back using my legs as easels and my body as a partial blockade to the intense winds of freefall.

4. I release paint until it is time to roll over to my belly and deploy my parachute.

5. In the air, once I'm safely under canopy, I release paints into the wind again to produce the punctuated accents that you see in my artwork.

6. After landing and once the artworks are dry, I engrave their conception information into the back of their canvas frame with a wood-burning tool. This information includes the date the piece was jumped, its name, the amount of "sky captured"—that is, the amount of time the piece spent at **terminal velocity**—and a brief description of the sky when the piece was caught.

What is terminal velocity? The maximum speed attained by a falling body when the resistance of the air has become equal to the force of gravity.

UP IN THE AIR

LOVE LETTER > A 60-year-old love letter that was sent to a thrift store by mistake was returned to the writer following an appeal on Facebook. Louie Edyvean, of Cornwall, England, had written the letter to her future husband Derek in the 1950s and later put it in a sugar jar for safe keeping, but the jar was then accidentally given to a charity shop. In another accident, in 2018 the jar was smashed by its new owner, Lizzie Dixon, who, finding the letter, successfully traced its author via social media.

POTATO CURRENCY > During the Great Depression, Marshall University in Huntington, West Virginia, sometimes accepted potatoes toward tuition payment.

BUS WEDDING > Kara Mullins and Osvaldo Jimenez first met on an M14 Manhattan crosstown bus in 2004—and 13 years later they got married on the same bus, watched by 50 guests and passengers.

MATCHING OUTFITS > Identical twins Elores Stephens and Dolores Swint, of Dallas, Texas, still wear matching outfits from head to toe despite being 71 years old.

In 1999, skydiver JOAN MURRAY survived a 14,500-FT (4,420-M) DROP after landing on a mound of FIRE ANTS, whose stings kept her alive!

There are 5,000 AIRPLANES in the sky above the United States at any one time.

MILES DAISHER of Twin Falls, Idaho, invented "SKYAKING"—skydiving while sitting in a kayak and landing on water.

In May 2017, 101-YEAR-OLD D-Day veteran BRYSON WILLIAM VERDUN HAYES became the OLDEST person in the world to skydive, completing a dive from 15,000 FT (4,570 M) in Honiton, in Southwest England.

JOSH MIRAMANT of San Francisco, California, base jumped off a 377-FT (115-M) CLIFF using a PARACHUTE ATTACHED TO HIS FLESH with metal hooks.

In December 2014, a group of rocket enthusiasts successfully launched a PORTABLE TOILET into the sky over southwest Michigan, and it landed in one piece!

STOLEN CAR > A blue Peugeot 104 that was stolen in 1979 was reunited with its owner 38 years later after French police pulled it from a murky swamp in Chalons-en-Champagne. The car was in surprisingly good condition, although it was crawling with crayfish.

NEEDLES REMOVED > Doctors in Uttar Pradesh, India, removed 70 metal nails and needles from the legs of 35-year-old Anusuiya Devi. She says that for over five years she has developed cysts that grow bigger until they burst and discharge a needle or nail.

OMINOUS TITLE > On August 28, 1974, former British Prime Minister Edward Heath helped publicize a novel by John Dyson titled *The Prime Minister's Boat Is Missing*. Five days later, Heath's yacht, *Morning Cloud III*, was lost at sea.

PENN CURSE > In late November 2017, superstitious construction workers placed a William Penn figurine atop Philadelphia's new tallest skyscraper, the 1,121-ft (342-m) Comcast Technology Center, to protect the NFL-leading Philadelphia Eagles from a jinx. And it appeared to work, because less than three months later, the Eagles won the Super Bowl. The curse of Billy Penn was said to have doomed the city's sports teams for decades after Philadelphia's first skyscraper rose higher than the Penn statue topping City Hall. In 2007, the situation was addressed when a statuette of Penn was placed atop a taller skyscraper, and the following year the Phillies won the World Series.

AVOCADO ACCIDENT > After catching fire, an 18-wheeler truck spilled 40,000 lb (18,100 kg) of avocados onto Interstate 35E near Waxahachie, Texas.

GARDEN LABYRINTH

⬅ Measuring a whopping 2.5 mi (4 km) long, the paths of the Pineapple Maze at the Dole pineapple plantation stretch across 2 acres of native plant growth, forming the largest plant maze in the world!

Originally debuting in 1998, the maze boasts more than 14,000 plants and contains eight stations that visitors pass by on their way to successfully navigating the labyrinth. To get an idea of the competition, the maze posts fastest finish times on the sign at the entrance, although the ultimate record remains a hard-to-beat 7 minutes.

$TILETTO$

⬅ The potent mix of high heels with gold and diamonds has produced the Passion Diamond Heels—the most expensive shoes in the world. Designed by Jada Dubai in collaboration with Passion Jewellers, each pair contains only the rarest diamonds and costs a cool $17 million. While gold-and-diamond-studded stilettos might seem like a splurge, they do come with a lifetime warranty for the lucky wearer.

HOLE N' THE ROCK

Located along U.S. Highway 191 in southwestern Utah, Hole in the Rock is a 5,000 sq ft (464.5 sq m) home carved out of rock, and took more than 20 years to build beginning in the 1940s. The vision of Albert Christensen, he and his wife, Gladys, also operated a popular diner from its subterranean depths. Today, Hole in the Rock endures as a popular roadside attraction. During the tour, visitors get a firsthand look at the fireplace with its 65-ft (20-m) chimney, 14 rooms arranged around massive stone pillars, and deep rock-carved bathtubs.

LODGED LENS > A woman from Dundee, Scotland, unknowingly had a contact lens lodged inside her eyelid for 28 years. At age 14, she had been playing badminton and was hit in the face with the shuttlecock. Unable to locate her lens afterward, she thought it must have fallen out due to the impact. Instead it had migrated to her left upper eyelid, where it remained undetected for decades until she began to experience swelling there.

WINNING TICKET >
A lottery ticket that won Fred and Lesley Higgins, of Aberdeenshire, Scotland, $75.5 million was initially torn in half and thrown out by the store clerk because he mistakenly thought it was worthless.

POTHOLE GUARD > Acting on his own initiative, Ernest Barnes, from Summerford, Newfoundland, Canada, goes out for up to five hours a day and spray-paints orange circles around potholes in the island's roads to warn drivers of their presence.

LATE DEVELOPER > Napoleon Bonaparte finished almost bottom of his class at military school when he was 16 years old, graduating in 1785 from France's École Militaire in 42nd place out of 52.

BOTTLED AIR ➲ How much would you pay for a breath of fresh air? The New Zealand–based company Kiwiana sells a two-canister pack of their "Pure Fresh New Zealand Air" for $65. Each canister contains between 130 and 140 deep breaths, and the two-pack even comes with a mask that fits over your mouth for convenient delivery. Despite the $0.24 per deep breath price point, Kiwianas' maintains that this is the freshest air you'll ever breathe.

PURE FRESH NEW ZEALAND Air

THE PUREST AIR YOU WILL EVER BREATHE...

PEACH DIET > Micah Gabriel Masson Lopez, a young boy from Montreal, Canada, lives only on fresh peaches. He has a rare medical condition called *food-protein-induced enterocolitis syndrome*, which causes him to suffer a severe allergy to almost every other food.

BITING THERAPY > New Jersey masseuse Dorothy Stein bites the backs of her clients to improve their blood circulation.

BOTTLE MESSAGE > Kym and Tonya Illman, of Perth, Western Australia, found a 132-year-old message in a bottle. The gin bottle, found on a beach north of Wedge Island, contained a message dated June 12, 1886. It had been tossed overboard in the Indian Ocean from a ship named *Paula*, which was on a voyage from Cardiff, Wales, to Makassar, Indonesia.

IDENTICAL TWINS > Wearing matching outfits, identical twin sisters Brittany and Briana Deane married identical twin brothers Josh and Jeremy Slayers in Twinsburg, Ohio, on August 4, 2018—and the ceremony was officiated by identical twin ministers. The couples met at the 2017 Twins Day Festival and plan to live and raise their families together all in the same house.

OVERSIZED HAND > Tajbir Akhtar, a five-year-old boy from Bangladesh, has a rare condition that has resulted in his left hand being three times larger than the right. His left hand weighs 14 lb (6.3 kg) and is bigger than his head. He probably has elephant foot disease—or elephantitis—which is often caused by a parasite carried by mosquitoes.

MISSING WALLET > Dennis Helmer, of Westmont, New Jersey, had his wallet stolen during a burglary at his parents' home in 1970—but 47 years later it was returned to him intact after a contractor found it in the ceiling of a home in Bellmawr.

TEAMS MERGED > The Philadelphia Eagles and the Pittsburgh Steelers merged to form the Steagles for one season in 1943. The merger came about because both NFL teams had lost so many players to military service during World War II.

FATEFUL DATE > When King Louis XVI of France was a child, an astrologer warned him to be on his guard on the 21st day of each month. Consequently, he never conducted any business on that date. Even so, on June 21, 1791, following the French Revolution, Louis and his queen, Marie Antoinette, were arrested in Varennes while trying to flee France. Then on September 21, 1792, France abolished the monarchy, and finally on January 21, 1793, Louis was executed by guillotine.

GREEN FACE > A thief painted his entire face green in an attempt to avoid being identified while stealing a woman's purse at a train station in Krasnodar, Russia. A 23-year-old man was quickly arrested because he was the only person in the vicinity with a green face.

WHITE OBSESSION > Turkmenistan banned all black cars from the capital, Ashgabat, in 2018 because President Gurbanguly Berdymukhammedov prefers white. Police towed away black cars and only returned them if the owners signed a document promising to paint them white or a light color. The president considers the color white to be lucky, so he dresses in white, rides white horses, and has draped Ashgabat in white marble.

SPLIT TOWER

⊃ The ancient Ganying Temple Pagoda in Quwo county, Shanxi Province, China, was split in half by an earthquake—which hit the structure more than 700 years ago. Constructed in 1165 during the Song Dynasty, the seven-story brick building survived the destructive earthquake in 1303 that evenly ripped it apart—but no other natural disaster nor World War since has been able to topple the durable octagonal pagoda.

BUBBLE LIZARD

⮌ A certain species of water anole native to Costa Rica uses an oxygen bubble hidden in its nose to breathe underwater—sometimes for more than 15 minutes! The hidden air pocket may allow the lizard to exchange stale air for fresh air or possibly just to expel carbon dioxide. The behavior is not yet well understood, but it is believed that this species of lizard adapted it so it would be able to hide from predators that hunt primarily on land.

ZIT CAKE > Malaysian bakery The Cakescape creates cakes that are decorated to look like zit-infested faces, featuring pus-filled spots that you can squeeze. . . and eat.

TREE RESCUE > A man in Berkshire, England, was rescued by firefighters after getting stuck up a tree while trying to catch his escaped parrot.

BLOOD SUCKER > After every race, gold medalist runner Ruwiyati of Indonesia sucked blood from her coach's finger because it helped her feel refreshed. The ritual started at Indonesia's national games in 1993 when Ruwiyati bit the neck of her coach, Alwi Mugiyanto, before a race. It took a week for Mugiyanto's wound to heal, but Ruwiyati went on to win both the marathon and the 10k.

DRUNK RIDER > A 53-year-old woman was arrested for being drunk while riding a horse along a busy road in Lakeland, Florida.

THREE BRIDES > Fifty-year-old Mohammed Ssemanda, from Katabi, Uganda, married three women in a single ceremony in November 2017 because he could not afford to marry them separately.

ALTERNATIVE PAYMENT > In October 2017, New Mexico State University in Las Cruces allowed students and faculty to pay parking fines with peanut butter.

EXPENSIVE FARE > A drunk reveler racked up a $2,175 taxi fare on New Year's Eve 2017, after ordering the driver on a 372-mi (595-km) journey through three countries. The ride took more than six hours from Copenhagen, Denmark, through Sweden and on to Oslo, Norway, where the passenger refused to pay and fell into bed.

WHIRLWIND ROMANCE > Nigerian furniture maker Chidimma Amedu married makeup artist Sophy Ijeoma on January 6, 2018, only a week after he had advertised for a bride on Facebook. She had originally commented on his post as a joke, but two days later they went on their first date after he traveled 500 mi (800 km) from his home city of Abuja to meet her.

SECRET GUEST > A 20-year-old man managed to live undetected in an elderly woman's house in Himeji, Japan, for five months. He was only exposed when the woman's son visited and heard strange noises coming from the second floor. On opening the door to one of the upstairs rooms, the son found the mystery squatter sleeping on a futon.

CORPSE CATCH > An angler taking part in a 2018 fishing competition on the Citarum River in Bandung, Indonesia, reeled in a human corpse.

LIGHTNING STRIKE > In 1971, Edwin Robinson lost his sight and hearing after sustaining a serious head injury in a road accident. Nine years later on June 4, 1980, he was struck by lightning outside his house in Portland, Maine, and after being knocked unconscious for 20 minutes by the bolt, he recovered to find that his central vision and hearing had amazingly been restored. He could even hear without his hearing aid, which had been burnt out by the lightning.

TRUFFLE MONEY

⮌ In November 2018, a truffle weighing almost 2 lb (850 g) was sold for €85,000 (around $100,000) at the World White Truffle auction in Alba, Italy. The city has hosted a two-month-long white truffle fair every year for 88 years, but this was its 19th auction. We have to wonder if the buyer intends to cook with or simply admire the expensive fungus.

➲ Two salt lakes in the Australian Outback resemble runny eggs when seen 0.62 mi (1 km) above the ground!

Photographer Alex Ham of the United Kingdom snapped the photo while in a plane above Wheatbelt region, east of Perth, Western Australia. The color of the lakes depends on the salinity of the water.

No Yolk

SUNNY SIDE UP!

GLASS GLOW

➲ Believe it or not, radioactive uranium glassware was once all the rage and is even sought after by collectors today. When viewed under a blacklight, they are positively radiant! But it's not the radioactivity that makes it glow—uranium glows under UV light no matter how radioactive it may or may not be. The use of uranium in glass to achieve a lovely shade of yellow or green took off in the early 1830s, but mostly died off in the early 20th century.

The levels of radiation in uranium glassware are so low that it is safe to handle, but it is not recommended for holding food or drink.

BURP CURE > Neil Ribbens, from London, England, was unable to burp for 34 years until a surgeon cured him by giving him Botox injections in his throat. Ribbens lost the ability to burp when he was a baby due to a condition so rare it does not even have a name. His larynx would become so tensed that it prevented gases from escaping through his throat, causing him severe pain, persistent hiccups, and bloating.

CAR REWARD > Emmanuel Elliott, 81, and his partner, 79-year-old Hilda Farmer, offered a $130 reward to anyone who could find their car. They had parked it "within a mile and a half" of Cheltenham General Hospital in Gloucestershire, England, but could not remember exactly where and had spent four days searching for it without success.

TANK BIKE ➲ This massive motorcycle is powered by a World War II tank engine! The 5-ton behemoth was built by German mechanics Tilo and Wilfried Niebel and can reach speeds of up to 50 mph (80 kmph). The bike is decorated with old gas masks, and the exhaust pipes, one of which is a converted missile, shoot flames. Talk about a wild ride!

harzer-bike-schmiede.de

RETRO TRICYCLE

⮕ This strange and fascinating tricycle was invented and photographed by Charles W. Oldrieve in 1882. The photo shows the amazing machine into which a rider would actually climb and sit inside the third wheel while peddling. Looking somewhat like a penny-farthing or high-wheeled bicycle—but much weirder—it's hard to imagine that the rider of this tricycle wouldn't get a few confused looks while rolling down the street.

BAD MOVE > Off-duty FBI agent Chase Bishop was charged with assault after accidentally shooting a bystander while dancing in a bar in Denver, Colorado. The man was shot in the leg when the agent tried to pick up a gun that fell from its holster as he performed a back handspring on the dance floor.

UNDERGROUND TEMPLE > In 1985, Levon Arakelyan's wife asked him to dig a potato storage pit under their house in Arinj, Armenia—but after finishing the pit he kept chiseling away at the rock for another 23 years, eventually creating an incredible underground temple covering an area of 3,014 sq ft (280 sq m). The temple consists of seven rooms connected by a network of corridors and staircases, and the walls are adorned with mosaics and sculptures. He did it all by hand, working 18 hours a day and excavating about 450 truckloads of rubble, and work on the project only stopped when he died in 2008.

NO JURORS > Two trials at Forsyth County Court, North Carolina, were postponed in February 2018 because officials had forgotten to invite any jurors. After nobody showed up for jury duty at the start of the week, sheriff's deputies tried to recruit volunteers by visiting local shopping malls, while court officials made pleas on local television.

EXPENSIVE SNACK > When a 37-year-old Russian woman, Olesja Schemjakowa, used her credit card to pay for coffee and cake at a café near Zurich, Switzerland, she accidentally typed in her PIN code as the tip and ended up paying $7,732 for a $23.76 bill.

WHITE LIE > Jiang Jingwei, a police officer from Shanghai, China, has posed as a stranger's dead son for over five years to protect her from the painful truth. In 2003, Liang Qiaoying, from Shanxi Province, lost her son, Liang Yu, in a freak accident that left her paralyzed and brain damaged. Whenever she asked about her son, her husband, Xia Zhanhai, rather than tell her he was dead, said he had gone to work in another city. Then in 2010, while watching a TV show about police work in Shanghai, Xia was amazed to see an officer who looked just like his dead son. Three years later, he finally tracked down the officer, and on hearing the family's tragic story, Jiang Jingwei agreed not only to meet them but also to pretend to the mother that he was their son. She accepted the kindly imposter immediately, and he began regularly phoning them and sending food parcels, even though he has a life and parents of his own.

ACCIDENTAL CODEBREAKER > A typo helped the Allied forces crack the famous Enigma code and ultimately defeat the Germans in World War II. The U.K. Ministry of Defense recruited Geoffrey Tandy to work at its top-secret Bletchley Park headquarters in Buckinghamshire, England, in the belief that he was an expert cryptogramist—someone who deciphers codes—when in fact he was a cryptogamist, an expert on mosses, algae, and seaweed. Despite the mistake, he stayed, and when a German U-boat was sunk in 1941 and its cryptic documents captured, his knowledge of preserving water-damaged specimens proved invaluable in making the papers readable.

HYGIENE PROBLEM > In 2018, a Taiwanese man filed to divorce his wife because he said she only bathed once a year. In his petition to New Taipei City District Court, he claimed psychological torture due to her lack of hygiene.

YOUR UPLOADS

Long Tooth

Melanie Misselbrook of the United Kingdom contacted Ripley's about her 8-year-old son's milk tooth (or baby tooth) that measured 1 in long (2.6 cm)—longer than the current world record holder! A dentist had to extract the tooth after it wouldn't come out. She says the top of the tooth measures 0.28 in (0.7 cm) and the root measures an astonishing 0.7 in (1.9 cm).

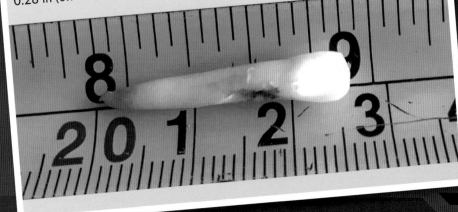

TRACTOR WHEELIES

⊃ Gaggi Bansra, a farmer from Punjab, India, performs wheelies on his father's one-ton tractor and can drive the vehicle on just its back wheels for more than 330 ft (100 m)!

Bansra, 21, became a local celebrity and amateur stuntman after videos of his tractor wheelies went viral online.

UNSUCCESSFUL CANDIDATE > Since 1988, K. Padmarajan, from Tamil Nadu, has run in more than 180 unsuccessful elections in India.

TETRIS LOVER > Noorul Mahjabeen Hassan, a 20-year-old math student from Orlando, Florida, announced that she was going to "marry" a Tetris video game after her relationship with a calculator called Pierre ended when he short-circuited while she was cleaning him. She had previously formed romantic relationships with other inanimate objects—including an iPod, a treadmill, and a GPS system—a condition known as *objectophilia*. She loves Tetris so much that she plays it for up to 12 hours a day. She also has a Tetris necklace, Tetris-shaped lamps, T-shirts, and magnets, and she sleeps with Tetris pillows and rare hard drive editions of the game.

HUMP DAY > Washington Nationals manager Dave Martinez arranged for three camels to be brought to spring training camp in 2018 as a visual aid to help the players get over the baseball team's notorious playoff hump!

NOT DEAD > A woman was hurriedly transferred to a hospital after being discovered alive in a mortuary fridge in Carletonville, South Africa. She had been declared dead by paramedics following a road accident, but when a morgue worker went to check on the body in the fridge several hours later, he noticed that she was breathing.

WRONG BODY > For more than seven years, Juana Escudero has tried to prove to Spanish authorities that she is not dead. She was registered as deceased due to an administrative error after a woman of the same name died in Malaga in 2010. Unable to renew her driver's license or arrange a doctor's appointment, a frustrated Escudero wants her alleged grave dug up and the remains DNA tested so that she can prove she is not the one buried there.

SECOND HOME > Including pre-tournament practice days, American tennis player Venus Williams has spent more than a year of her life at Wimbledon. She made her debut there as a 17-year-old in 1997.

SOCCER URINAL ⮑ Just
when you thought the global soccer craze couldn't get more fanatical, there's this: soccer-themed urinals. A mall in Xuhui District, Shanghai, China, renovated their men's bathroom to celebrate the FIFA World Cup in Brazil, accessorizing each urinal with a screen mat featuring a miniature green soccer field, white soccer goal, and a soccer ball. What's more, for $7 or less, you too can purchase a soccer-style urinal screen mat.

MAYOR PUNISHED > On February 25, 2018, the people of San Buenaventura, Bolivia, put their mayor, Javier Delgado, in wooden stocks for an hour because they thought he was doing a bad job.

SMILING CORPSE > Two months after Buddhist monk Luang Phor Pian died in Bangkok, Thailand, at age 92, his followers removed his body from his coffin as part of a ritual and found that not only had his corpse not decayed, but he even appeared to be smiling!

COUNTING CASH > A few minutes after robbing a bank in Anchorage, Alaska, a man was arrested outside the very same bank while in the act of counting the money he had just stolen. He had also given the bank teller a hold-up note bearing his real name and birthdate.

LAST REQUEST > In his obituary, storm chaser Jim Sellars, of Springfield, Missouri, told friends that he wanted them to launch his ashes into a tornado.

ROMAN GLOVES > In 2017, a pair of 2,000-year-old Roman leather boxing gloves were discovered by archaeologists near Hadrian's Wall in northern England.

ODD PREDICAMENT > A young woman got her head stuck in a truck's oversized tailpipe at the 2018 Winstock Country Music Festival in Winsted, Minnesota.

GARLIC CHOCOLATE > During World War II, garlic-infused chocolate bars were given to soldiers dropped behind enemy lines in France and Spain so that they would smell like local people.

CLOWN INTRUDER > A man arrived home in Marlboro, Vermont, to find a stranger intoxicated and fast asleep in an upstairs bedroom and wearing a clown costume.

BRIDAL BALL > To demonstrate their love of soccer during the 2018 World Cup, two teams of Russian women played a 30-minute-long game on a gravel pitch in one of the host cities, Kazan, while wearing floor-length white bridal gowns and running shoes.

DUMB THIEF > A shoplifter in Leicester, Massachusetts, used a blob of Play-Doh to cover the lens of the store's security camera—but in doing so left detectives with a perfect impression of a fingerprint in the Play-Doh.

LOCAL HEROES > The England national soccer team's defensive back three who played in the 2018 World Cup semi-finals—Kyle Walker, John Stones, and Harry Maguire—were born within 20 mi (32 km) of each other in South Yorkshire.

4 TIMES AS TALL AS A GIRAFFE!

COLOSSAL CANVAS

⮑ A 76.5-ft-high (23-m) easel on three steel legs in Altona, Manitoba, holds a gigantic reproduction of a Vincent van Gogh sunflower painting. Created by local artist Cameron Cross in recognition of Altona's status as the sunflower capital of Canada, the painting measures 23 × 33 ft (7 × 10 m) and weighs 7,920 lb (3,600 kg). It took two and a half years to finish and used 17 gal (77 l) of paint and 24 sheets of plywood.

FAN'S FAREWELL > After Boston Celtics basketball fan Renard Matthews died in 2018, his family dressed his body in a Celtics jersey for his wake at a funeral home in New Orleans and positioned him in front of a TV screen showing a Celtics game. He also had a video game controller in his lap and his favorite snacks nearby.

CHILD DRIVER > Police officers who followed a car zig-zagging down a street in Des Moines, Iowa, found a nine-year-old girl at the wheel with a seven-year-old child as her passenger.

PRIMITIVE WEAPONS > After only 30 officers out of 130 passed their firearms control tests in 2018, the entire police department in Alvarado, Mexico, were stripped of their guns by the state governor and issued with slingshots and small rocks instead.

NEW CAR > On July 14, 2018, a man totaled a $300,000 McLaren 720S luxury sportscar in Great Falls, Virginia, by crashing it into a tree—just one day after buying it.

COLOR CHANGE > After winning only one home game in four months, the Guangzhou R and F soccer club in China decided to change their stadium color from blue to gold in an attempt to bring good luck. The gold makeover appeared to work, as the team won its next five home games.

An 18th-century Chinese vase that had been kept in a shoebox in an attic in France sold for $19 million at auction in Paris in 2018.

LONG-LOST BROTHERS > Political science students Kieron Graham and Vincent Ghant were classmates at Kennesaw State University in Georgia for three years before they discovered they are brothers. Graham, who is nine years younger than Ghant, had been adopted at the age of three months.

OVERCONFIDENT > Teddy Allen, from Staffordshire, had a tattoo of England soccer team captain Harry Kane inked on his left leg along with the words "World Cup Winners 2018". . . two days before England was knocked out of the tournament by Croatia.

STRANGE STABBING > A man with no arms was arrested in Miami Beach, Florida, in July 2018 for stabbing another man with a pair of scissors using his feet.

CREEK COMMUTE > For the 11th annual Tube to Work Day, about 1,000 people in Boulder, Colorado, entered Boulder Creek at 8 a.m. on July 11, 2018, and floated downstream to their places of work on inflatable inner tubes.

CHANGE OF LUCK > In 1999, Bill Morgan, a truck driver from Melbourne, Australia, was clinically dead for 14 minutes following a massive heart attack—but within a year he made a full recovery, married the girl of his dreams, and won the lottery twice!

MOTORBALL

⊃ **While the thought of soccer played from the back of motorcycles might sound improbable (and dangerous) today, Motorball enjoyed a real moment in 1920s London.**

Surprisingly, the rules were similar to soccer, although goals didn't contain nets, which would have proven dangerous to get tangled up in while riding a motorcycle.

Some of the colors included are Coca-Cola (red), Diet Dr. Pepper (white), Canada Dry Ginger Ale (silver), and Monster Energy Drink (gold).

Rarity N° 171446

Soda Can Art: Superman

Superman portrait made out of thousands of strips of soda cans.

JUST DESSERTS > A man was arrested in Pine Bluff, Arkansas, after apparently trying to pay for a meal with the waitress's stolen credit card. Flora Lunsford's purse, containing her card and driver's license, had been stolen from her car two days earlier.

MISSPELLED NAME > Johanna Giselhäll Sandström, from Kyrkhult, Sweden, changed her son's name because of a tattoo artist's blunder. She had requested a tattoo on her arm of her children's names, Nora and Kevin, but the artist mistakenly inked "Nora and Kelvin." So Sandström decided to rename the two-year-old "Kelvin."

BUCKET SEAT > When police officers in Norfolk, England, stopped a driver in a battered old car, they found he was using an upside-down metal bucket as a seat and a pair of pliers for steering.

POTTER TYPO > An uncorrected proof of J. K. Rowling's debut novel *Harry Potter and the Philosopher's Stone*, with the author's name misspelled as J. A. Rowling, sold for $13,000 at auction in London in 2017.

TOO HEAVY > A suspected credit card thief tried to hide from police by climbing into the ceiling panels of a convenience store in Spruce Grove, Alberta, Canada, only to come crashing down in the coffee aisle when the ceiling gave way beneath her weight.

QUICK THINKING > When an unoccupied boat caught fire in Tequesta, Florida, Bret Townsend put it out in 10 minutes by repeatedly riding a Jet Ski toward it at speed and then turning at the last moment to create a huge spray that doused the flames.

YOUR UPLOADS

Giant Veggie

Jill Wiens of Regina, Saskatchewan, Canada, sent Ripley's this photo of a giant zucchini that grew in her family's box garden! It weighs 11 lb (5 kg) and measured just over 24 in (61 cm) long. She commented, "It's bigger than my 2-week-old niece."

FREEZE *Beard*

➲ **Subzero temperatures can't stop Daniel Schetter of Marquette, Michigan, from catching a few waves on Lake Superior!**

Somewhat of a local legend, "Surfer Dan" tries every year to grow a bigger ice beard than the last. He surfs for up to four hours at a time and wears a wet suit designed to protect his body from the bone-chilling temperatures reaching as low as –24°F (–31°C) with the wind chill factor. However, his face remains exposed, which is great for growing an ice beard but leaves his face numb and in pain by the end of the surf session.

SPIDER PHOBIA > Demi Sweeney, a 22-year-old criminology student at Bournemouth University, England, called for KFC delivery just so that the delivery driver could help her remove a large spider that was outside her room. Unfortunately, the driver was also scared of spiders, although he eventually plucked up the courage to catch it.

BURIAL RITUAL > The body parts of Habsburg emperors, who ruled Austria from 1278 to 1918, were often buried at three different sites. Their intestines were kept in a copper urn in St. Stephan's Cathedral, Vienna, while the bodies were buried in the Imperial Vault at the city's Capuchin Church and their hearts were buried at the Augustinian Church.

LANGUAGE MYSTERY > O'Neal Mahmoud, a three-year-old Arabic-speaking boy from the Golan Heights, Israel, has learned to speak English with a British accent, despite hardly ever hearing the language. Named after basketball star Shaquille O'Neal, he did not speak at all until he was two and then began using phrases like "my dear" and "oh, my goodness" even though his parents don't speak English, he rarely watches English television, and has never traveled abroad.

POOP LOOT > Two hapless burglars attempted to steal a large plastic container from Central Bark, a business in Winnipeg, Manitoba, Canada, only to discover that it contained nothing more valuable than dog poop.

IRONIC CAPTURE > Two women who escaped from a prison in Edmonton, Alberta, Canada, were captured the next day in an escape room! They had inadvertently wandered into Sidequests Adventures, a business where participants are given a set amount of time to develop strategies to escape from a confined space.

BIRTHDAY GIFT > When Vikki Rutter, from Kent, England, bought a $180 ruby ring as a birthday gift for her cousin, she decided to present it tied to a helium balloon. But as she turned around to find something to weigh down the 36-in (0.9-m) inflatable, it drifted out of the house through an open door and soared away into the distance. . . along with the ring.

THE SMILE EXPERIMENT

This old, toothless man was a frequent subject of Duchenne's, as he had a condition that left his face numb so he did not feel pain from the electricity.

⊃ **In his search to unlock the secrets behind facial expressions, a 19th-century French neurologist used electricity to make people's faces move!**

Using a special machine, Guillaume-Benjamin-Amand Duchenne de Boulogne would apply small (and unfortunately painful) amounts of electricity to his subjects' faces to simulate muscle contractions and then catalog which muscles were used for which expressions. One of his more famous conclusions is that a genuine smile engages not just the lip and mouth muscles, but also the eye muscles. To this day, a smile like that is known as a "Duchenne smile." His work also led him to describe and develop treatments for multiple nervous and muscular disorders.

False laughter

NUCLEAR SHELTER > Bruce and Jean Beach have buried 42 school buses on their homestead in Horning's Mills, Ontario, Canada, as their own 10,000-sq-ft (929-sq-m) nuclear fallout shelter. The buses are encased in concrete and buried 14 ft (4.3 m) below ground. Called "The Ark Two," the shelter was originally designed in 1980 at the height of the Cold War to accommodate around 350 people for several weeks and is equipped with a full plumbing system, a private well, food supplies, fuel generators, and even a dentist's chair.

Surprise

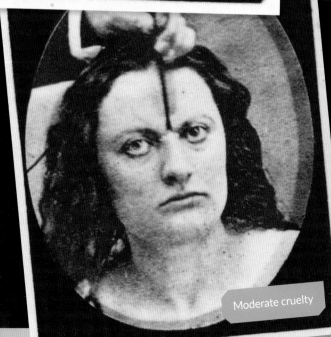

Moderate cruelty

Duchenne was one of the first to document his experiments with photographs, resulting in these images, which he labeled by expression.

DRY VALLEYS > No rain has fallen on the Dry Valleys in Antarctica for at least 2 million years. There is no snow or ice there either because the 200 mph (320 kmph) katabatic winds—which occur when cold, dense air is pulled down by the force of gravity—blow away all precipitation.

GLASS BRIDGE > A new 1,600-ft-long (488-m) glass bridge in Hebei, China, can hold 3,000 people simultaneously on its transparent walkway. The bridge, which is made from more than 1,000 thick slabs of glass, stretches between two steep cliffs 715 ft (218 m) above the valley floor at Hongyagu in Pingshan County and is designed to withstand a force 12 wind or a magnitude six earthquake.

MIRACLE SEEKERS > Every day for the past decade, an average of more than 20 people visit the Acapulco grave of Raulito, a Mexican baby who died in 1933 at the age of 10 months and is still credited with performing miracles more than 80 years later. They bring flowers, candles, and toys in the hope that Raulito will help them from beyond the grave, and on Raulito's birthday, April 2, there are as many as 100 visitors. Raulito's powers were first acknowledged in 2007 when a local woman arrived at the city's San Francisco cemetery with her young, dying daughter in her arms. Doctors had said the child would not live beyond the day, but after the mother prayed at Raulito's tomb for 90 minutes, the little girl made a complete recovery.

EQUATORIAL CROSSINGS > The Congo River in Africa flows in both a northerly and southerly direction across the equator.

DEVIL'S NUMBER > On Friday, October 13, 2017, Finnair's Flight 666 landed in HEL, the airport code for Helsinki, for the final time. The devil's number flight from Copenhagen began operating in 2006, but even though it has since flown without mishap, including 21 times on Friday the 13th, Finnair decided to retire the number.

CRICKET BREAD > The Fazer Bakery of Finland sells bread made from crushed crickets. In addition to wheat flour, each loaf contains about 70 dried and finely ground crickets, which are an excellent source of protein.

ELEPHANT BUILDING > The 32-floor, 335-ft-high (102-m) Chang Building in Bangkok, Thailand, is also known as the Elephant Building because it is shaped like an elephant, complete with eyes and a trunk.

SOCK DAY > May 9 each year is National Lost Sock Memorial Day, when people are encouraged to let go of all their remaining single socks and to hold a minute's silence for all socks that have been lost.

PIZZA OFFER > In December 2017, Tony Glorioso, co-owner of Mario's Pizza in Union Pier, Michigan, offered snowed-in customers a $30 "pizza and plow" service that included delivering a large, one-topping pizza and snowplowing the caller's driveway.

CHOCOLATE MUSIC > Croatian confectionery company Nadalina has created a chocolate record that plays real music. The grooved disc, which is made of 70 percent cocoa chocolate, plays a song recorded by chocolatier Marinki Biskic's band Fon Biskich.

GARLIC COFFEE > Yokitomo Shimotai, a coffee shop owner in Japan's Aomori Prefecture, has invented coffee made entirely of garlic. He has been perfecting the idea for more than 30 years—ever since he accidentally burned some garlic while waiting tables. When he mixed it with water, he found that it looked and tasted like coffee.

AX THROWING > At Les Cognées, a venue in Paris, France, customers unwind after work by paying $22 an hour to throw axes at a target on a wall.

DRONE DELIVERY > When heavy snow hit Ireland in 2018, Patrick Mungovan, of Quilty, County Clare, used his camera drone to deliver bread to neighbors within a 3-mi (4.8-km) radius.

VITAL INGREDIENT > Hundreds of KFC restaurants in the United Kingdom had to close temporarily in early 2018 because they had run out of chicken.

VEGETARIAN COMPLEX > Veda Village, an apartment complex in St. Petersburg, Russia, is for vegetarians only. Prospective residents must first undergo an interview with sales agents, and if they fail to convince them that they are genuine vegetarians, their application will be rejected.

Dancing HOUSE

⮕ **Known as one of the most beautiful cities in the world, Prague boasts a truly remarkable piece of architecture: the Dancing House.**

One of the most significant and popular pieces of post-1989 Czech Republic architecture, the Dancing House houses more than 32,292 sq ft (3,000 sq m) for offices, restaurants, a gallery, and a conference center. The curvy exterior—inspired by fleet-footed dancing legends Fred Astaire and Ginger Rogers—remains a local symbol of democracy.

A GLITCH IN THE MATRIX?

EIGHT-LEGGED EATS ⊃ Nothing satisfies quite like a chargrilled tarantula served atop a juicy beef patty, right? Believe it or not, the owners of North Carolina's Bull City Burger and Brewery offer the exclusive "Tarantula Burger" front and center on their menu. With just 15 farm-raised tarantulas available to the restaurant per year for the arachnid treat, guests must register for a lottery to earn their chance at the eight-legged eats. Besides the spidery concoction, Bull City serves other exotic meats, including alligator, camel, iguana, and a variety of other insects on a seasonal basis.

CLASS RING > A class ring found during a construction project at Comstock High School, Michigan, was returned to the woman who had lost it as a student 47 years earlier. The 1971 ring from Loy Norrix High School in Kalamazoo fell out of an old locker in the Comstock locker room and was then traced by its engraved initials to Angelita Olivares (now Angelita Kolodzieyczyk), who had transferred to Comstock for her senior year.

WAR BARS > Nine 103-year-old chocolate bars were found recently in a tin that belonged to Leicestershire Regiment soldier Richard Bullimore, who served with the British Army in France during World War I.

ARMPIT ADVERTISING > Japanese company Wakino employs young women as human billboards by sticking product adverts on their armpits, which can then be seen when the wearer reaches up to hold on to a hanging strap on public transportation.

CAMERA RETURNED > William Etherton, 10, was reunited with his video camera four months after it was swept out to sea by a huge wave in Yorkshire, England. It drifted before washing up 500 mi (800 km) away on the island of Süderoog, Germany, where the still-working camera was found by resident Roland Spreer, who posted a picture of it on Facebook to find the owner.

OVERDUE BOOK > A library book was returned to Hereford Cathedral School in England 130 years late. The 1,000-page *The Microscope and Its Revelations* was checked out by one of the students, Arthur Boycott, in 1886 and was only returned when it was discovered in 2016 by his 77-year-old granddaughter Alice Gillett while she was sorting through her late husband's possessions at her home in Taunton, Somerset. If the overdue book fine had been enforced, it would have totaled almost $10,000.

BLUE CHRISTMAS > In 1971, Adrian Pearce of Edmonton, Alberta, Canada, was given a Christmas gift by his girlfriend, who then immediately broke up with him. He held on to the unwrapped present for nearly 50 years when, on December 6, 2018, the two came together to unwrap it for a charity event—it was a book about love!

ICE DISK

⊃ On January 16, 2019, residents of Westbrook, Maine, awoke to a 300-ft-wide (100-m) spinning ice disk in the Presumpscot River. After aerial photos taken by a drone revealed the moon-like, circular configuration, it set off a social media frenzy. While some online fans speculated it was a winter crop circle of extraterrestrial origin, scientists say the rare natural phenomenon hints at what's going on beneath the surface—a circular river current or whirlpool. When ice crystals in this spinning water merge, they create a round mat of ice whose edges get polished by the surrounding shoreline and other ice chunks it bumps into as it rotates.

CAN-DO

⊃ Artist Noah Deledda of Tampa, Florida, takes ordinary aluminum cans and—using just his fingertips and nails—converts them into geometric works of art, some of which sell for more than $2,000 apiece!

Deledda uses only his hands to create the dents and grooves, turning regular cans into delicate sculptures. He says this action elevates an item we'd normally throw away, but he also wants to show people how art can turn a discarded object into something extraordinary.

NOAH'S BLANK CAN-VAS

CONSTIPATED SUSPECT > Mounkadir Mustapha, from Surrey, England, did not go to the toilet for nine days in order to avoid passing illegal drugs that he had hidden up his butt. After arresting him and discovering the hidden stash, police officers kept him under round-the-clock surveillance waiting for him to pass the drugs naturally. When he finally did, he was jailed for three years and five months.

CAR CASKET > A Nigerian man named Azubuike buried his father in a brand new $100,000 BMW car instead of a traditional coffin. A 6-ft-deep (1.8-m) grave was dug in the village of Ihiala and the car was then lowered into the hole by villagers and the dead man's family.

MACARONI WEDDING > Emma Mykytyn and Mark Murphy, from Glasgow, Scotland, had a macaroni-themed wedding, with confetti, cufflinks, and earrings all made from macaroni. The bride also had macaroni sprinkled in her bouquet and their guests enjoyed a macaroni cheese cake. The best man was Mr. Macaroni, the mascot for a local pasta company.

FACEBOOK CHALLENGE > Wanted suspect Michael Zaydel messaged Redford Township Police Department in Michigan, promising to hand himself in if the department got 1,000 shares on its next Facebook post. It got over 4,000, so he kept his side of the deal and turned himself in, bringing officers a dozen donuts and a bagel for good measure.

FUNERAL TRAGEDY > Samen Kondorura was crushed to death by his mother's coffin after he and other pallbearers lost their footing while carrying the casket up a bamboo ladder to a ceremonial plinth at the funeral in North Toraja, Indonesia.

ICE GAME > When the *Titanic* first hit the iceberg, passengers had no idea of the impending disaster and began playing football with the chunks of ice that fell on the ship's deck.

BIRTHDAY LINK > Psychologist Dr. Linda Gilmore, from Brisbane, Australia, has connected with over 150 women from around the world—including Iraq, Norway, the United States, and England—who were born on the exact same day as her—Tuesday, June 12, 1951.

LUCKY DAY > On the same day—April 28, 2018—Ping Kuen Shum, from Vancouver, Canada, celebrated his birthday, marked his retirement from work, and won the $1.5 million jackpot in the BC/49 lottery.

DÉJÀ VU > On March 6, 2018, Millwall soccer player George Saville scored after just 51 seconds of the English League game against Hull City—and four days later he repeated the feat, scoring in the 51st second of the game against Brentford.

DUEL DEATHS > Between 1861 and 1878, Henri Tragne, of Marseille, France, took part in five duels, winning the first four without needing to fire a shot as in each case his opponent died suddenly of a cardiac arrest. On the fifth occasion, it was Tragne himself who dropped dead before a shot was fired.

PARALLEL LIVES > When two American women named Patricia Ann Campbell were wrongly given the same Social Security number, they discovered that, in addition to sharing the same name, both were born on March 13, 1941, both of their fathers were named Robert Campbell, both had married in 1959 to men who served in the military, and both had children aged 21 and 19 at the time. Furthermore, both women had studied cosmetics, worked as book-keepers, and had an interest in oil painting.

YOUR UPLOADS

ERASER COLLECTOR

Khushboo Marda Malani of New Delhi, India, started an eraser collection in 1992—and today she has the world's biggest collection of erasers! The 39-year-old owns more than 14,000 erasers of all shapes and sizes: transport vehicles, food, electronics, currency, animals, famous people, space, musical instruments, and much more. She told Ripley's, "Name it, think of it, and I have an eraser for it."

HUMAN COLOGNE > Ani Liu, a graduate of the Massachusetts Institute of Technology, has bottled the scent of her parents. She creates her range of human-scented colognes by extracting volatile molecules from clothes they have worn and fixing that into a solvent.

FULL MARX

⮞ The city of Trier, Germany, celebrated the 200th birthday of Karl Marx—author, philosopher, and political theorist—in a quite unusual way. In the town's center, pedestrians can now find a traffic light that offers both a green and red Marx telling them when to cross or not to cross. Marx was born in Trier on May 5, 1818.

CEMETERY LOTTERY > Due to lack of space, the town of Berchtesgaden, Germany, staged a lottery so that people could win coveted burial spots in the picturesque local cemetery.

GENEROUS TIP > Enjoying a vacation after his country's elimination from the 2018 World Cup, Portuguese soccer star Cristiano Ronaldo left a $23,000 tip for hotel staff at the luxury Costa Navarino resort in Greece.

STOPPED TWICE > A 31-year-old Iowa woman who was ticketed for speeding at 92 mph (147 kmph) in a 2018 Ford Mustang near North Platte, Nebraska, was then arrested after deputies clocked her driving at 142 mph (227 kmph) as she accelerated away from the police stop.

DREAM WIN > Frederick Knox, of Hampton, Virginia, won a $100,000 lottery prize after the five winning numbers came to his wife in a dream.

PLASTIC DEPOSITS > Ear wax removal specialist Dr. Neel Raithatha, from Leicestershire, England, discovered 22 tiny plastic items buried deep in a patient's ear canal. They were identified as ear wax filters for a hearing aid that apparently kept falling off the patient's device.

WRONG LISBON > Two tourists who were trapped in an elevator in Lisbon, Portugal, called the wrong Lisbon police department for help. They searched online on their phones for "Lisbon police" and called the first number listed, only to be put through to the Lisbon Police Department in Maine, more than 3,000 mi (4,800 km) away.

PASSPORT BLUNDER > A bank robber in Moscow, Russia, was easily arrested after leaving his passport with the clerk. He handed his passport to the female cashier with a note inside demanding money, but when she immediately fainted behind the protective glass screen, he was forced to flee without the incriminating document.

SECRET WELL > After more than 20 years, Colin Steer found a hole beneath the living room floor of his house in Plymouth, England. He started digging and discovered the wall of a well, and with the help of a neighbor, he has now dug more than 17 ft (5 m) down and has still not reached the bottom.

CAR WASH > A man drove his expensive Land Rover SUV into a river in Dujiangyan, China, just to save $3 on a car wash, but had to be rescued when the flood gates of an upstream dam were opened, causing the water level to rise dramatically and turning the river into a raging torrent that threatened to sweep the vehicle away.

DOUBLE DUNNE > Soccer players James Dunne of Swindon Town and James Dunne of Accrington Stanley were sent off after clashing in an English League Division Two game on May 5, 2018.

SOFT LANDING > A three-year-old girl survived with only minor injuries after falling five floors from an apartment window in Stamford, Connecticut, because she landed in a cushioning layer of freshly spread garden mulch.

ROYAL TRIBUTE > British Airways celebrated the wedding of Prince Harry and Meghan Markle by operating a London to Toronto, Canada, flight on their wedding day (May 19, 2018) crewed entirely by people who share the couple's names—two men named Harry, seven women named Megan, and one Meghan.

YOUR UPLOADS

Swallow This

Nick Penney of Augusta, Maine, has been swallowing swords for more than a decade, and has been told many times that he'll do it until he's in his grave. As a playful response to those worried for his well-being, he swallowed a sword while buried alive in sand up to his neck!

YIKES SPIKES

⟳ **In December 2018, a factory worker in Zhuzhou, China, was impaled by 10 steel spikes and still managed to survive!**

The 49-year-old worker known as Zhou was working at a porcelain factory when a piece of machinery malfunctioned and he was struck by a falling robot arm covered in steel spikes. Each of the spikes measured about 1 ft (30 cm) in length and 0.6 in (1.5 cm) in diameter, with six of them entering his right shoulder, chest, and arm—narrowly missing an artery by just 0.04 in (0.1 cm)! Zhou was taken to a local hospital by his coworkers and then transferred to Xiangya Hospital of Central South University due to the severity of his injuries. Amazingly, he survived the harrowing ordeal.

Doctors were unable to X-ray Zhou, making the spike removal and surgery extremely risky.

INDEX

Page numbers in *italic* refer to images.

INDEX

ACKNOWLEDGMENTS

COVER © Albert Russ/Shutterstock.com; **10** (t) Courtesy of Travel Channel; **10–11** Photo by Colton Kruse; **11** (t) Photo by Matt Mamula, (b) Courtesy of Norm Deska, (br) Pictorial Press Ltd/Alamy Stock Photo; **12–13** (dp) HECTOR RETAMAL/AFP/Getty Images; **14** (tl) PA Images/Alamy Stock Photo, (tc) Public Domain {{PD-US}} Bog body from Denmark, "Borremose Man," circa 1946, Danish National Museum, (bl) PA Images/Alamy Stock Photo; **15** (t) Jeff J Mitchell/Getty Images, (b) Tim Graham/Contributor via Getty Images; **16** (sp) Zen Rial via Getty Images, (bl) Auscape/UIG via Getty Images; **17** (t) Photo by Jessica Firpi and Jordie R. Orlando, (b) Imaginechina; **18** Ken Howard/BIPs/Hulton Archive/Getty Images; **19** REUTERS/Arnd Wiegmann; **20** (bl) Nora Carol Photography via Getty Images; **20–21** (dp) Guillaume Payen/LightRocket via Getty Images; **21** (tc, tr) Images courtesy of Boaz Rottem, (tr) Neil Setchfield/Alamy Stock Photo; **22** (sp) Neil Setchfield/Alamy Stock Photo, (cl) Christopher Price/Alamy Stock Photo; **23** (t) OLI SCARFF/AFP/Getty Images, (b) Waltraud Grubitzsch/picture alliance via Getty Images; **24** (t) PACIFIC PRESS/Alamy Stock Photo, (b) Reproduced by permission of the National Library of Scotland; **25** (l) Library of Congress, Prints & Photographs Division, photograph by Harris & Ewing, LC-DIG-hec-31631, (r) Library of Congress, Prints & Photographs Division, photograph by Harris & Ewing, LC-DIG-hec-31633; **26** (t) Jakub Czajkowski/Shutterstock.com, (b) © Olga Ernst & Hp.Baumeler, Wikimedia Commons//CC-BY-SA 4.0; **27** RARESHOT/CATERS NEWS; **28** (t) Eric Catalano, Eternal Ink Tattoo Studio, Hecker, Illinois, (b) PA Images/Alamy Stock Photo; **29** (t) Urs Flueeler/EPA-EFE/REX/Shutterstock, (b) Franck Fotos/Alamy Stock Photo; **30–31** (dp) Heinz Kluetmeier/Sports Illustrated/Getty Images; **31** (t) Ralph Crane/The LIFE Picture Collection/Getty Images, (cr, b) Bettmann/Contributor via Getty Images; **32** (sp, cl) Bettmann/Contributor via Getty Images, (br) World History Archive/Alamy Stock Photo; **33** (tc) Kypros/Getty Images, (tr) Bettmann/Contributor via Getty Images, (b) ABC Photo Archives/ABC via Getty Images; **34** Bettmann/Contributor via Getty Images; **35** Alina Smurygina; **36** (t) MARTY MELVILLE/AFP/Getty Images, (b) Buyenlarge/Getty Images; **37** (sp) Twitter: @ride_hero_ (Yuasa Riku); **38** (t) Nationaal Archief/Collectie Spaarnestad, (b) Lee Bandoni; **39** (tr, cl) GIUSEPPE CACACE/AFP/Getty Images, (br) Photos by Matt Mamula and Steve Campbell; **40** (t, b) Nationaal Archief/Collectie Spaarnestad/Het Leven/Fotograaf onbekend; **41** (tr) Nationaal Archief/Collectie Spaarnestad/Fotograaf onbekend, (b) Nationaal Archief/Collectie Spaarnestad/Het Leven/Fotograaf onbekend; **42** Mario Tama/Getty Images; **43** (b) Public Domain {{PD-US}} Library of Congress Prints and Photographs Division Washington, D.C. 20540 USA http://hdl.loc.gov/loc.pnp/ppmsca.31948; **44** (t) Caters News, (b) © Colin Monteath/Hedgehog House/Minden Pictures; **45** Andrew Myers Art/Solent News/REX/Shutterstock; **46** Ben Churchill/Cover Images; **47** © John Mcevoy/Solent News & Photo Agency; **48–49** (dp) HECTOR RETAMAL/AFP/Getty Images; **49** (tr) MIGUEL ALVAREZ/AFP/Getty Images, (b) HECTOR RETAMAL/AFP/Getty Images; **50–51** FRED DUFOUR/AFP/Getty Images; **52–53** ITAR-TASS News Agency/Alamy Stock Photo; **53** (tr) Arijit Sen/Hindustan Times via Getty Images, (b) Panther Media GmbH/Alamy Stock Photo; **54–55** MARIUS VAGENES VILLANGER/AFP/Getty Images; **55** (t) Abdul Momin/Solent News/REX/Shutterstock, (br) REUTERS/Marko Djurica; **56** (tr) Tim Graham/Getty Images, (tl) Pam McLean via Getty Images; **57** (sp) DMITRY SEREBRYAKOV/AFP/Getty Images; **58** (tr) Ian Dagnall/Alamy Stock Photo; **58–59** (t) Imaginechina; **59** (bl) Li Zhihao/VCG via Getty Images; **60** MARCO LONGARI/AFP/Getty Images, **61** IndiaPictures/UIG via Getty Images; **62** (tl) Dominic Lipinski/PA Images via Getty Images, (tr, b) © Tom Harrison/Solent News & Photo Agency; **63** (t) STR/AFP/Getty Images; **64** (tl) Images & Stories/Alamy Stock Photo, (tr) Sharkawi Che Din/Alamy Stock Photo, (b) Nokuro/Alamy Stock Photo; **65** (t) VCG/VCG via Getty Images, (b) Imaginechina; **66** (t) Koichi Kamoshida/Getty Images; **66–67** YOSHIKAZU TSUNO/AFP/Getty Images; **67** (t) Richard Atrero de Guzman/NurPhoto via Getty Images, (b) TOSHIFUMI KITAMURA/AFP/Getty Images; **68** REUTERS/Michaela Rehle; **69** (tr) Imaginechina, (bl) REUTERS/Michaela Rehle; **70** (sp) Donna K. and Gilbert M. Grosvenor/National Geographic/Getty Images, (tr, cr, br) ERIC LAFFORGUE/Alamy Stock Photo; **71** (t) 28Lab/Caters News, (b) China Daily via REUTERS; **72** (t) Three Lions/Getty Images, (br) robertharding/Alamy Stock Photo; **73** (tl) Neil Setchfield/Alamy Stock Photo, (br) Imaginechina; **74** AFP/Getty Images; **75** (sp) REUTERS/Heino Kalis, (tl) Morell/Epa/REX/Shutterstock; **76** (sp) © John Riddell, Wikimedia Commons//CC-BY-SA 4.0 International, (cr) © Novemberscot, Wikimedia Commons//CC-BY-SA 4.0 International; **77** (t) VCG/VCG via Getty Images, (b) Seetheholyland.net, Wikimedia Commons//CC-BY-SA 2.0 Generic; **78–79** (t) DANIEL MIHAILESCU/AFP/Getty Images; **79** (tr) Andrei Pungovschi/Anadolu Agency/Getty Images, (b) Raymond Boyd/Getty Images; **80–81** (dp) Photos by News Examiner, Used with permission.; **82** Philipp Guelland/Getty Images; **83** James D. Morgan/Getty Images; **84** (tl) Imaginechina, (b) Matthew Chattle/Barcroft Media/Barcroft Media via Getty Images, Steve Back/Getty Images, Kirsty O'Connor/PA Images via Getty Images; **85** (tl) AP Photo/Jessica Hill/FILE; **86–87** DOMINIC RODRIGOUS/CATERS NEWS; **88** (sp) REUTERS/David Mercado, (bl) José Luis Quintana/LatinContent/Getty Images, (br) Andia/UIG via Getty Images; **89** (t) © Tropical studio/Shutterstock.com, (br) Rene MATTES/Gamma-Rapho via Getty Images; **90–91** (b) FRED DUFOUR/AFP/Getty Images; **92–93** Mark J. Barrett/Alamy Stock Photo; **94** © Felipe Gomes, Wikimedia Commons//CC-BY-SA 2.5; **95** (b) Chris Mattison/FLPA/Science Source; **96** (bl) SERGEI SUPINSKY/AFP/Getty Images; **96–97** Helen Olive/Caters News; **97** (tr) Panther Media GmbH/Alamy Stock Photo, (c) © Edwin Giesbers/NPL/Minden Pictures; **98** (sp) NOAA Fisheries/Brittany Dolan; **99** (t) Yasuda Mamoru via Minden Pictures, (c) The History Collection/Alamy Stock Photo, (bl) Public Domain {{PD-US}} Dr. Julius Neubronner, (br) Science History Images/Alamy Stock Photo. **100** Palaninathan M/Caters News; **101** (t) Ignacio Yufera/Biosphoto via Alamy, (b) Steve Chapple/Caters News; **102** (t) © Annie Gilbert/Solent News & Photo Agency, (b) Auscape/UIG via Getty Images; **103** Todd Ryburn Photography via Getty Images; **104** (sp) Public Domain {{PD-US}} before 1890, Author Unknown; **105** (tr) Lynda Christison/Solent News/REX/Shutterstock, (b) © Chien Lee/Minden Pictures; **106** REUTERS/Alexandros Avramidis; **107** (t) Imaginechina, (b) Courtesy of Benjamin Hicks; **108–109** Marcio Cabral/Caters News; **110** (t) © Michael and Patricia Fogden/Minden Pictures, (b) jiGGoTravel/Alamy Stock Photo; **111** Willows Veterinary Group; **112** (tl) Mark J. Barrett/Alamy Stock Photo; **112–113** (t) Wara Art/Cover Images; **113** (br) Caters News; **114** (t) Lacey FD/Rex Features, (br) Courtesy of Ugly Shyla; **115** (tr) © Michael D. Kern/naturepl.com, (b) George Grall via National Geographic; **116** Dirk Theron/Caters News; **117** (t) Armin Weigel/picture-alliance/dpa/AP Images; **118** MUNIR UZ ZAMAN/AFP/Getty Images; **118–119** (b) MUNIR UZ ZAMAN/AFP/Getty Images; **119** (t) Anthony Pierce/Alamy Stock Photo, Courtesy of Harold Moses via Flickr; **120** Jamie Hulit/Cover Images; **121** (t) Auscape/UIG via Getty Images, (b) CATERS NEWS; **122** (tr) Grahm S/Columbus Zoo and Aquarium/Cover Images, Tomo/Columbus Zoo and Aquarium/Cover Images; **123** MANJUNATH KIRAN/AFP/Getty Images; **124** (t, b) ASIF HASSAN/AFP/Getty Images, (br) Sabir Mazhar/Anadolu Agency/Getty Images; **125** Dinh Công Tâm/Solent News/REX/Shutterstock; **126** (t) Katmai NP&R/Cover Images, (b) SWNS; **127** Photography by Shin.T via Getty Images; **128–129** (b) Life on white/Alamy Stock Photo; **129** (cl) Dr. Del Rae Martin DVM and Dr. Elizabeth Kraft DVM, Heart River Animal Hospital, Mandan, ND, (cr) William Turner via Getty Images; **130** (sp) Al Fenn/The LIFE Picture Collection/Getty Images, (bl) Ethel Purtle and King riding in a lion drome for a Clyde Beatty circus show. 19--. Black & white photonegative, 35 mm. State Archives of Florida, Florida Memory. <https://www.floridamemory.com/items/show/115468>, accessed 3 January 2019; **131** (b) © Peter Scoones/naturepl.com; **132** Kevin Ebi/Caters News; **133** (t) Wu Yung-sen/Caters News, (b) RSPCA/Cover Images; **134–135** Adam Myers/Caters News; **136** James O'Neal/Cover Images; **137** (t) WENN, (b) Justin Poulsen/Cover Images; **138–139** WENN; **140** ANDREAS VRONTI/CATERS NEWS; **141** REUTERS/Kim Kyung-Hoon; **143** Cover Images; **144–145** Jane Labowitch (aka Princess Etch) princessetch.com, @princessetch on social media; **146** Images courtesy of Bryanna Marie; **147** (t) Jack Dredd/REX/Shutterstock, (b) Todd Sumlin/The Charlotte Observer via AP; **148** (tr) Matteo Bazzi/EPA-EFE/REX/Shutterstock, (tl) REX/Shutterstock, (b) Michael Bezjian/Getty Images; **149** GIOVANNI CONTARDI/CATERS NEWS; **150** (tl, bl) Jim Holden/Alamy Stock Photo, (tr) Imaginechina; **151** (t) www.foredgefrost.co.uk; **152–153** Arun Kumar Bajaj/Cover Images; **153** (r) AF archive/Alamy Stock Photo; **154** (t) Callie Scardina Instagram: @miss_callie_marie, (b) José Mauricio dos anjos; **155** Simon Stacpoole/REX/Shutterstock; **156–157** Supplied by WENN.com via Cover Images; **158** ANDREAS SOLARO/AFP/Getty Images; **159** (t) Supplied by WENN.com, (b) The Big Fresno Fair; **160–161** Jessica Leigh Clark-Bojin, Instagram @thePieous, www.PiesAreAwesome.com; **162** (tr) Cookie 63/Alamy Stock Photo; **162–163** Stephanie Pokorny Crochetverse; **164** Brett Stanley/Barcroft Images/Barcroft Media via Getty Images; **165** Uwe Anspach/picture alliance via Getty Images, Sebastian Willnow/picture alliance via Getty Images; **166** Jian Yang/Cover Images; **167** LEGO/Cover Images, Independent Photo Agency Srl/Alamy Live News; **168** (t) CHRISTIAN MOULLEC/CATERS, (b) Leon Neal/Getty Images; **169** (l) Xinhua/Alamy Stock Photo, (cr, br) Richard Lautens/Toronto Star via Getty Images; **170** (t) MERCURY PRESS via Caters; **171** Steve Casino/Solent News/REX/Shutterstock; **172** Adam Myers/Caters News; **173** TIMOTHY A. CLARY/AFP/Getty Images; **176** (tl) Courtesy of Barbara Neiman, (br) SWNS; **177** (tl) INDRANIL MUKHERJEE/AFP/Getty Images, (b) SWNS; **178** MAURO PIMENTEL/AFP/Getty Images; **179** (tl) Courtesy of Tiffany Villarreal, (br) Bettmann/Contributor via Getty Images; **182** Print Collector/Getty Images; **183** (tr) CATERS News, (b) REUTERS/Raneen Sawafta; **184** (sp) REUTERS/Mike Blake; **185** (bl) Daniel Teetor/Alamy Stock Photo; **186** (t) SWNS, (cl) Alex Socci/Barcroft Media via Getty Images; **186–187** Pitaya Filmes/Barcroft Images; **187** (t) Pitaya Filmes/Barcroft Images; **188** (sp) Alex Socci/Barcroft USA/Barcroft Media via Getty Images; **189** Alex Socci/Barcroft USA/Barcroft Media via Getty Images; **190** (sp) CHRISTOPHE SIMON/AFP/Getty Images, (bl) Alastair Grant/AP/REX/Shutterstock; **191** Mansell/Contributor via Getty Images; **192** (tl) DAN JAMES/CATERS NEWS; **193** (tr) John Phillips/The LIFE Picture Collection/Getty Images, (c) THE WIZARD OF ODD TV/CATERS NEWS; **194** (b) MERCURY PRESS; **195** GraphicaArtis/Getty Images; **196** The Adventurists/Richard Brandon Cox/Cover Images; **197** (tr) SIPA Asia/ZUMA Wire/Alamy Live News; **198** (tr) ANDREW CUTRARO/AFP/Getty Images, (bl) Bettmann/Contributor via Getty Images; **199** (b) The Real Life Guys/Caters; **200** (b) Abhisek Saha/Solent News/REX/Shutterstock; **201** REUTERS/Sheng Li; **202–203** (bkg) LIONEL BONAVENTURE/AFP/Getty Images; **202** (cl) Joerg Mitter/Red Bull via Getty Images; **203** (l) Red Bull via Getty Images, (r) Charles McQuillan/Getty Images; **204** (t) RUSS FOXX/CATERS NEWS, (b) Michael Scott/Caters News; **205** Barcroft Media/Getty Images; **206** (t) Eric Lafforgue/Art in All of Us/Corbis via Getty Images, Courtesy of Natasha Soyini; **207** (t) REUTERS/Brendan McDermid; **208–209** TORU YAMANAKA/AFP/Getty Images; **210** (l) NICOLAS DATICHE/AFP/Getty Images, (b) TOSHIFUMI KITAMURA/AFP/Getty Images; **211** dpa picture alliance/Alamy Stock Photo; **212** (tr, l) CESAR MANSO/AFP/Getty Images; **213** (tl) CESAR MANSO/AFP/Getty Images, (tc) Pablo Blazquez Dominguez/Getty Images, (tr) Joaquin Gomez Sastre/NurPhoto via Getty Images, (b) Randy Duchaine/Alamy Stock Photo; **214** (t) Matthew Horwood/Caters News, (b) AP photo/The Reporter, Patrick Flood; **215** (sp) Imaginechina, (b) PictureLux/The Hollywood Archive/Alamy Stock Photo; **216** (t) TORU YAMANAKA/AFP/Getty Images, (b) Mirrorpix via Getty Images; **217** (bl) Chronicle/Alamy Stock Photo, (br) Photo 12/UIG via Getty Images; **218** (t) Franck Fotos/Alamy Stock Photo, (b) Cosplay by Mira Coy @beebinch. Photography by Erik Jaworski; **219** ITAR-TASS News Agency/Alamy Stock Photo; **220** Nationaal Archief/Collectie Spaarnestad/Fotograaf onbekend; **221** (t) Courtesy of Devin Smith, (b) Supplied by WENN.com; **222–223** (dp) Courtesy of Michelle Nirumandrad; **224** (r) Caters News; **225** (bl) Courtesy of Michelle Nirumandrad; **226** (t) Design Pics Inc/Alamy Stock Photo, (b) REUTERS/Satish Kumar; **227** (t) David Wall/Alamy Stock Photo, (b) Kiwiana NZ/Cover Images; **228** Imaginechina; **229** (t) Caters News, (b) MARCO BERTORELLO/AFP/Getty Images; **230** Alex Ham/Caters News; **231** (t) © Raimond Spekking/CC BY-SA 4.0 (via Wikimedia Commons), (tr) © Realfintogive, Wikimedia Commons//CC-BY-SA 3.0, (b) dpa picture alliance/Alamy Stock Photo; **232** (t) Public Domain {{PD-US}} Library of Congress Prints and Photographs Division Washington, D.C. 20540 USA http://hdl.loc.gov/loc.pnp/pp.print, (b) Courtesy of Melanie Misselbrook; **233** RARESHOT/CATERS NEWS; **234** (t) Colin Edwards/Alamy Stock Photo, (l) Jordan McAlister/Contributor via Getty Images, Nationaal Archief/Collectie Spaarnestad/Het Leven/Fotograaf onbekend; **236** (b) Jill Wiens; **237** Devon Hains/Solent News/REX/Shutterstock; **238** (sp) © W. Bruce and Delaney H. Lundberg Fund, in Honor of the 25th Anniversary of Photography at the National Gallery of Art/CC0 1.0 Universal (CC0 1.0) (via Wikimedia Commons), (br) Experiments in physiology. Facial expressions: False laughter' by Guillaume Benjamin Amand Duchenne de Boulogne. Credit: Wellcome Collection. CC BY 4.0; **239** (cl) Experiments in physiology. Facial expressions: surprise' by Guillaume Benjamin Amand Duchenne de Boulogne. Credit: Wellcome Collection. CC BY 4.0, (b) Experiments in physiology. Expression: Moderate Cruelty' by Guillaume Benjamin Amand Duchenne de Boulogne. Credit: Wellcome Collection. CC BY 4.0; **240** Insights/UIG via Getty Images; **241** (t) Ethan Hyman/Raleigh News & Observer/TNS/Alamy Live News, (b) Tina Radel/AP/REX/Shutterstock; **242** Noah Deledda/Caters; **243** Courtesy of Khushboo Marda Malani; **244** Thomas Lohnes/Getty Images, Courtesy of Nicholas Penney; **245** Imaginechina; **MASTER GRAPHICS** Exhibit Tags: Created by Luis Fuentes, Abstract Background Texture: From https://drawingpen99.com; Infographics: Icons made by Freepik from www.flaticon.com, "Loch ness monster png" by https://ya-webdesign.com, Wheel icon made by dmitri13 from www.flaticon.com

Key: t = top, b = bottom, c = center, l = left, r = right, sp = single page, dp = double page, bkg = background

All other photos are from Ripley Entertainment Inc. Every attempt has been made to acknowledge correctly and contact copyright holders and we apologize in advance for any unintentional errors or omissions, which will be corrected in future editions.

Connect with Ripley's — Online or in Person

30 ZANY LOCATIONS

There are 30 incredible Ripley's Believe It or Not! Odditoriums all around the world, where you can experience our spectacular collection and go beyond the bizarre!

Amsterdam THE NETHERLANDS	**Genting Highlands** MALAYSIA	**New York City** NEW YORK	**San Francisco** CALIFORNIA
Atlantic City NEW JERSEY	**Grand Prairie** TEXAS	**Newport** OREGON	**St. Augustine** FLORIDA
Baltimore MARYLAND	**Guadalajara** MEXICO	**Niagara Falls** ONTARIO, CANADA	**Surfers Paradise** AUSTRALIA
Blackpool ENGLAND	**Hollywood** CALIFORNIA	**Ocean City** MARYLAND	**Veracruz** MEXICO
Branson MISSOURI	**Jeju Island** KOREA	**Orlando** FLORIDA	**Williamsburg** VIRGINIA
Cavendish P.E.I., CANADA	**Key West** FLORIDA	**Panama City Beach** FLORIDA	**Wisconsin Dells** WISCONSIN
Copenhagen DENMARK	**Mexico City** MEXICO	**Pattaya** THAILAND	
Gatlinburg TENNESSEE	**Myrtle Beach** SOUTH CAROLINA	**San Antonio** TEXAS	

Stop by our website daily for new stories, photos, contests, and more! **www.ripleys.com**

Don't forget to connect with us on social media for a daily dose of the weird and the wonderful.

  /RipleysBelieveItOrNot

 @Ripleys

 youtube.com/Ripleys

 @RipleysBelieveItorNot